How the stock market really works

How the stock market really works

Fifth edition

Leo Gough

**Financial Times
Prentice Hall
is an imprint of**

Harlow, England • London • New York • Boston • San Francisco • Toronto • Sydney • Singapore • Hong Kong
Tokyo • Seoul • Taipei • New Delhi • Cape Town • Madrid • Mexico City • Amsterdam • Munich • Paris • Milan

PEARSON EDUCATION LIMITED

Edinburgh Gate
Harlow CM20 2JE
Tel: +44 (0)1279 623623
Fax: +44 (0)1279 431059
Website: www.pearson.com/uk

First published in Great Britain in 2001
Fifth edition published 2011

© Pearson Education Limited 2001, 2011

The right of Leo Gough to be identified as author of this work has been asserted by him in accordance with the Copyright, Designs and Patents Act 1988.

Pearson Education is not responsible for the content of third-party internet sites.

ISBN: 978-0-273-74355-2

British Library Cataloguing in Publication Data
A catalogue record for this book is available from the British Library

Library of Congress Cataloging-in-Publication Data
Gough, Leo.
  How the stock market really works / Leo Gough. – 5th ed.
    p. cm.
  Includes index.
  ISBN 978-0-273-74355-2 (pbk.)
  1. Stock exchanges. 2. Stocks. 3. Investments. I. Title.
  HG4551.G68 2011
  332.63'2–dc23
                              2011024733

10 9 8 7 6 5 4 3 2 1
15 14 13 12 11

Typeset in 9pt Stone Serif by 30
Printed and bound in Great Britain by Ashford Colour Press Ltd, Gosport, Hampshire

Contents

Introduction

For the last few years the financial news has been dominated by the series of financial crises that began in the US in 2007, spread to the international banking system and, by 2011, had become a threat to the solvency of a number of sovereign states, particularly in the West. Does this mean that the good times for investors are finally over, and that we should keep our savings under the bed from now on? Almost certainly not! Although the financial crisis (discussed in detail in Chapter 13) has been a serious shock, the financial markets still offer good opportunities to ordinary investors to make their assets grow respectably in the long term.

This book is an introduction to the complex world of the financial markets. These days, anyone can participate in them, even if they only have a small amount of money to start with. Few people get rich quick through financial investment, but a lot of people do badly by trying to do this; it is a much better strategy to build your wealth steadily over the long term, adding to your investments by saving from your income and reinvesting the money that your investments generate. If you do this for many years, following a disciplined and well-founded set of rules, you won't need to be particularly lucky or to have any amazing talent for spotting winning investments – the chances are that you will be able to build up a considerable sum of money to help support you in your old age and to provide your children with a good start early in life.

The 'guerrilla investor' concept, as outlined in this book, is all about being sceptical and self-reliant. Many people become so overwhelmed with all the strange terminology and bland assurances offered by the financial services industry that they throw up their hands in despair and sign their money over to the first scheme that looks plausible. This book argues that it is very important to learn as much as possible about the financial markets and about the extraordinary progress that has been made during the last few decades in the theoretical understanding of how stock markets work. This doesn't mean that guerrilla investors should try to do everything themselves

– for many people, the most sensible way to invest is through funds, such as index funds, unit trusts and investment trusts – but it is very important to develop the ability to discriminate between good deals and bad deals, more risky and less risky investments, and situations where your own actions can make a difference compared with ones where they cannot. Think of this book as a first step on the road to a lifetime of learning about investment while you put what you learn into practice in a steady, disciplined way.

Investment can be fun, and it shouldn't take over your life completely. Take it at your own pace, and enjoy the process. Don't be too worried or in too much of a hurry to make money, and you should be pleasantly surprised with the results you can achieve in the long run.

What's new in this edition

Since the major financial crisis began in 2007, there has been a lot of reckless talk about the evils of the financial markets, and a general disillusionment with investment. This is understandable, given that the UK, along with many other countries, had a good economic run for more than a decade, and that the preceding investment crisis, the dotcom bubble that burst in 2000, did not affect the general public very directly. Following the crisis that began in 2007, however, not only has the public been affected directly in terms of bank collapses, low bank lending, unemployment and public sector cuts across the board, but also some major international schemes, such as the EU's common currency, the euro, have come under threat in ways that seem to have come as an enormous surprise to many people.

In this new edition, throughout the book efforts have been made to show how investment issues and topics have been affected by the financial and economic turmoil, and to demonstrate that the fundamental principles of investing have not changed, despite new products, new problems and new market conditions. This new material includes:

- Updated tax information, including changes to ISAs and other tax-sheltered investment vehicles.
- New case studies of major investment scandals and collapses, including Icesave, Bernie Madoff and Greece.
- A detailed analysis of what happened in the series of crises between 2007 and 2011.

- A discussion of how major issues, such as climate change, global economic development, demographic change and population growth may affect investment in the future.
- More on the joys of index investing.
- A discussion of the life-stages approach to investment (Chapter 14), and how to develop a long-term financial plan.
- More on good ways and bad ways of buying overseas property or retiring abroad.

All investors pay attention to current events, but guerrilla investors need to think even more deeply about the long term. Crises and crashes come and go, even the big, nasty, long-lasting ones. So do booms and bubbles. Try to develop strategies that will enable you to survive as an investor through the vast range of market conditions that you will encounter during your investing lifetime. Use this book as a springboard to get started on this exciting and rewarding journey.

1

The 'guerrilla investor'

This book is for people who want to make money. If you think that having money is wrong, or unfair, this book is not for you. Don't despair, though, if you don't have any money yet. It is possible to accumulate capital if you are determined to do so, whatever your disadvantages when you are starting out. In this chapter we will look at the basic issues and concepts you need to know about to prepare yourself for the stock market, namely:

■ The 'guerrilla investor' concept

■ What can you realistically expect to get out of the stock market?

■ Guerrilla strategy and tactics

■ Asset allocation – a powerful strategy

■ Choosing a financial adviser

The 'guerrilla investor' concept

Private investors – that is, individuals who are not stock market professionals who invest their own money – have vastly superior forces arrayed against them in the struggle for wealth; the large investment companies have better information, better equipment, more experience, incomparably more money, and political influence, so the prospect of beating the big players at their own game may seem daunting.

In this respect, the private investor is in a similar position to a real guerrilla; the way to fight back is to exploit the opportunities of being small. Guerrillas are frugal and in the game for the long haul. So it is with the private investor: what would be a small gain to, say, a merchant bank is a large gain for an individual. You cannot compete on the same terms as the huge financial institutions and companies that dominate the world's economy. You must adopt a survival strategy entirely different from the way that the big boys operate. You might be surprised to know that private investors have a number of real advantages over the financial institutions. The key to making the most of these is to refuse to play the game on their terms.

> **❝private investors have a number of real advantages over the financial institutions❞**

Like most large corporations, financial institutions don't enjoy a great deal of loyalty from their employees, who move from company to company in search of better-paid jobs. Managing in this environment means constantly checking on your employees' performance, and being judged on your own. This is one of the factors behind the tendency towards 'short-termism' amongst the institutions – they tend to focus on quick profits. People don't get fired for making profits! What's more, many professional traders can afford to think short term, since they only pay a tiny fraction of the share dealing costs that you and I must pay.

Let's look at the private investor's main advantages:

- As a private investor, you don't have to justify your decisions to a board. You don't have angry customers telephoning you to ask why you haven't invested in the latest craze.

- Unlike many investment funds, you are not restricted to only investing in the safest investments.

- You're not in competition with anybody, and no one need ever know how well, or badly, you are doing. Contrast this with companies and funds, which have to publish their performance several times a year.

■ You aren't under pressure to produce huge gains every quarter, which inevitably exposes you to high risk – you can afford to buy something and sit on it for years, if you believe in it.

■ You don't have to worry about your reputation. You can take a position in an unknown but promising company that many institutions simply aren't allowed to touch because of the rules that govern them. You can purchase shares abroad in any market that will allow you to do so. You can go against the grain and ignore conventional wisdom.

All this points to the need for private investors to concentrate on medium- to long-term investing, not short-term trading. To do this well, you need to do research, which simply means developing an understanding of the businesses and industries that you are following, and you can use the internet to help you do this – many corporate websites now have useful 'investor relations' sections.

It is often pointed out that investors only really need one or two big successes in their lifetimes to become really well off. Getting to know a winning company over a decade or two, watching it grow and grow and grow beyond all expectations, and continuing to purchase more of its shares out of your income, could give you the results you want. Notice the time frame – decades, not months, or a year or two. Keeping your big winners, and buying more, for a very long time, is likely to serve you better than endlessly churning your portfolio in search of a quick profit.

There are professional investors who do take the long view and refuse to be swayed by all the pressures of corporate life, but they are in a small, and decreasing, minority. Most of them own their own firms, have autonomy within a larger organization, or work for a small firm that has loyal clients who respect their investment philosophy. For example, Warren Buffett, the famous investor and one of the world's richest people, has only a handful of staff working at Berkshire Hathaway, his holding company in Omaha, Nebraska. In turn, Berkshire Hathaway owns a large number of firms in a wide range of industries, from insurance to building materials, that employ hundreds of thousands of people. By insulating himself from the pressures of running these businesses from day to day, and from the demands of a fickle stock market, Warren Buffett is free to do what he does best: thinking very carefully, and very independently, about his investments. He is, of course, answerable to his shareholders, but they adore him – he has made a lot of them very, very rich.

What can you realistically expect to get out of the stock market?

Equities have produced better returns than other kinds of investment over the long term, but this does not mean that most investors in equities become staggeringly rich. People who are new to the stock market often think that you can get rich simply by trading frequently in 'hot' shares, but this is very unlikely to work, for reasons that are discussed throughout this book. If you are determined to become very rich, you may be able to achieve this by a combination of earning a big salary, doing property deals, running a business, and working in parts of the world that are booming economically. You will almost certainly not be able to achieve this by frequent trading in the stock market.

Private investors should aim to invest in the stock market from any capital they have and, very importantly, by saving from their income, in order to accumulate a substantial sum for their retirement. If they can live off their pension and other income while they are retired, they can continue to invest in equities with the aim of achieving further capital growth, or they can draw down some of the income from their investments for living expenses with the aim of preserving the value of their capital so that they can pass it on to their relatives after they die.

But we often think of the stock market as the domain of the very wealthy; how can it be that most investors are not fabulously rich? To understand this, think about the millions of people around the world who own shares; when you add up the value of all shares owned by private investors, it comes to a staggering amount, but remember that this is spread across millions of individuals, many of whom only have a few thousand pounds' worth of shares.

The business of managing people's money has mushroomed in recent years as more and more countries have liberalized their financial markets. Financial firms employ many thousands of people to handle this business, which is of many kinds, not just equities: the markets for bonds, derivatives and foreign exchange, for example, are also very active. The financial industry is still growing, and it pays its employees quite well, especially through bonus schemes – we have all heard about the wet-behind-the-ears traders who have just bought Porsches with their annual bonuses. What many people do not realize is that these high salaries and large bonuses are not necessarily the result of high investment returns; in fact, most of this money comes from the fees that firms charge to investors and other customers. In times when financial markets are booming, bonuses can be high but during bad times many firms lay off large numbers of their employees.

There are, however, some people who do make vast fortunes in the stock market. This is not usually done by picking the right shares, seeing them go through the roof, selling at the right time and repeating the process again and again (which is probably nearly impossible to do consistently for a long period of time). More usually it is done either by:

- being a senior executive in a large publicly quoted company who enjoys a high salary, generous options on buying the company's shares at a special rate, other bonuses, and sometimes the opportunity to gain control of a spin-off company; or by

- being a major shareholder in a privately owned firm that is later floated on the stock market. In this case the shares can be sold at a very large profit.

In other words, the people who get really rich in the stock market are, by and large, senior businesspeople working either in the financial markets or in other industries who make money from their salaries or on deals connected with the sale of ownership of the firm they own, control or manage. They are not usually people who have unusually good stock-picking abilities.

You might think that someone like Warren Buffett is an exception to this rule, since many people think of him as having an uncanny ability to choose the right shares, but in fact most of his wealth has been achieved by being in business, acquiring substantial interests in businesses and influencing how they are managed – this is quite different from simply owning a portfolio of shares.

So, the point of investing in the stock market is to make your assets grow substantially by saving and investing carefully over many years. This is a realistic proposition. In contrast, trying to make a quick fortune by frantically buying and selling stocks and shares is not a realistic proposition.

Guerrilla strategy and tactics

Traditionally, investors are supposed to fall into two categories: those who want capital growth (i.e. to get more money) and those who want to live on the income they get from investing the money they already have. The notion of 'widows and orphans', middle-class people with no job but a little capital, was once used as a symbol for the investors who wanted income – advisers felt that it was their duty to keep such individuals in the safest possible investments because they were unlikely to be able to recover if they suffered a serious loss. With the advent of social welfare, the situation has changed – widows and orphans will not starve in the gutter if they lose their capital – so these traditional categories are probably less helpful than they used to be. After all, we all want capital growth if we can get it. Strictly speaking, a private investor who wants to get as rich as possible should never spend any of the income he or she receives from investments, but should reinvest it. That's a lot easier to do if you have a substantial income from other sources; the fact is that most investors do spend some of their investment returns, especially after they have retired and their other income has dropped.

Some people reading this book will not have any money to invest. Others will have acquired a small nest egg, perhaps through inheritance. Others will be earning a large salary and wanting to invest their savings in the best possible way. Still others will be hoping to use investments to help provide them with an income in retirement. These different situations and objectives require different investment strategies, all of which will be examined in this book.

As a guerrilla investor, it is a good idea to keep records – as well as allowing you to keep track of your current position, it will also help you to analyse how you have performed in the past, and identify any mistakes that you have made. Many investors also keep an investment diary to record their ideas and plans; this can be very helpful in showing you how you are affected by changes in your circumstances and in the market, and can teach you the great investment virtue: self-discipline.

Here is a list of basic questions that you could ask yourself regularly (say, once a year) and record in your investment diary:

- What is my net worth?
- What is my total income and expenditure?
- Am I getting richer or poorer? Why?
- What are my future employment prospects?

Net worth

Net worth is simply the difference between the value of all the things that you have and all the money that you owe. Most people on this planet have no net worth. Even in the richest countries of the world, most people only have some clothes, a car and a few sticks of furniture – not much to show for a lifetime's toil. The reason why this is so is that the system is constantly ripping them off. They buy life assurance products and then give it up after a couple of years, making a loss. They buy consumer goods at retail prices and borrow money at high interest rates to do so. They run up expensive overdrafts and live off credit cards. They buy things to make themselves feel they are richer than they really are. They borrow too much money in boom times to buy houses and fail to anticipate the inevitable bust. When they are old, they are put into a retirement home and their last remaining assets are spent on nursing costs. On and on it goes. Financially speaking, most people are abused and pushed around all their lives. The guerrilla fights back by exploiting the advantages and opportunities that are available, and resisting becoming victimized by the consumer mentality.

To fight back, you have to be in command of your own resources; you need to develop some Scrooge-like tendencies. First and foremost this means knowing what you've got and how much it is worth. Naturally, it is hard to estimate the value of some things, particularly houses, so take the trouble to get realistic valuations and be conservative. The market value of assets goes up and down all the time, which is why you must frequently take a 'snapshot' of how you are doing. Make your net worth the benchmark by which you measure your performance.

Companies have to work out their net worth regularly too; it's called a 'balance sheet'. The principle is exactly the same, whether you are an ordinary person or a large firm:

1 List all the things you own and put a realistic but conservative resale value against each of them.

2 List all your debts.

3 Subtract (2) from (1) to find your net worth.

Example

Julia is 32 and owns her own home.

Her assets are:

A flat	180,000
A car	2,000
A pension fund	10,000
Cash in a building society	5,000
	Total 197,000

Her debts are:

A mortgage	160,000
A bank loan	2,000
A bank overdraft	500
Credit card loan	1,000
Sundry bills	2,000
	Total 165,500
Net worth	Total 31,500

Knowing your net worth is vital, because it gives you your 'score' in the game of increasing your wealth. Of course, not all of Julia's £31,500 can be spent right away – much of it is tied up in her home and her pension – but it is still 'real' money.

Comparing your own wealth with other people's isn't very helpful in the struggle to build up your assets. As a guerrilla investor, you need to focus on your own goals, both in the short term and in the long term – trying to keep up with the Joneses is simply a diversion. Suppose, for instance, your long-term goal is to amass sufficient wealth to live in comfort in later life and to be able to pass on money to your children. Some people might already have enough money to do this, others may feel that this is a rather modest aim, while yet others may feel that it is a very challenging goal indeed. It doesn't matter what other people think: decide for yourself what your financial goals should be, and then work out a strategy of how to get there.

Think about how much money you would need to possess in order to generate an acceptable income, after adjusting for inflation. For example, suppose you were able to obtain an average annual return, after inflation, of 4 per cent in the long term – so if you had £1 million, this would give you an income, before taxes and after inflation, of £40,000. Whether or not you think this sum is adequate really depends on your lifestyle and your personal circumstances; if you are a confirmed bachelor and you want to live for nine months of the year on a tropical island, £40,000 a year might be plenty, but if you are the sole wage earner in your family and you are putting three kids through their education, you might feel that such a sum was insufficient for you to give up working. Most people in the UK, of course, do not have such large sums in cash available for investment in the stock market – even if their house is worth £1 million – but guerrilla investors do not have to stay put. For example, as is discussed in Chapter 9, it is possible, if you arrange things carefully, to move to a low tax country where your money will grow faster, and the goal of amassing £1 million becomes more realistic. In much of the Far East, for example, income tax rates are remarkably low, and some expatriates are able to save up much larger sums than they ever could have done back home in high tax Britain. The really important point, though, is that it is not the exact numbers that matter, but how you manage your finances in order to reach your long-term financial goals.

Income and expenditure

Working out how much you earn and how much you spend is a mundane housekeeping activity that many people do reasonably well (of course, there are also many people who do not!). However, even good money managers don't usually go far enough. Simply aiming to cover your bills leaves you exposed: you need to be able to save too. This is a cardinal principle for accumulating capital. Engrave it on your mind:

Don't consume more than you earn

Most people waste their money on things they don't need. By all means buy the best you can afford – the best quality is usually the best value in the long run – but look for bargains and ways of reducing your expenditure. Examine each category in your regular budget, and try to think of ways of cutting it down. A guerrilla has few resources, and must put them to the best use. Don't worry if you don't buy all the things that your peers do. Your goal must be to generate regular savings out of your income.

> **❝the foundation of successful investing is to save money out of your income❞**

The foundation of successful investing is to save money out of your income. It is your savings that you use to add to your investment holdings. This may appear obvious, but in practice it is easy to start to think of your investment gains as extra cash you can spend. The real secret of long-term investment gains is to stay invested for as long as possible.

Conventionally, people are told that in retirement they can expect to start drawing out money from their investments. This is true enough, if you are no longer earning an income. Nevertheless, successful investors often manage to make their assets grow substantially during retirement. The more income you have from other sources, such as a pension, the easier this is, since you are not under pressure to keep dipping into your funds to pay for your living expenses.

Employment

Investors need income from non-investment sources to pay for their living expenses. Trying to live on investment gains severely reduces your chances of making your investments grow satisfactorily. For most people, this non-investment income has to come from working.

The world of employment is uncertain. If you have a good salary, there is no excuse not to save, but many high earners manage to get into debt nevertheless. In old age you may not be able to get a job – so don't rely on your pension alone, start saving!

Many of us don't earn as much as we'd like. If you are able to re-train and get a better job, do so. Self-employment is an option, and has tax advantages, but it is not something to be taken on lightly. The whole mentality of the self-employed is different: it's lonely, you must bear more responsibility, it is uncertain, and it often takes years of struggle to get established. Most people who start businesses fail within five years – and this is true all around the world – and the vast majority of small businesspeople work longer hours and earn less than they would as employees. If you get it right, though, it can be very rewarding.

Educate yourself about money

Sportspeople often say that people's general unfitness and lack of body awareness is as great a form of ignorance as not being able to read and write. I believe that the same holds true for financial matters. Unless you were lucky enough to have been born into a business-minded family – and most people are not – you will have to learn it all for yourself. Talk to people who are richer than you are and know something about the subject. Read widely. When you have run though your local library, try using university libraries and talking to people who have studied economics and investment. There are many uncertainties and unanswered questions in the world of investment. Developing a deep appreciation of this will help your judgement. Read the serious financial press, like the *Economist* magazine and the *Financial Times*, but avoid the financial news on television, which is just a source of confusion.

Should you own your own home?

For UK residents, buying a property is usually a good investment in the long term. We all have to live somewhere, and if the alternative is renting at market rates, you usually find that the cost of servicing a mortgage is roughly equivalent to the rent you would otherwise pay, although this varies according to economic conditions. In the long term, property has been a good hedge against inflation, and if prices go up you are using the 'leverage' of your mortgage to increase the value of your equity. At the time of writing (early 2011) the UK property market has entered a stagnant phase, and it is difficult for people to obtain mortgages. This does not necessarily mean that this is not a time to buy. House prices are the national obsession because so many of us have so much money tied up in our homes, and you can read all kinds of scare stories about 'plummeting property' in the press. However, unless there are radical changes to the structure of the property market in the future, which would be very difficult politically, there is good reason to believe that property prices will recover within a few years.

Example

> If you buy a £160,000 flat with a £140,000 mortgage and £20,000 of savings, and after a few years the flat's value increases to £190,000, your equity will increase from £20,000 to £50,000, or 150 per cent. If you had bought the flat entirely with your own money, your equity would have increased by a much lower percentage – from £160,000 to £190,000, or 15.79 per cent.

Another good thing about property is that it is a way of forcing yourself to save. As you pay off your mortgage, your equity in your home increases. This is tough in the early years, but gets easier as time goes by. Sometimes people argue that they cannot consider selling their homes, so their equity is useless. That is their choice. There is nothing necessarily wrong with moving down the housing ladder in order to release some capital for other investment purposes.

People are often nervous about property because of the potential problems when values crash and interest rates go up.

There are two things to do to stay safe:

■ Don't borrow more than you can afford, taking into account possible interest rate hikes.

■ Be careful what you buy. Location is the most important factor – is the area growing or dying? Soundness of the property is also important – do all the searches and surveys properly before you buy.

Preparing for the stock market

Let's assume that you have a regular income, a home of your own, and that by saving regularly you have accumulated a capital sum of, say, £10,000. You have practised all the bourgeois virtues and now you feel ready to spread your wings. Investing in the stock market will probably give you a better return on your money than any other kind of passive financial investment; but try not to be greedy. Trying to 'beat the market' almost always means taking more risk, so you are much more likely to lose money. The safest way to invest in shares is to buy ones in good companies and hold them for a long time. Constantly buying and selling shares is expensive because of the commissions you pay.

To understand how shares (also known as 'equities') compare with other types of investment, we should compare their average performance over the long term.

The rewards of share ownership – what can you realistically expect?

Investors are free to invest their money in whatever is available, so why should we choose shares rather than, say, property or cash in the bank? Most people think of equities as being more risky than other types of assets, so why does anyone buy them? The idea of risk in investment is a little different from our normal definition, so we will consider it in more detail on page 24; for now, let's just assume that what we mean by 'risky' is that an investment changes its value more frequently – either up or down – than other investments.

People invest in shares because in the long term, they have produced better returns on average than other types of asset. A celebrated study by academics at the London Business School[1] has demonstrated this: in a comparison of the performance of equities and bonds (the other main type of financial asset, see Chapter 3) in all the major industrialized nations between 1900 and 2003, the inflation-adjusted annual returns on equities ranged from 1.9 in Belgium to 7.5 in Sweden and Austria. Bonds, in contrast, ranged from –2 in Germany to 3 in Denmark. These results can be treated with more confidence than earlier long-term studies because the study uses more accurate long-term data for countries outside the USA than was previously obtainable. It is worth noting that the USA, although it still comprises more than half of the monetary value of all the world's stock markets, performed well in equities

[1] Dimson, Marsh and Staunton, ABN AMRO/LBS and *The Triumph of the Optimists*, Princeton University Press, 2002.

(6.5), and rather less well in bonds (1.9). The most recent version of the study, which is updated frequently, shows no really substantial changes when the period is extended to the end of 2009, by which time the latest financial crisis was in full swing: for example, average US equity performance for the period only dropped from 6.5 to 6.1.[2]

So, if equities perform better than other kinds of financial asset in the long term, why should we believe that they have performed better than non-financial assets than, say, residential property? The short answer is usually that we should take it on trust that this is the case. To my knowledge, there are no high-calibre long-term studies of the global returns on residential property to use for comparison; property in the UK and parts of the USA has performed well over the long term, and although it has various disadvantages (for example, the time and trouble of managing tenants), we should not rule out this kind of investment – see Chapter 10 for a more detailed discussion.

For the private investor, stock market investing is really a place for cash savings that you are not going to need to spend for at least five years, and preferably that you will not need for much longer. The longer you keep your money invested, the better chance it has of producing solid returns. This may sound obvious, but in practice a lot of investors are attracted into the stock market during a boom and then drop out during the next bust. This is called buying high and selling low – we all know we are not supposed to do it, but many, many people do it anyway, because in practice it is difficult to avoid the temptation unless you have a thorough understanding of how it really works.

What can the private investor really expect? In the long term, going by the study mentioned above, about 5.3 per cent annually for a portfolio of UK equities, adjusted for inflation. To a lot of people, this sounds distressingly little. During booms the returns seem to be much more, and people start to expect, and even demand as their right, returns of 10 per cent or more. For example, during the world-wide boom of the 1990s, many countries, including the UK and the USA, did achieve returns above 10 per cent a year. People started to think that their pensions – which are generally invested for a much

---

[2] Credit Suisse *Global Investment Returns Yearbook*, 2010.

longer time period than 10 years – would perform equally well. Then the dotcom frenzy collapsed and during 2000–2003 equities did badly around the world; in some countries, bonds even outperformed equities. Which period would have given you a more 'realistic' opinion of the future performance of equities? Neither – they were both unrepresentative of the long-term record. Subsequently, equities boomed again between 2004 and late 2007, dropped badly in 2008 and then recovered substantially in 2009.

We are all in a hurry and have an appetite for life, so the thought of keeping cash (since most equities are so easy to sell, they are almost like cash) stuck in the markets for a century may seem quite unappealing. Nevertheless, in the long term, they will beat savings in cash or bonds hands down. Remember, though, that equities are 'volatile' (the prices change frequently and sometimes dramatically), and the soundest way to mitigate this volatility is by holding for a long time. Later we will look at volatility in more detail as a tool for measuring risk.

Adjusting for inflation

People get confused about inflation-adjusted figures; the 'nominal' return is the money figure, the amount you would receive, say, as bank interest into your account, The 'real' or inflation-adjusted figure is the same, less the annual rate of inflation. If you don't adjust for inflation – and some financial services firms have an unpleasant habit of always quoting nominal figures – you may get a very unrealistic picture of your returns, particularly over the long term. Inflation rates tend to vary a lot, but they eat into the purchasing power of your assets even when they are low. If you want to know if the real purchasing power of a sum invested has been preserved, and how well it has performed as an investment, you need always to look at the inflation-adjusted figures – don't guess, ask!

Memorize the terms:

Nominal rate = not inflation-adjusted
Real rate = inflation-adjusted

Sometimes a country experiences 'deflation', which is a general drop in prices, but this is much less common than inflation. In general there is some inflation every year, and in the long term this has been about 3–4 per cent a year, which means if you wanted to achieve a 5 per cent return, you would need to be getting an average nominal return of 8–9 per cent over the long term.[3] For most of us, low and stable inflation rates are best, because they make life easier to plan. Periods of high and volatile inflation tend to hurt ordinary people and most businesses because they cause panics and elicit emergency government measures that can be very damaging.

Asset allocation – a powerful strategy

It may not suit everyone, but there is a lot to be said for an investment approach called asset allocation that some professional investment funds use. Asset allocation involves looking at all your wealth as one big lump of money, and deciding how to invest parts of it to get the best returns at a risk level with which you feel comfortable.

In asset allocation, you worry less about how specific investments perform, and focus on your overall return. Different kinds of asset, such as shares, bonds and property, tend to be out of sync with one another. By spreading your wealth between asset types whose performance is not closely correlated, the aim is to achieve a balanced portfolio that produces a more reliable and less volatile return each year. Sometimes, for instance, bonds will do badly while shares are doing well, and vice versa – the idea is to have a portfolio that is more stable in its returns than one that was invested 100 per cent in shares.

Throughout this book we will return to the idea of asset allocation in various contexts; it really is a very good way to think strategically about your investments.

Why spreading the risk may be a good idea

This is a key concept in investment; if you are a wild-eyed hedge fund manager on the make, you may not follow it, but as a private investor it is generally not a good idea to be too eager for risk. If you put all your money in one investment, you are completely exposed to

---

[3] Dimson, Marsh and Staunton, ABN AMRO/LBS and *The Triumph of the Optimists*, Princeton University Press, 2002.

that market. For instance, if all your money is in your house, and you live in the UK, you might feel reasonably confident that in the long run you will make a good profit, but there are drawbacks. For example, the market might be stagnant for a few years, as it is at the time of writing, or even go down, and you will have to go to the trouble of borrowing or remortgaging if you need cash – and at the time of writing, many people are finding this difficult to do because of the bank credit crunch (see Chapter 13). If you put all your wealth into a single company's shares, the price might go down for a long time, and if you sold some of your holdings you would realize a loss. The same goes for funds: if you invest all your money in a single fund, you are taking the risk that the fund may collapse, which happened to many investors who were caught in the recent Bernard Madoff scandal (see Chapter 8). In general, although not always, investments of different asset types, and in different industries and countries, tend to perform very differently. By spreading your investments across a wide range of investments you protect yourself against the shocks of a drop in the value of a given investment.

A lot of people who are starting out in the stock market are tempted to ignore this principle. It is easy to get the feeling that you have a superior instinct, better knowledge, or better trading skills than most of the other investors who make up the market. You almost certainly don't, however, and in Chapter 5 we will look at the theoretical basis for this.

Choosing a financial adviser

In many ways, your best financial adviser is yourself – you know yourself, and care more than anyone else what will happen to your money. Before seeking professional advice on a matter, read everything you can about it

❝your best financial adviser is yourself❞

first and try to understand it. This will help you to get the best out of your advisers. A very experienced businessman once told me that there are two kinds of customers who get the best treatment: the ones who spend a lot of money, and the 'difficult' ones who never stop badgering, looking for a bargain, insisting on their rights and making demands. Be a difficult customer – it's your money, and you are the person who cares most about it. Don't be afraid to be rude or pushy if necessary, and don't let yourself be pushed around – there is always someone else ready to help if your adviser doesn't want your business.

Nevertheless, you do need professional help – even stock market professionals use advisers when investing in areas outside their own area of expertise. The investment world is enormous and complicated, and even if you understand the principles, you need to be guided through the details in specialist areas to avoid making silly mistakes.

Good advice is not free. Often the cost is included in the charges and commissions on investments you buy, or it may be identifiable as a separate fee. The quality of the advice is not necessarily closely linked to its cost. As with any other service you purchase, the quality of advice varies considerably. A high cost is not a guarantee of high quality: in other words, not all expensive advice is good, and not all cheap advice is bad, so it is important to take some trouble over selecting the right advisers.

Financial regulators allow many professions to give financial advice, but some of them are only allowed to advise on a small range of investments, or to give very restricted kinds of advice. The first thing to do is to find out what kind of advice they can give, and if the adviser is tied to specific investment products and companies. Tied advice may be good, but you would need to compare it with that of the competition.

Tied agents

Tied agents represent a company, most often an insurance company, and only sell the products offered by that company. There are also 'multi-tied' agents, who sell products offered by several companies. They don't necessarily have to tell you how much commission they are making, but they do have to tell you that they are tied. The high street banks and most building societies are tied agents, since they will only sell financial products offered by a particular company. Before dismissing tied agents out of hand, you should recognize that since they are backed by large companies, they are unlikely to go bust, and they may, sometimes, be able to give you the best deal on a particular product. Never sign an agreement that contains a penalty clause specifying that if you allow, say, an insurance policy or mortgage to lapse you will pay a percentage of the sum to the agent.

Independent financial advisers (IFAs)

IFAs can be stockbrokers, accountants, insurance brokers, solicitors and some building society managers. They may also be individuals without professional qualifications other than having passed the Financial Planning Certificate exams. IFAs have to tell you about their charges and any commissions they make, if you ask them, and are obliged by law to give you the best advice for your circumstances. IFAs who live on commissions are arguably less independent than ones that only charge fees. The latter type may rebate any commissions they earn to you. Never rely on the regulation of IFAs to give you complete protection; check them out very thoroughly before you part with any money. Such checks would include getting references, confirming that they are members of the relevant regulatory bodies (usually the Financial Services Authority, or FSA), making sure that you have obtained, and understood, all the relevant paperwork, and verifying that they are insured against professional negligence.

Remember to be careful when writing cheques. A cheque should be made out to a company, not an individual, to minimize the chances of fraud.

Here is a brief review of the characteristics of the different kinds of IFA.

■ Solicitors and accountants. Although they are not usually tied to specific products, solicitors and accountants rarely make investment their main business, so they may not have enough expertise to recommend the best investment of any given type. They may be useful for tax considerations (for example, how to mitigate inheritance tax) and on general strategic issues.

■ Banks. In some countries, such as Hong Kong, banks can offer a very wide range of sophisticated advice and other services. In the UK, with the exception of some of the 'posh' banks who offer special services for wealthy customers (so-called 'private banking'), they are limited in the type of advice they can offer, and may pass you on to stockbroking companies they own. In the UK, investors don't generally obtain much advice from banks, but you should be aware that in financial centres in other parts of the world they may well offer the best advice you can get.

■ Stockbrokers. The days of the old-fashioned stockbroking firm are disappearing, but you can still find a few brokers who have not been swallowed up by the mega-corporations. Stockbrokers make their money from commissions on the investments you buy and sell, so it is in their interests to get you to buy and sell as often as possible. This isn't quite as sinister as it sounds, as good stockbrokers take pride in their work and often go out of their way to protect you from doing anything silly. Often they have sensible advice to give about all kinds of investment matters, not just shares.

There are three types of service generally on offer, discretionary, advisory and execution-only.

■ The discretionary service is the poshest. You leave all the decisions to your broker while you go off skiing with the royals or on safari in Kenya. Not surprisingly, it tends to cost the most. Unless your portfolio is worth at least £150,000, you will probably not find a broker to offer you this service, although some may take you on if you have as little as £50,000.

■ The advisory service is where you are allowed to nag your broker for advice during office hours – and sometimes at night, too! It costs less than the discretionary service, but make sure you understand all the charges.

■ The execution-only service is the cheapest and gives no advice at all. You issue your instructions and the broker obeys them without comment. Some specialist execution-only brokers have websites chock full of research for you to digest on your own. Commission costs are low, but the quality of service varies greatly. You need to make sure that you are buying the right shares (some companies have more than one kind) and that you have done all the calculations correctly; for instance, if a company has altered the number of shares in issue and you haven't checked, you could make a nasty mistake. It is probably not a good idea to use an execution-only service when you are starting out.

Some investors like to use both an advisory broker and an execution-only service. This may be a bit rough on the advisory broker, who loses some commission, but it enables you to have the best of both worlds. Brokers never know everything, so sometimes you have to go elsewhere. For example, you might use an execution-only service to buy the latest hot high-tech stock in the USA that your London broker doesn't want you to touch, and your London advisory broker to trade in a British blue chip company. If you do embark on this approach, remember to keep the advisory brokers happy by putting some deals through them – they'll get upset if you just milk them for advice and use it for your execution-only deals.

The fact-finding meeting

In the UK, many advisers are required to ask for full details of your circumstances. This is a good rule that is designed to protect you. It is in your interests to tell them everything (except for any crimes you may have committed, perhaps!) so that they can advise you appropriately. In most countries, you will need to prove your identity because of the regulations against money laundering. Often the 'fact-find' is a questionnaire that you complete at a meeting with your adviser. There may be questions on it about how much risk you are prepared to take, and if you have any special goals in investing. These often seem rather nebulous questions to the uninitiated, but when you have finished reading this book you should have a better understanding of their purpose – remember, 'risk' has a rather different meaning in investment than it does in everyday speech.

Some investments are much more risky than others; for instance, it is possible in derivatives trading to lose much more money than you started out with. The financial regulators are wisely trying to keep these kinds of investment away from the foolhardy, and so you will probably be asked to prove that you have enough expertise to take on this kind of exposure. Don't be offended if a broker tells you she will not let you open an account trading, say, international copper futures because you don't know enough about it – she really is doing you a favour!

The paperwork

You will be given the adviser's terms of business, which should tell you:

- the services to be provided
- commissions, charges and fees

■ the adviser's regulatory authority (this is usually the FSA)

■ how the adviser is insured against negligence and bankruptcy

■ warnings about the risks of investment

■ how your money will be kept by the adviser (usually in a separate client account).

Paperwork is boring, but it will protect you against problems because you will be able to prove what happened. Keep copies of everything on file, and try to get verbal advice in writing as well. If you buy and sell shares very often, your conversations may be recorded by the broker to protect you both against misunderstandings, which are more common than you might think.

Is the advice any good?

A good investment adviser will:

■ Be reachable. Good advisers want to have a long-term relationship, not just sell you a product and ignore you. You need to be able to reach them when you wish.

■ Listen. Bad advisers push standardized products at you and treat you as if you are an idiot. Good advisers will try to tailor your portfolio to your own needs, and will give you advice even when they might lose out – for example, if you want to put £10,000 into shares and you also have £10,000 in credit card debt, a good adviser will tell you to clear the debt first.

■ Regularly review your investments. Every six months or so, you and your adviser should look at your portfolio and decide whether it has performed in the way you planned, or whether you need to change your approach.

■ Rebalance. Rebalancing a portfolio means adjusting your invest-ments to return to your specified asset allocation. For instance, let's say you have determined that you are keeping 50 per cent of your wealth in shares, and 50 per cent in bonds. After a year or two, your shares may have gone up in value to the point where the proportion is 60 per cent shares and 40 per cent bonds. The total wealth is more, but the portfolio is now out of balance with your original strategy. You should talk this over with your adviser, who may suggest rebalancing by selling 10 per cent of your shares and putting them into bonds. You can also rebalance within types of asset – for example, by rebalancing the spread of utility, transport and retail shares you hold, depending on market expectations.

■ Defend you against churning. 'Churning' means selling investments and buying others in order to generate commission. It is bad for you because the transaction costs will diminish your returns. It is often hard to spot churning unless you are an expert. A good adviser will be eager to keep your transactions costs down. Sometimes gung-ho investors churn their own portfolios constantly in their lust for high profits; frequent trading is fun, but it is not thought wise to do it with all the money you have allocated to equities. If you can't resist the thrill, earmark some separate gambling money for frequent trading when you do your initial asset allocation; if you do turn out to be lucky, you will have more to play with and if you are wiped out, you will not have damaged your wealth too much. So, if you get a new adviser who wants you to rebalance your portfolio, how do you know that it isn't just churning? I remember some time ago an elderly relative of mine, who wasn't very disciplined about her investing, decided that life would be easier if she gave everything to her bank to manage. The bank sprang into action, recommending that she sold most of her perfectly ok shares and bought another bunch of perfectly ok shares, which would have immediately generated several thousand pounds' worth of commission for the bank. To her credit, my relative was very unimpressed, and decided to keep on managing her shares on her own. Was the bank trying to churn? We can't prove it, but it did look suspect. Rebalancing should only be done when you understand the rationale fully and agree with it; any new adviser who tries to patronize you should be ignored. In fact, the capacity to ignore people is a very important asset in investing!

■ Clearly explain all charges. Good advisers hide nothing about the charges, and will tell you if one investment has higher charges than another.

■ Give tax advice. Good advisers will be knowledgeable about tax issues, and will try to keep you out of trouble. They will also put you in touch with specialist tax lawyers if necessary.

What is a risky investment?

Risk is a truly fascinating subject, and it is surprising how few people are willing to contemplate risks in a sober and rational fashion. As an investor, if you train yourself to become a better judge of risk, you may be able to achieve good returns by finding investments that are less risky than they appear to be

Some types of asset are inherently more risky than others, in the sense that they are more likely to sustain big losses suddenly:

■ **Least risky:**
  - cash at the bank (but it depends on the bank – see the Icesave saga, page 179)
  - bonds
  - second-hand endowment policies

■ **Medium risk:**
  - property
  - shares
  - unit trusts and investment trusts

■ **Very risky:**
  - your own business
  - derivatives and commodities
  - some kinds of hedge funds.

It is important to understand that borrowing, say, £150,000 to buy a house is inherently less risky than borrowing £150,000 to start your own business. This is because businesses are unpredictable and much harder to control than houses. Lending to buy house is also less risky for the lender than lending money to start a business, because a house loan is secured on the property, so it can be recovered by the lender. That makes the lender willing to offer much better terms to the borrower.

Don't assume that an investment is not risky just because most assets of its kind are not thought risky. A bad bank, a problematic house or a troubled corporation may all turn out to be bad investments. Remember to consider worst-case scenarios and how you would act if they occurred.

If you want to be good at investing, don't be silly about risk, either by taking wild plunges that are almost certain to fail or else by dismissing everything as too risky. There is risk in not saving and not investing too – the risk of ending up with no money at all! Successful

> **if you want to be good at investing, don't be silly about risk**

risk-takers take carefully considered gambles with which they can live comfortably. To master risk, you need to master your own emotions. If a certain investment will keep you up worrying every night, it is not worth having – stick to investments that won't make your life a misery, and you'll make better decisions.

In investment theory, risk is defined and measured in terms of volatility. This is discussed in detail in Chapter 5.

Summary

Before you begin investing, then, you need to take stock of where you are and how much you can realistically save on a regular basis to add to your investments. Even if you already have a lump sum, it is a good idea to get into the habit of saving to invest, because by doing this the value of your portfolio will grow substantially if you hold it for a long time. Once you are ready to take the plunge, you need to decide on what kind of broker you are going to use, or whether you are going to stick to collective investment funds (see page 36) which generally allow you to buy direct from them; although execution-only brokers are the cheapest, many people find that the guidance they receive from a discretionary service is well worth the extra money you pay. As well as a broker, it is generally a good idea to find other financial advisers to guide you through issues such as mortgages and insurance, and because they are required to do a thorough 'fact-find' about your overall circumstances, you will discover plenty of matters that you will need to consider in order to develop a long-term investment plan. Investment is all about doing your homework first, so don't worry if it takes a few years before you make your first investment – all that reading and learning will stand you in good stead when your money is really on the line.

In the next chapter we will look at the basics of how the market for shares works, and discuss some of the options open to the private investor.

2

Shares

In this chapter we will look at the basics of share ownership and stock markets. These are important, because by developing your understanding of the principles of how the markets work, you will be able to follow and act on any advice you receive from your brokers or other advisers much better. The stock markets are truly a place where knowledge is power – make it your business, as a guerrilla investor, to keep learning as much as you can. If you are a UK taxpayer you should read the section on Individual Savings Accounts (ISAs), carefully. These can be an attractive way to invest in shares. The topics covered in this chapter are:

- What are shares for?

- Why shares exist – the capital markets

- Stock exchanges

- Buying and selling shares

- Collective investments

- The world's stock markets

- Stock indices

- Individual Savings Accounts (ISAs)

What are shares for?

A company that is quoted on a stock exchange offers shares in its ownership to anyone who wants to buy them. A large company may have issued millions of shares. There are several types of shares, but the most common are called 'ordinary' shares. If you buy one, you are a part owner, or shareholder, in the company, with the right to share in its profits, to attend board meetings and to vote on key issues and appointments. You can sell your shares if someone is willing to buy them.

The price of a share changes all the time: it may bear little relation to the cash value of the company if you were to sell all its assets. There have been many cases, for instance, where the buildings owned by a company were grossly undervalued in its accounts and its share price was much lower than it 'should' have been. However, these days, when the stock markets of the world have become more important than ever, many companies are valued at much higher prices in the stock market than their 'real' value. And there are new challenges to valuation – how, for example, do you value a high-tech company whose products change every few months and whose real earning power resides in the brains of its talented employees? The constantly changing difference between the market capitalization – which is the total value of all a company's shares at the current market price – and 'real' value is one of the great themes of stock market analysis.

Share prices are volatile – they go up and down all the time as people buy and sell them. All sorts of factors influence the prices of shares, including company analyses, political change, natural disasters, wars and economic fluctuations, but one of the main influences is the behaviour of people who buy shares, or, as some would have it, 'the madness of crowds'. If many investors think that the price of a share is going to go up and buy it, the price of the share will go up until they stop buying. This may have nothing to do with the essential soundness of the company. As we will see, this kind of volatility is temporary. In the long term, shares in good companies are thought to be better investments than those in bad ones, which might seem obvious, but in the intense world of the stock market, it is often forgotten!

This capitalist system of financing big business is fundamental to the world's present economic system. Following the collapse of the USSR, there is no other system that is a serious contender with it. Thus, like it or not, people who want to increase or preserve their assets must learn how it works, and will probably decide to participate in it at some time in their lives.

Shares are also called 'equities'. Outside the UK, shares are often called 'stocks'. This can cause confusion since, in the UK, bonds are traditionally referred to as 'stocks'.

How shareholders make profits

There are two main ways:

- by selling their shares at a higher price than they paid for them
- by receiving 'dividends', which are a distribution of profits that the company has made.

Another way to make a profit is to sell 'short', which means, in effect, to bet that a share's price will drop. This is neither easy nor advisable unless you are a very experienced investor.

The quality of shares

The soundest, best-established companies are known as 'blue chips'. The term 'blue chip' comes from the world of the casino, where blue chips are those with the highest value. Next come the 'secondary issues', which are shares in solid companies. These receive slightly less confidence than the blue chips. 'Growth stocks' are shares in newer companies which are expected to do well in the future, but which may not do so. Finally, there are 'penny shares' which are those of companies with a low value, but which may increase for some reason.

❛❛ don't become fixated on the apparent safety of blue chips ❜❜

Growth stocks may become blue chips, blue chips may become dinosaurs that can no longer achieve business growth and increased profits, and the stock market jungle is always throwing up new possibilities. Don't become fixated on the apparent safety of 'blue chips'; an American friend of mine likes to refer to them as 'blue gyps' (a slang term for a swindle in the US). It is not unheard of for very large companies to suffer major setbacks; for example, during the oil spillage scandal in the Gulf of Mexico in 2010, the oil company BP's share price dropped from 650 to 300 between April and June. At the time of writing (early 2011) BP's shares have recovered to above 450. Imagine that you were a very timid investor who felt that you knew nothing about the stock market except that it was safe to keep your money in big companies like BP. How would you feel if you saw the value of your investment drop by more than half between April and June 2010? Actually, BP, like other large firms, tends to do reasonably well over the long term, but if there is a bad drop in price, you have to be willing to hold on to your shares until they recover. Thus, even if you only invest in the shares of major blue chip companies like BP, it is not the same at putting the money in a savings account: in a savings account, the nominal value of the investment will not fluctuate, except to grow modestly through the interest it earns, but with an investment in blue chip shares – as with other shares – the value of the investment may fluctuate dramatically on occasion.

Kinds of shares

Companies usually start out by being privately owned. When they get big enough the owners may decide to 'go public' and sell part of the shares of their company on a stock market. The rules for going public are quite strict, to make sure that the company is worth buying. The advantage to the original owners of selling their shares is that, if the offering is successful, they can realize very large sums of cash. Some owners, however, prefer to keep control by staying private, while others have been known to buy back all the shares and return the company to private ownership. Taking a company listed on a stock market back into private ownership is quite rare, and when it is done the aim is usually to increase control over decision-making; for example, a tycoon may decide that he or she can do a better job building the business by taking a company private because the red tape and potential for interference by other shareholders is much less.

Companies can issue several kinds of shares, usually labelled 'A', 'B', 'C', and so on. Each class of share will have different rules, different market prices and different dividends.

Most shares are 'ordinary' shares, putting the shareholders at the back of the queue of creditors if the company goes bust, and giving them equal voting rights and dividends to all other holders of ordinary shares in a company. Less common are 'preference' shares, which give the holder a slightly better chance of recovering some money in the event of a liquidation, often pay a fixed dividend, and usually don't give voting rights. The rights of preference shares vary from company to company, so you should always examine the rules in detail before buying. 'Convertible' preference shares give the holder the option to change them to ordinary shares at a fixed future price and date.

Companies sometimes issue warrants. These give the holder the right to 'subscribe' for shares at a fixed price at some point in the future. If the share price then rises higher than the subscription price, the warrant can be sold in the market. People who buy company bonds (see Chapter 3) are sometimes given warrants as an inducement to hold on to their bonds, thus helping the company to prosper.

Key terms

Market maker – market makers are 'wholesale' share dealers who deal with other stock brokers on a stock exchange. To be a market maker in most shares, you have to promise always to buy or sell whenever a broker asks – this 'makes a market' because it gives brokers the confidence that they can sell the shares that they buy. Usually market makers offer deals on a maximum quantity of shares, so if a broker is trying to offload a large number of shares, he or she may have to sell them in smaller lots over a longer period of time. The market maker makes a profit on the 'spread', which is the difference between the buy price and the sell price – on the shares of large, well-known companies the spread is usually very small.

When considering the purchase of obscure shares, always investigate the number of market makers in the share and its marketability before investing. A share with only one market maker may be very expensive, in terms of the 'spread', to buy and sell, and it may not be possible to sell the share at all for long periods of time. Most investors really appreciate the ability to buy and sell a share whenever they want, as is the case with well-known companies that are traded all the time throughout every day that the stock market is open (such shares are said to have good liquidity). If you take a punt on some little-known firm whose shares are only traded very infrequently, you must remember that it may be very expensive, or even impossible, to sell the shares when you want to.

Why shares exist – the capital markets

The stock market is one of three kinds of financial market that as a group are called the 'capital markets'. These exist so that owners of spare money, such as private individuals, trusts and organizations, can strike bargains with companies and governments who are in a position to put this money to productive use. When these markets fail, as they did to a large degree during the Great Depression of the 1930s, the owners of spare money didn't have confidence that companies could provide them with a better deal than they could get by buying bonds, so investment in shares slumped. Many companies had to close down, in part from lack of investment, and there was mass unemployment; the situation was only improved when governments stepped in to get the economy going again. While the world's financial system is more sophisticated today, the capital markets remain the principal way in which 'idle' money is put to productive use, but we should recognize that the system is not entirely stable and is vulnerable to shocks. See Chapter 13 for a discussion of the major financial crisis that began in 2007.

The capital markets consist of the share market, the market for bonds (which deals in mid- to long-term loans), and the money markets (which deals in large short-term loans). Unlike the other two capital markets, the share market does not deal in loans but in selling part shares of companies.

All the capital markets enable investors to buy and sell quite freely, usually at any time that the markets are open. This liquidity is a great benefit because it makes most of these investments almost as liquid as cash, although prices may change unpredictably.

Why do companies issue shares?

When a company needs extra money for its business – usually to expand it – it has a choice of either borrowing or selling part shares in its ownership. From the firm's point of view, there are pros and cons for each option, and these change according to specific circumstances. In general, however, the main benefit for a company in selling shares is that it never has to pay the money back; it may or may not pay dividends to shareholders, but these are much smaller sums and the firm retains control over the decisions of when and how much dividends to pay. The main drawback of selling shares, from a company's perspective, is that it widens the ownership. Some companies listed on the stock market have only a few majority shareholders who can control everything that happens, while many others have a much wider spread of ownership, with thousands of shareholders.

Companies are not very afraid of the ordinary private investors because individually they don't own many shares and it is relatively easy for a firm to push them around, even when they try to act collectively. The real pressure on firms comes from the financial institutions that invest very large sums in companies and sometimes are able to influence management policies. These financial institutions include banks, investment funds and pension funds, often investing on behalf of thousands of ordinary customers.

> **Key terms**
>
> **Liquidity** – how quickly an asset can be turned into cash.
> **Negotiability** – the freedom to trade a financial instrument with third parties.

How companies are structured

Companies can be seen as rather uncomfortable alliances between many different interest groups, sometimes known as stakeholders, which include employees, customers and suppliers as well as the owners and managers of the firm and the banks that lend them money. In investment, the focus is primarily on the owners, managers and lenders, who are the most directly involved in the firm's finances. These three groups do not have the same motives or objectives, and can easily come into conflict. For example, suppose that a company receives a huge bid from another firm to buy up its shares and take it over. The shareholders may be delighted at the prospect of a fat profit, while the managers may be fearful that the takeover would result in a complete change in senior management personnel. A situation can arise where senior executives are doing their best to prevent the takeover, in direct conflict with the wishes of the majority of the owners (shareholders) of the company. In many large companies, senior managers usually only own a small number of shares in the firm they manage, so their interests may not coincide with the interests of the owners (shareholders). In a few firms, a small group of senior managers may own a sufficiently large proportion of the shares that enables them to control shareholder decisions; these arrangements are quite rare in the UK, but more common in other parts of the world, including the USA and the Far East.

To cope with problems that arise from conflicts of interests between different stakeholders, formal structures have evolved for how companies are governed, to try to ensure that there are clear procedures for making decisions, that responsibilities are clearly defined, that senior managers are accountable for their actions, and that much of the important information about the company is publicly available. Companies have boards of directors to oversee this process. The directors are voted in by shareholders in proportion to the voting rights they hold (not all shares have voting rights). In the UK, USA, Australia and some other former British colonies, the model for corporate governance is different from the one used in much of continental Europe. On the Continent, companies often have two boards, a management board to oversee the daily running of the business and a supervisory board, which may include shareholder representatives, workers' committees, politicians and bankers.

Companies listed on a stock exchange have much stricter governance rules than private companies. They have to hold annual general meetings where shareholders vote, and they have to publish very detailed financial statements regularly that are publicly available. Investors and lenders rely heavily on these statements for their knowledge of the company, because they do not know as much as the managers about the inner workings of the firm. Although these financial statements are very important, it is very difficult to use them to make accurate comparisons between firms, especially if they are in different countries, because there is no universal standard for accounting (see page 85); in practice, the average private investors is not equipped to make good judgements using the financial statements, which is one reason why many people prefer to invest in professionally managed funds.

Stock exchanges

The most important stock exchanges in the world are based in the USA, UK, Europe and the Far East, but there are also many smaller exchanges. In terms of the total market value of their companies, the US markets are the largest. The basic purpose of a stock exchange is to provide an arena for the buying and selling of shares in a fair and orderly way. Exchanges have a governing body to oversee the rules, which are highly detailed, and only allow approved people and organizations to participate. It is very expensive to become an approved member of a stock exchange, so many brokers are only members of one stock exchange – for this reason, you will find that many UK brokers are reluctant to assist you in buying shares of companies listed on another stock exchange, say in New York or Hong Kong. If you want to buy shares listed on foreign stock exchanges, you may have to have several brokers in different countries, and you will find that their terms of business will vary greatly. Some of the large institutions, however, such as Citibank, may be able to offer broking services on all the major exchanges.

Stock exchanges decide which companies may have their shares traded on the exchange, and which ones to eject if their circumstances change. They also oversee the back office work of settling all the bargains made during day-to-day trading and, announce important news that may affect the market.

The global growth in investment

Only a few decades ago, most people knew little about stock exchanges, which were often regarded as only for the very rich. Even in the USA, private investors had a very narrow range of investments from which to choose. Today there has been an explosion in investment around the world as a result of the globalization trend, which has involved a tremendous liberalization of financial rules in many countries. Money can now flow in and out of many – but not all – countries very freely, which enables investors to buy shares in foreign companies with the confidence that they can get their money home again when they wish. The internet has made information-gathering and communication much easier and cheaper, and the professional investment fund business has become internationalized. Private investors are much more sophisticated than they used to be. They can choose from a much wider range of investment products and instruments than ever before, and the professional fund business has changed to reflect this, offering a huge variety of funds that invest in almost anything you could imagine.

It is best to regard globalization as a trend rather than a permanent change; it is unpopular in many quarters for many different reasons, and there is nothing to prevent political moods swinging in the future back towards more 'protectionist' strategies (which in investment essentially

> **"it is best to regard globalization as a trend rather than a permanent change"**

means nations trying to prevent foreign investors and companies from making money in their country). In addition, future politico-economic circumstances may give rise to radically new systems for running international business and investment. What this means for the average investor is that it is important not to go to sleep at the wheel, and to keep up to date with economic news. The only thing we can be fairly sure of is that things do change quite radically from time to time, and as investors we need to be able to respond intelligently if this occurs. For example, at the time of writing there are calls for major reforms of the world's banking systems, in the wake of the financial crisis that began in late 2007 (see Chapter 13). It remains to be seen what, if any, reforms will be made, so investors need to follow developments as they are reported in the financial press.

Although there is a lot of excitement about the newer stock markets around the world, it is important to keep this in proportion. According to the Bespoke Investment Group, as of mid-2010 the US markets held about 29.7 per cent of the total stock market wealth, in terms of 'market capitalization', which means the paper value of the shares traded on the exchanges. In contrast, the UK had about 6.72 per cent, Japan 8 per cent and Germany 2.8 per cent. The overall trend in recent years is for the market capitalization of the USA and Europe to fall, and for some newly developed countries, notably China and India, to rise. The markets of the Far East, however, although they may have a very exciting future, are still only a very small proportion of the total; as of mid-2010, China's total market capitalization was only slightly more than the UK's, at 6.89 per cent (although this does not include Hong Kong, which is much more international than China, and has 4.97 per cent of the world's market capitalization). For the time being, the USA remains by far the largest country in terms of market capitalization.

Buying and selling shares

Except for new issues, you must usually buy shares through a broker. In recent years, traditional full service brokers have found that increased costs have made it difficult to offer an ideal service to everyone, so, unless you have £50,000 or more to invest, the cheapest deal available is the 'execution only' service which means that the broker just does what you ask, without offering any advice. Not all brokers offer this service, so you will have to shop around. If you are investing £10,200 or less each year, you should consider using an ISA scheme, which limits the field further (see below for how these work).

> **Key terms**
>
> **Earnings per share** – earnings per share (EPS) is simply the total dividends paid out by the company in a year, divided by the total number of ordinary shares. This is not the same as profits, since some profits are not paid out as dividends.
>
> **Yields and price/earnings ratios** – these are the two main ways that investors judge shares and both are published in the financial pages. The yield tells you the rate of income, as dividends, that you will get at the current share price. The p/e (price/earnings) ratio is the market price of the share divided by the company's earnings per share. It is a measure of how much the market is prepared to pay for the company, given the profits that it makes. It is often said that the actual number of a p/e ratio is irrelevant, and that it is whether that number is right that is important.

Collective investments

For a number of technical reasons, the average private investor does not usually do particularly well by trying to select individual shares by him- or herself, and so many people use professional funds to do the work for them. It is not entirely clear that professional fund managers as a class do particularly well either, although there are some outstanding performers; however, professional funds do get the technical matters right and do not as a rule make silly mistakes like buying the wrong class of share or misunderstanding the information given, which private investors can easily do when they are operating on their own. However, if it is true, as it seems to be, that professional fund managers do not perform particularly well overall, there is a strong case for avoiding all types of collective investment except for 'index tracking funds', which mechanically follow the performance of a major stock market index, such as the FTSE 100 (see page 109).

Collective investments, or 'managed funds' are based on a fairly simple idea that has been around for a long time – the first one appeared in 1820. The principle is that a large number of people put savings into a fund that is managed by professionals. The idea is that the professionals will be able to get better deals and discounts on their stock market and other investments because of the huge size of the fund (which is true) and that they will make better investment decisions than private investors (which may not be true, see page 106).

Managed funds come in different varieties, which are discussed below. Guerrilla investors should appreciate that the companies and individuals who manage such funds often make most of their money from deducting charges from the funds. Depending on the contract, a manager can draw down huge sums from the fund, irrespective of whether or not the fund is profitable.

A report in late 2000 by Professor Merlin Stone of Bristol Business School[1] suggested that financial advisers recommend products that are overpriced and that the 'mass affluent' in the UK have paid £3.8 billion in unnecessary investment charges for packaged products that often include managed funds. The 'mass affluent', it is argued, are hit in two ways, both by being overcharged and by being steered into investments that produce poor returns in the name of safety. In the last few years the quality press in the UK has become increasingly vocal about the unfairness of charges, especially of managed funds, without much apparent effect on the industry. Unit trusts and OEICs (see below), in particular, come in for a lot of criticism for making high charges, which is another reason to consider index tracking funds, which have substantially lower charges (see page 109).

[1] Stone, *Stealth Financial Charges and the Mass Affluent*, Bristol Business School, 2000.

If you invest in a fund, you buy a share in the portfolio of the fund, not a share in the company itself. Funds are well-regulated in the major markets to protect the private investor and are often barred from making specified high-risk investments. Many of them are not allowed to borrow money.

The varieties of funds

❛❛the goals of individual funds vary very widely❜❜

The fund industry has grown massively, and today there is a staggering range available across the world. The goals of individual funds vary very widely, and some are much more risky than others. Funds have to invest in the ways that they say they will in their prospectuses, so that investors know what they are getting into; investors should choose the funds that are right for them.

Some of the more general types of fund you will encounter include:

- Bond funds, which invest in bonds. These funds are usually more stable in performance than funds that invest in shares.

- Balanced funds, which invest in both shares and bonds, and are intended to produce a more stable performance than funds that invest only in shares. Some of these are known as 'income funds', and are intended to provide investors with a fairly predictable stream of income to live on without reducing the value of their investment.

- Guaranteed funds, which promise that the value of your investment will not drop if you hold your investment to maturity – but remember to take inflation into account! Also, check the value of the guarantee by investigating the guarantor – what measures have they taken to ensure that the money exists to make good any guarantee?

- 'Small cap' and 'large cap' funds, which invest in companies by their market capitalization, calculated as: share price × number of shares in issue. Large cap funds invest in companies with market capitalizations of billions of pounds, while small cap funds pick companies with a much lower market capitalization. These choices reflect expectations about the future performance of the two different types of company.

■ Growth funds invest in companies that the fund managers think will grow extremely well in the future. Generally they argue that you need to hold the investment for many years. The evidence that this strategy works is not entirely convincing (see page 116).

■ Value funds look for bargain companies that the market hates and therefore undervalues. When choosing such a fund, you need to read and understand its aims and methods very carefully.

■ Global funds invest in companies across the world, often on grounds of growth potential for both the companies and the countries in which they are based.

You also may encounter much more focused funds, including:

■ Index tracking funds, which aim to perform very closely to a specific market index such as the FTSE 100. See page 109 for more details.

■ Commodity funds and precious metal funds, which invest mainly in mining companies. Their performance is often highly volatile because they depend on fluctuating world prices.

■ Money market funds, which invest in short-term lending contracts. They are less volatile that bond funds, but generate a low return.

■ Regional funds, which invest in a particular region of the world, such as South America, usually on the grounds that the overall economy in that region is improving.

■ Country funds, which invest in a single country. They may invest in local bonds and shares and also in the shares of foreign companies working in the country. Their performance is very variable, depending on the country.

■ Emerging market funds, which invest in countries that are just becoming industrialized. The performance of these funds tends to fluctuate a lot.

■ Sector funds, which invest in a specific industrial sector. If you think, say, that world food prices are likely to rise substantially over the next 10 years, you might invest in a fund focused on the food sector.

■ Funds of funds, which invest only in other funds. Be careful about the extra layer of charges.

■ Hedge funds, which are different from other funds because they are allowed to use exotic financial instruments and high risk strategies that may involve massive risk. For example, they may invest heavily in derivatives (see Chapter 7). In general such funds' performance is not correlated with that of conventional funds. Hedge funds use methods that are hard to understand, and the information they provide is less transparent than you might expect.

Unit trusts and 'oiks' (OEICs)

Before we look at what unit trusts are, you should be aware of the following points:

■ Unit trusts that are closely linked to stock market indices are one of the safest ways to invest in shares; the reasons for this are examined in detail in Chapter 5.

■ Investment trusts (see below) frequently offer better value than unit trusts.

■ Unit trusts are heavily marketed financial products aimed at the general public. Their literature and sales approach is designed to put fearful savers at their ease and is generally bland; the image projected is paternalistic and reassuring. You pay for all this 'service' in the charges.

■ You hear a lot in financial advertising about how advantageous it is for you to put your money into the hands of the professional unit trust manager who will invest it so much better than you can. As will be discussed in Chapter 5, there is considerable evidence that this is not really the case.

Unit trusts were introduced into the UK from the USA, where they are known as 'mutual funds', in the 1930s. The fund is professionally managed and spread across a range of investments, including shares and bonds in the UK and in foreign markets. The value of the units fluctuates with the value of the investments of the funds. Since you pay charges to buy and hold units, they are medium- to long-term investments. In other words, you should expect to hold them for at least three years.

Traditionally, the main advantages of unit trusts are considered to be:

- Good diversification for the small investor – possibly better than you could do on your own.

- Less worry, and less work, than holding your own portfolio.

- At times it has been difficult for small investors to find brokers to handle their business. In such conditions, which do not exist currently, unit trusts were virtually the only way a small investor could get into the stock market.

- Unit trusts have been well-regulated and far freer from scandal than other investments.

The money is held by a trustee, such as a bank or an insurance company, and not by the unit trust company itself. The trust is regulated by a Trust Deed, which lays down all the rules of how the money is to be handled.

Offshore trusts

This is a British definition meaning a trust which is not an 'authorized unit trust' in the UK. Many of them are run from places like the Channel Islands, Bermuda and the Cayman Islands, and are run on the same lines as 'onshore' unit trusts. They are harder to buy and sell in the UK, and are, in some cases, less well regulated, so you should check the companies out very carefully before investing. Their charges tend to be higher and there are often no direct tax advantages for UK taxpayers.

Savings schemes

Many trusts allow you to pay in a monthly sum, and you can miss a few months, or reduce or increase your payments, without any penalties. Such schemes should outperform financial products such as endowment and unit-linked insurance policies.

Unit trust net asset value (NAV)

The net asset value of a unit trust is: total assets – total liabilities. Suppose a fund has assets with a current market value of £500 million and liabilities of £200 million; its NAV is £500 million – £200 million, which is £300 million. You will find that NAVs can change frequently, so usually the fund will calculate its NAV at the end of each trading day.

If you want to know how much your own investment is valued at, you can calculate it by:

Fund's NAV ÷ number of shares or units issued = NAV per share/unit

You can find the NAV per share in the financial press each business day.

Buying and selling unit trusts

There are many ways to buy unit trusts; you can buy through a newspaper advertisement, a bank, a solicitor, an accountant, a stock broker or an insurance broker. If you buy through an intermediary, you will be expected to hand over a cheque once the units have been bought. You will then receive a contract note recording your purchase. Some weeks later you should receive a unit trust certificate which is your proof of ownership. As with all business documents, you should always check both the contract note and the certificate to see that the right type of unit trust is recorded, that the number of units are the same on the contract note and the certificate, and that your name and address appear correctly. If all is well, you should then store the documents somewhere safe where they will not be lost or destroyed.

When you come to sell, you contact the organization from whom you bought the units, and send them the certificate, having signed it first. Normally you should get the money within 10 days. If you lose the certificate, you must apply for a new one, which will take several weeks. You can still sell units in the meantime, but you won't receive the money until you have surrendered the duplicate certificate.

Check newspapers for the bid and offer prices; remember that the higher one, the offer, is the one you must pay when buying, and the lower one, or bid, is the one you get when selling. Check the difference between the bid and offer prices; normally they are around 6 per cent, but they can be more than double this. The majority of unit trusts quote prices every day, but some may do so once a week or even once a month. You may find that the trust has rounded up a buying price or rounded down a selling price by 1.25p or 1 per cent, whichever is the smaller; they are allowed to do this.

The charges

The two main charges are the 'front-end load' or fee that you pay when you buy, and an annual management fee. The front-end load is included in the published offer price. If you buy into a unit trust and sell soon after, you will probably lose 5 per cent or so. The idea is to hang on until the units grow enough to cover the front-end load. These charges are in addition to the bid/offer spread discussed above.

Check the annual management fee before you buy. It is usually 1 per cent or less, but VAT is added. This fee is usually taken from investment income automatically by the management.

The cost of investing in mutual funds varies a lot. Sales charges can include:

- a charge when you purchase units in the fund
- a redemption charge when you sell units
- a transfer fee if you switch to another fund in the same group.

Management fees for expenses also vary, and it is important to realize that the lower the expenses, the more of your money goes into the investment. For funds that invest in shares, the expenses are typically 1.5 per cent to 2.5 per cent of the value of the fund. Nobody likes these management expenses, but the essential question is; could you do better on your own? In general, the answer is probably 'no'; if you only want your investments to perform roughly in line with a stock market index, however, you could choose a tracker fund (see page 109) which should have lower charges since there is less work for the management to do.

Open ended investment funds (OEICs)

OEICs, or 'oiks', are similar to unit trusts, but instead of buying units you buy shares in the company. The main difference between oiks and investment trusts (see below) is that oik managers can increase or decrease the number of shares whenever they wish, just as unit trust managers can with units. Oiks are generally offered by the same companies that operate unit trusts, and the current trend is to convert the remaining unit trusts to oiks. As with unit trusts, you really need to look at the charges of oiks, especially the initial charge – which can some-times be a disgracefully high 6 per cent. Sometimes it is possible to avoid the initial charge altogether by buying through a fund supermarket – and often, the most expensive route is to buy direct from the company.

Investment trusts

❝generally, investment trusts are better value than unit trusts and OIECs❞

Investment trusts are similar to unit trusts in that they are pooled funds which are profes-sionally invested in a wide range of shares. They are not trusts, however, but companies whose shares are quoted on the stock market; you buy shares, rather than units, in an invest-ment trust. They are taxed in much the same way, and offer a similar variety of categories, including monthly sav-ings schemes. Generally, they are better value than unit trusts and oiks because the buying costs are often lower and the shares can often be bought at a discount to the value of the fund. The bid/offer spread, which is the difference between the buying and selling price, is around 2 per cent, as opposed to 5 per cent in unit trusts, annual manage-ment fees are about half, and the initial charges are lower too. Another feature is that they are allowed to borrow money to invest; this makes them slightly riskier and more volatile than unit trusts. All this helps to boost their performance.

You buy the shares in the same way as you would any company listed on the stock market, through a stockbroker. Some large investment trusts also run schemes where you can invest small amounts on a regu-lar monthly basis.

When you buy and sell, you pay the stockbroker's commission, plus stamp duty on purchases. Investment trust managers do make charges, which you can find in the accounts. As mentioned earlier, these tend to be lower than the charges on unit trusts.

All pooled investments are judged by their net asset value per share or unit, but investment trusts are traded on the market like any other company, so their share price will fluctuate according to supply and demand. They calculate their net asset value per share at regu-lar intervals, generally every three months. For a number of reasons investment trusts tend to trade at a discount to the NAV. Remember that while the published NAV is historical (recorded at the last valuation date), the share price is current, so you may not be able to calculate the precise difference between the two.

With the growth of giant financial conglomerates, the industry is becoming 'vertically integrated', which means that a group may own banks, stockbrokers, unit trusts, investment trusts, bond traders and so on. This is not wildly good news for the guerrilla investor, but there are ways of exploiting it. There are a number of independently owned investment fund groups that buy control of investment trusts trading at a huge discount to NAV and 'crack them open' by converting them to unit trusts, a very profitable strategy for shareholders in the raiding company. Vertical integration has created huge conflicts of interest within financial groups, and raiders have many interesting opportunities to exploit inefficiencies amongst the giant financial institutions.

Investing in funds through asset allocation

Because there is such a wide range of funds available, it is possible to take an asset allocation approach even if you are investing exclusively in funds. The aim here is to choose investments with the minimum risk (volatility) for the level of return you seek by combining different funds with different characteristics. This works because not all investment types rise and fall in tandem (known as 'positive correlation'); if you spread your investments between funds that invest in assets that are 'negatively correlated', in other words that they tend not to rise and fall in tandem, it may be possible to reduce volatility while still getting a high return. For example, for some periods you find that a portfolio that combined, say, 20 per cent shares with 80 per cent bonds, which you would have expected to have a higher volatility than a 100 per cent bond portfolio, actually had the same volatility but produced higher returns.

You will need specialist advice in order to calculate the optimal mixture of funds for your purposes using this method, because it will be based on estimates of how different asset classes are likely to perform over the next few years. As always, though, remember that nobody can be absolutely sure about the future. Also, although there are periods when, say, bonds do relatively well, in the long run an investment in volatile equities is likely to produce a superior performance.

How to pick funds

Most funds publish information regularly about their aims and performance. These are worth reading; they contain:

■ the fund's asset allocation

■ the benchmark against which the fund's performance should be judged – this is often a stock market index such as the FTSE 100

■ the NAV and size of the fund

■ details of the charges

■ the specific investment goals of the fund

■ how the fund has been affected by the market

■ major investments that the fund holds.

Using this basic information you can develop a shortlist of funds that fit the types that you are looking for. The next step is to obtain fuller prospectuses and the annual reports for the funds on your shortlist and study them very carefully. Check for:

■ sales and settlement procedures – find out how long it takes to receive your money when you sell

■ full details of all charges, including switching funds within the group and penalties for early withdrawal

■ gains and losses made by the fund, any liabilities, and income generated from the portfolio

■ all the expenses incurred by the fund.

Comparing funds

Selecting and comparing funds can be tricky, especially because past performance really is not – just as all the warnings tell you – a good guide to future performance. These issues are discussed in more detail in Chapter 5; for now, here is a brief list of points to consider:

■ Charges are important, but should not be the primary reason for selecting or rejecting a fund. If you find two funds that are very similar, however, then pick the one with the lower charges.

- Funds that invest in a very focused way, for example only in the shares of an emerging market, or only in one or two industrial sectors, are likely to be highly volatile in their performance.

- Examine the benchmarks that the fund wants to be compared with. Is the benchmark really the right one? To take an extreme example, a fund that only invests in, say, Chinese plastics companies is not likely to perform in a similar way to the FTSE 100, the index of the top companies in the London market. Some funds have a fairly diversified portfolio and suggest a well-known index as their benchmark, but on closer examination of their investments it becomes clear that the funds really are not likely to have a similar performance because their investments are too different from the companies used for compiling the index. As well as the benchmarks that the fund says it wants to be used for comparison, look at other funds with a similar portfolio to compare their performance.

- Use independent industry ratings handbooks (there are many of them, such as Standard & Poor's) for opinions on the quality of the management of the fund.

- Check the Sharpe ratio of the fund (see page 115). The higher the ratio, the better the performance to date.

- Check the volatility of the fund. High volatility means that its price will fluctuate a lot over time.

- Use the risk-adjusted return (see page 112) to compare performance. This measure adjusts for the different levels of risk inherent in different types of investment so that you can compare the performance more fairly.

The world's stock markets

There are now more than 60 countries in the world with stock exchanges. The biggest one of all is the New York Stock Exchange (NYSE) where about a third of the total value of the world's shares are traded. Many of the newer stock exchanges are tiny, such as the one in Croatia which trades only a handful of stocks and shares. Some countries, such as Germany, finance their industries more by bank lending than through shares, and their stock markets are smaller than you might expect. Then there are the highly internationalized stock markets, such as London and Hong Kong, where the total value of shares far exceeds the country's gross domestic product (GDP). Different countries have different rules for managing their stock exchanges. Most of the big ones now allow unrestricted foreign investment. Dealing costs and tax arrangements vary considerably, and if you buy or sell shares worth less than £10,000 in some markets you may be hit with a wide bid/offer spread.

The USA

The most important stock exchanges in the USA are based in New York.

The New York Stock Exchange (NYSE)

The NYSE is the best-known of the New York stock exchanges, trading tens of billions of shares in nearly 2,000 companies. It is well-regulated by the Securities and Exchange Commission (SEC), and individual investors get preferential treatment over institutions when buying and selling thanks to the Individual Investor Express Delivery Service (IIEDS). The main index used is the Dow Jones Industrial Average, which is the arithmetic mean of the share price movements of 30 important companies listed on the NYSE.

The American Stock Exchange (AMEX)

Until 1921, brokers who didn't have a seat on the NYSE would trade in the street. Eventually, they were organized into a proper exchange where companies not large enough to qualify for listing on the NYSE are listed.

National Association of Securities Dealers Automated Quotations (NASDAQ)

NASDAQ began in 1971. It has no central dealing floor, but works as an international system of trading in shares and bonds via computer screens. It has information links with the London Stock Exchange and was the first foreign exchange to be recognized by the then Department of Trade and Industry in the UK. In recent years, investors across the world have become very excited about NASDAQ because so many fast-growing high-tech companies, based both in the USA and abroad, have listed there. The wild booms in new sectors such as the dotcom industry have made NASDAQ a hair-raising, speculative ride.

Continental Europe

Shares have been traditionally regarded with some suspicion by continental Europeans, and not without reason. Nevertheless markets have existed for centuries in most countries. The world trend towards liberalization has encouraged European governments to reduce taxes on dealing and to move towards standardizing their regulations. The principal markets are described below.

Euronext

Euronext was formed by mergers of the Amsterdam, Brussels, Lisbon and Paris stock exchanges, and is currently merged with the New York Stock Exchange. It has also opened a market in London and owns LIFFE, the London futures exchange (see Chapter 7). More than 1,200 companies are listed.

Germany

There are eight regional stock exchanges in Germany which together make Germany the next biggest market after New York, Tokyo and London. The biggest of these regional centres is Frankfurt, owned by Deutsche Börse. At the time of writing, there are hopes that Deutsche Börse will merge with NYSE Euronext.

The Far East

Eastern Asia is the fastest growing area in the world and is likely to remain so for many decades despite the occasional crisis. Japan is the most powerful economy, but until the crisis of 1997, the 'Tigers' (Hong Kong, Taiwan, Singapore and South Korea) were catching up. Not far behind were the 'Dragons' (Thailand, the Philippines, Malaysia and Indonesia). Today, the 'Dragons' are troubled and the excitement has moved to China.

People in these countries tend to save a large proportion of their incomes which is one of the reasons why economists believe that their growth is sound and will continue. Most of the Far Eastern markets are 'thin', which is to say that shares are less frequently traded than on, say, the NYSE. This has the effect of making the markets vulnerable to manipulation, and to financial shocks.

The Tokyo Stock Exchange (TSE)

There are eight stock exchanges in Japan but the TSE is the largest, rivalling the NYSE for the title of 'world's biggest'. Companies are listed in three sections, the first for over 1,000 of the biggest issues, the second for a few hundred smaller companies, and the third for non-Japanese companies. There is also an over-the-counter market which is separate from the TSE. The main Japanese index is the Nikkei Stock Average, which is price-weighted and includes over 200 Japanese companies from the first section of the TSE. Although there are still some limitations to foreign buying on the TSE, it is possible for a small investor to buy and sell quite freely.

The Stock Exchange of Hong Kong (SEHK)

Hong Kong has had a stock exchange since the last century but it wasn't until the 1970s that the market began its rapid expansion. It suffered badly in the 1987 crash and its regulation has subsequently been tightened. It has two main indexes, the famous Hang Seng Index and the broader Hong Kong Stock Index. Hong Kong was leased from China by the British in the imperial era and was handed back in 1997. While it seems that China will try to maintain Hong Kong as a world financial centre, long-term investment in the market looks risky. At present, though, there are no restrictions on foreign investment in shares.

Shanghai and Shenzen

These are two new exchanges in mainland China. Shanghai was a great business centre in pre-Communist days, and is booming rapidly today. Together with Shenzen, it lists more than 1,000 companies with a market capitalization of over US$500 billion. Not for the fainthearted, but at the time of writing this is arguably the most exciting growth market in the world. Fasten your seatbelts for a bumpy ride!

Korea Stock Exchange (KSE)

South Korea's exchange is large and modern and is increasingly opening up to outsiders. Since the 1997 crash, the country has been mired in efforts to reform its banking and industrial sectors.

Stock Exchange of Singapore (SES)

This market is almost entirely open to foreign participation – only large stakes in certain important companies are prohibited. The SES has trading links with US dealers and many Malaysian companies are quoted on it.

Taiwan Stock Exchange

Trade in shares grew in Taiwan after a land reform in the 1950s gave owners stocks and shares in government-run companies. The market is very liquid and dominated by a few investors.

American Depositary Receipts (ADRs)

With the advent of the internet and the general liberalization of capital flows around the world, it is becoming easier for the UK private investor to purchase shares on foreign stock exchanges. However, it always takes more effort than purchasing UK shares because there are fewer dealers who will deal on foreign exchanges. Of the brokers that do offer foreign share dealing, most will offer to deal for you on the major US exchanges, which can let you deal in major non-US and non-UK firms through 'ADRs' (see below) on the US exchanges.

Many excellent foreign companies choose to be quoted in the US instead of, or as well as, on their home exchange. The reason is simple – the USA is where the big investment money is. A foreign company that is fully listed in the USA has to jump through the same hoops, and provide the same information, as a domestic American firm, which is reassuring to investors. There is also a class of security in the USA called the American Depositary Receipt, or ADR. Here is how ADRs work.

A major bank purchases shares in foreign markets which are kept on deposit by a custodian bank in the company's home country. The bank then sells ADRs which are evidence of the ownership of these shares. They are denominated in US dollars. In total there are over 1,600 companies listed in the USA under the ADR scheme from more than 60 countries. An ADR represents ownership in shares of a non-US company. The ADR holder usually receives the same benefits enjoyed by the ordinary shareholder in the company. Currently there are over 100 British companies with ADRs trading in the US including GlaxoSmithKline and Barclays Bank. ADRs may be listed on the NYSE, AMEX or NASDAQ.

The first ADR was created in 1927 by JP Morgan for Selfridges, the department store in London. Traditionally, the advantage of ADRs to Americans has been that they can purchase them on their home markets, rather than having to cope with the difficulties and uncertainties of opening accounts with foreign brokers. Until recently there were many foreign exchanges where outsiders were not allowed to invest, so ADRs were sometimes the only way for a private person to participate. Although today the trend is for stock exchanges across the world to abolish such barriers, there are still places, such as Russia and India, where it is simply too difficult, or too risky, to open a local account.

There are two main types of ADR:

■ Level I ADRs, which are traded on the 'over the counter' market. These require only minimal US regulation and are to be avoided unless you are an expert.

■ Level II and III ADRs are listed directly on the US securities exchanges and generally enjoy greater liquidity. Companies that have a listing for their ADRs must comply with the full registration and reporting requirements of the US Securities and Exchange Commission (SEC).

For investors in the UK, it can sometimes make sense to purchase a 'foreign' share – in other words, one that is not British or American – in its ADR form in the USA. There are a large number of ADRs available and there are now also newer variants, IDRs, EDRs and GDRs, which are sold on one or more international markets. Take a close look at the prices, though – ADRs and their variants often trade at a premium to the underlying share, which may be worthwhile because of their increased liquidity, or may simply reflect unwarranted investor enthusiasm.

You can find out more about ADRs at **www.adr.com**.

Stock indices

A stock index is a mathematical measurement of the performance of a number of shares as a group. Today, the most widely followed indices include:

- The Standard & Poor's 500 Index (S&P 500), which follows 500 shares quoted on the New York Stock Exchange, American Stock Exchange and the over-the-counter market in the USA. Dominated by stocks of large blue chip companies, the S&P 500 Index accounts for roughly three-quarters of all US stock market value. It provides a solid foundation for investing in US stocks.

- The Wilshire 5000 Total Market Index, an index of all regularly traded US common stocks. The Wilshire 4500 Completion Index, a subset of the Wilshire 5000 Total Market Index, excludes the stocks in the S&P 500 Index.

- The Russell 2000 Index covers small-capitalization stocks in the US.

- The FTSE 100 (Financial Times Stock Exchange 100 Share Index) measures 100 of the largest companies quoted in London and was introduced principally for options and futures trading.

- The FT-30 Share Index (also known as the Financial Times Ordinary Share Index) measures 30 blue chip companies quoted on the London stock market.

- The FT Actuaries Indices, which examine the performances of different industrial sectors so you can judge the relative performance of, say, shipping and energy.

- Morgan Stanley Capital International Europe, Australasia, Far East (MSCI EAFE) Index is the dominant standard for the major international markets.

■ The Morgan Stanley Capital International Select Emerging Markets Free Index consists of stocks in 15 countries – Argentina, Brazil, the Czech Republic, Greece, Hong Kong, Hungary, Indonesia, Israel, Mexico, the Philippines, Poland, Singapore, South Africa, Thailand, and Turkey.

There are many more indices, and they are a very helpful tool against which to compare the performance of individual companies. Anyone can run an index, and you may see obscure indices advertised by private investment firms.

In Chapter 5, stock market indices are shown to be extremely important in the analysis and measurement of the risks of investment. Indices provide strong evidence that shares are a good investment over the long term, and fund managers are always trying to get their funds to 'beat' the performance of the indices. There are even funds and portfolios that are tied to an index, and move up and down with it, the idea being to reduce risk. Investing in funds that 'track' the indices, by spreading money in the same proportions as the index uses to produce its measurements, is more popular in the USA than here, possibly because the realities of the risk/reward relationship are better understood there. The charges for index trackers are lower too, so for many people they are probably a better bet than other forms of collective investment.

In important stock markets, such as those of New York and London, most of the investing is done by pension funds, unit and investment trusts and insurance companies. Along with banks and building societies, they are known as the 'institutions'. Most of the money in these funds is owned indirectly by ordinary people so, in effect, the institutions are intermediaries. The funds are run by managers who decide how the money is invested. These managers are under enormous pressure to 'outperform' the averages of the market, as indicated by the market indices – this is principally because they want to do well in their personal careers, and the way to do well as a fund manager is to think in the short term and try to produce spectacular results. The net result is that most of these funds don't outperform the market. In fact, since they make up such a large proportion of the market's capital, one could say that they *are* the market, and can't outperform themselves – they are just too big.

Indices are constructed to provide a measuring point for portfolio comparisons, but they are more useful for assessing large funds than for individual shares. For instance, the FTSE 100 is rebased (adjusted) every three months – companies that have fallen below 100th in market capitalization are dropped, whilst those rising into the top 100 UK companies replace them. If an investor does not sell a share because it has dropped out of the index, the value of the portfolio declines, while the index advances.

Individual Savings Accounts (ISAs)

The Individual Savings Account (ISA) is a tax-free scheme designed by the government to encourage people to save. Like its predecessors, the PEP and the TESSA, it is likely to be tinkered with endlessly, so by the time you read this book, some of the rules and rates may have changed. For updates, check HM Revenue's website at: **http://www. hmrc.gov.uk.**

The reason for the scheme? ISAs are intended to encourage a wider range of people to save while modestly reducing the benefits for those who already did so during the PEP era.

> **ISAs are intended to encourage a wider range of people to save**

Since ISAs are a tax-sheltered scheme, if you don't pay tax in the UK, you don't need one. Most of us do pay tax, however, and despite the restrictions that ISAs impose, it will usually be worthwhile to have a scheme.

The principle of ISAs is simple – you put in your money, up to certain limits, and during its life it grows tax-free, which makes it grow much faster. You can have an ISA for cash, shares, bonds or insurance subject to certain restrictions.

You can invest less in an ISA than you could in the final version of the PEP scheme, but it is still attractive: for 2011/2012 you can invest up to £10,680, and this limit is likely to increase in subsequent years. Currently there are two types of ISA, one for cash, and one for stocks and shares. At the moment, the rules say that you cannot put more than £5,340 in a cash ISA, so you can either do this and put the remainder of the £10,680 into a stocks and shares ISA, or put the whole £10,680 into a stocks and shares ISA, or distribute the money between them in other proportions, so long as you don't exceed the limit for cash ISAs.

The tax advantages are not great, but still worthwhile for UK taxpayers:

■ income from investments is tax-free with the exception of income from UK dividends, which is subject to a 10 per cent tax credit

■ ISAs are free of capital gains tax.

ISAs are provided by approved financial services companies. You can withdraw money at any time without losing the tax relief you have already enjoyed. Some fixed term ISAs may impose a penalty for early withdrawal as may some life assurance schemes.

Permitted investments

For the cash component, you can invest in:

■ bank and building society accounts

■ units in authorized unit trust money market funds ('cash funds')

■ National Savings products that are specifically designed for ISAs.

For the stocks and shares component, you can invest in:

■ shares and company bonds listed on a recognized stock exchange anywhere in the world

■ gilt-edged securities ('gilts') and similar securities issued by governments of other countries in the European Economic Area

■ UK authorized unit trusts that invest in shares and securities

■ shares in UK open-ended investment companies (OEICs)

■ shares and securities in approved investment trusts (except for property investment trusts)

■ units or shares in Undertakings for Collective Investment in Transferable Securities (UCITS) funds based elsewhere in the European Union (these are similar to the UK authorized unit trusts and OEICs listed above).

For the life insurance component, you can invest in:

■ 'unit linked' or 'investment linked' policies

■ 'with profits' policies, where you share in the profits the insurer makes from investing your premiums. If the insurer makes such profits, a bonus is paid, normally annually.

Choosing a manager

The trouble with consumerism and investment is that they don't mix well. Consumerism is about selling one-size-fits-all products to mass markets, while successful investing is about pursuing a highly individual strategy. As a state-sponsored scheme, ISAs present investment managers with the challenge of providing products that will appeal to large numbers of people who are not investment-literate, while making profits for both themselves and their clients. The clients' profits often suffer.

Check if the ISA manager will charge for running your ISA, including any charges for withdrawals and transfers. CAT-standard ISAs have limits on charges (CAT stands for 'Charges, Access and Terms'; the CAT standards are voluntary, drawn up by the government and provide some assurance of a fair deal for customers). Some managers offer ISAs restricted to their company's own products while others offer a choice of their own and other companies' products.

When selecting an ISA, the two key points to remember are:

1 Check all charges and penalties and seek to keep them as low as possible.

2 Check all restrictions on transfers, choice of investment, withdrawals and so on. Ideally you should choose ISAs which give you the widest choices at the lowest cost.

ISAs cover a broad range of investments, not only shares, and are intended to provide something for everyone, but in the case of shares, self-select ISAs (see below) may be the most attractive.

As we will see later (page 109), there is evidence that investment managers are not superior in their ability to choose winning share portfolios, so experienced investors tend to question the value of being charged fees by managers to do something which they might do as well, or better, themselves.

Transfers

If you want to transfer the money you have put into your ISA in the current year, you must transfer all of it. If you do this, any more money you want to put in during the current year must go into the new ISA. You can also transfer some or all of the money you put into your ISA in earlier years. Some managers may not allow you to transfer part of your ISA. Your existing ISA manager will be able to tell you how much you can transfer.

Normally, you may transfer your ISA by applying to a new manager. The existing ISA manager may charge a penalty, or insist that you sell any existing ISA investments and transfer cash. ISA cash, savings and investments must always remain in the same component. For instance, you cannot move funds from a cash ISA with one manager to a stocks and shares ISA with another.

If you want to transfer the money you have put into your ISA in the current year, you must transfer all of it. Any extra money you contribute in the current year must go into the new ISA. You can also transfer some or all of the money you put into your ISA in earlier years, but some managers may not allow you to transfer only a part.

'Self-select' ISAs

'Self-select' ISAs are intended to give investors freedom from the restrictions imposed by providers' stock and share investments. This implies a degree of responsibility on the part of the investor, not least to trade judiciously, since every transaction on the stock market costs money. Some self-select ISAs have high charges, and all plans will have restrictions on the range of permitted investments. Self-select ISAs don't allow you to invest in life insurance, and most only offer the stocks and shares component.

You should check:

■ the investment restrictions

■ the charges

■ the capacity of the manager to cope with clients' demands. There is no point in investing with the cheapest provider if it transpires that they cannot administer the scheme efficiently because they are swamped by demand. The most common problem is that the manager does not answer the telephone during busy periods, but it is more serious if the manager makes errors in your portfolio records. This can escalate into a time-consuming nightmare, and is definitely to be avoided if possible!

A few self-select ISAs make an initial charge but most plans have an annual charge, usually based on a percentage of the value of your portfolio, expressed as a percentage charged per quarter with a minimum sum. You can expect this charge to range from 0.5 per cent to 1.5 per cent a year with a minimum of £25 to £50. Charges, apart from dealing costs, attract VAT.

Dealing costs are the price you pay for buying or selling shares. You do this through the manager. Normally there will be a minimum dealing charge, which will have a disproportionately large effect on small deals. Minimum dealing costs range from around £9 to £45, with maximum rates of between 0.9 per cent and 2 per cent. ISAs are not really intended for the very active trader – if you want to buy and sell shares every day, don't do it through an ISA.

There may also be charges for ad hoc portfolio valuations, annual reports and accounts, attending meetings, dividend collection and transfers. In the case of annual reports, you can obtain them free from the relevant company's registrar, or, often, from the internet. You can value your portfolio yourself if you keep records of your holdings, and few people have the time to attend company meetings, so you should be able to avoid most of these charges.

The outlook for ISAs

With very long-term growth of equity investments averaging less than 6 per cent annually, reducing the tax-bite will have a positive effect on your returns, even if you are being skinned alive by managers' charges. In the medium term (say, 10 years), future governments may introduce better schemes or improve ISAs.

❝don't expect to buy and sell shares within an ISA frequently❞

Use ISAs to save and to invest in blue chip companies that are unlikely to go bust. Don't expect to buy and sell shares within an ISA frequently – many people find that they only deal once or twice a year. As we will see later, there is substantial evidence that infrequent trading helps to improve your returns.

Investing in an ISA depends on how optimistic you are about the performance of your investments and how much you are investing. If you think that the annual capital gains tax (CGT) exemption might not be enough to cover your capital gains, then you should make use of an ISA. For instance, if you are saving to repay a mortgage, it wouldn't do you much good if you had to pay CGT when cashing in your investments at the end of your 25-year term. However, this only helps if you would be liable for CGT outside the ISA.

If you are still unsure whether or not you need an ISA, remember that your investment plan should come first. Decide on a detailed medium- to long-term investment plan. This might be simply to pay £100 a month into a UK fund for the next five years, or it could be a much more elaborate scheme involving investments in different countries and asset types. Once you have a clear idea what you want to do, then see if the plan can be made to work through an ISA, and if it will be efficient to do so. In some cases you will find that there are no ISA providers offering a scheme to suit your needs, or else that their charges and restrictions outweigh the tax advantages. More often, investors will take advantage of ISAs for some of their more simple UK-based investments, but will also make other investments outside the scheme.

Summary

Shares as a class are probably the best performers of all financial assets in the long term, but they are volatile, which means that the prices of individual shares – and whole markets – go up and down unpredictably and dramatically in the short to medium term. The stock markets are fundamental to the functioning of the world's big businesses, because they provide a way for people with some money – that's you and me, as well as big time investors – to put it in a business that can use it productively to make profits. If you own shares, you are a part-owner of the company that issued the shares, and the company has many heavy obligations towards you, including reporting its performance fully so that you know what is going on (see page 84).

Many investors find that the hard work of managing individual shares isn't for them, and prefer to invest in collective investment funds, such as unit trusts, that do the work for them. Collective investment funds are not all the same, and you do need to select and monitor them carefully. One way to do this is to compare them against an appropriate share index, which is an indicator of the performance of a specified group of shares, such as the top 100 UK companies (the FTSE 100). UK taxpayers should consider taking advantage of the ISA schemes to invest in shares because of the tax advantages that ISAs offer.

After having looked at the basics of shares, in the next chapter we will consider another very important type of financial asset, bonds. As we will see, bonds have very different characteristics from shares, and investors use them to achieve a different set of financial objectives.

3

Bonds

A bond is an IOU issued by a government, local authority or a company in return for the loan of cash the investor is making. In most cases, a fixed rate of interest is payable to the bond holder (the investor), and the bond issuer promises to pay back the amount borrowed (the face value of the bond) at a certain time in the future. This is different from investing in shares because you do not buy any share of the ownership of the lender. Another important difference is that bonds are generally issued for a fixed period of time, and the money you have lent is repaid in full at the 'par value' when the term of borrowing expires.

In the UK, bonds are traditionally called 'stocks' and equities are called 'shares'; in the USA, fixed-interest securities are called 'bonds' and equities, 'stocks'. It is worth noting that a lot of new financial products are being described as 'bonds' (for example, certain structured products, see Chapter 7) when in fact they bear little relation to the bonds described here.

In this chapter we will look at:

- Bonds for guerrillas

- The market for bonds

- Rating bonds

- Gilts

■ The other risks of bonds

■ The varieties of bonds

■ Auctioning new issues

■ Understanding yields

■ How to use bonds

Key terms

Par value – this is the value of the bond when it was issued (the face value). Par values vary considerably, and some bonds are issued for very large sums to attract institutional investors.

Maturity date – the day the bond expires

Yield – the total return you make on the bond

Bonds for guerrillas – using bonds for specific goals

Bonds are also known as fixed-income securities. They usually pay a fixed amount of interest twice a year until they expire. This feature – a very reliable cashflow – can be a powerful tool in controlling your finances, for example if you have a commitment, such as school fees, that you will have to fund at some point in the future. Top-grade government bonds usually offer a better interest rate than a bank deposit, but on average will not perform as well as shares in the long term.

Why buy bonds? The principal reasons are:

■ to put aside a large sum of cash to fund a particular objective in the future

■ to be sure of a regular income for a number of years

■ to diversify your assets and reduce the volatility of your returns.

In the very long term, bonds are not a good place to park a very large proportion of your assets for the simple reason that they do not produce a good return in real terms (i.e. after taking inflation into account)

over the long term. In the UK, the average annual real return for bonds has been 1.3 per cent[1] since 1900, and for many European countries they actually produced a negative return between the First World War and the 1990s. Bonds depend upon the longevity and strength of the borrowers (the bond issuers), and although governments are generally perceived as being secure borrowers, a little reflection on the upheavals of the twentieth century will remind us that this has not always been the case. In the 'Forsyte Saga' novels by John Galsworthy, the Victorian upper classes are depicted as keeping their wealth almost entirely in British government bonds because they think shares are too risky and they believe that the return on bonds will be enough to live on. Jane Austen, too, seems to have thought of government bonds as the best investment in her novel *Pride and Prejudice*, published in 1813. The times and economic conditions have changed, and few modern investors would agree with them in today's market!

So, bonds are best seen as a tool for specific purposes, and not as the answer to protecting your wealth and providing you with a good income in your retirement. To understand more about how useful they are as a tool, let's look at the following example:

Example: A roof fund

Jane has a thatched cottage, and she knows that within five to seven years she will have to pay for a new roof. She thinks this will cost about £50,000. Luckily, she has the money, but she decides not to put it into shares in case there is a market drop just when she needs to fix the roof. Instead, she buys 'zero-coupon' bonds (see page 74) which accumulate the interest until they mature in five years' time. The price of the bonds is discounted to reflect the interest accumulation, so Jane pays less than £40,000 for the bonds. When the bonds mature in five years' time, she will receive £50,000. With zero-coupon bonds, therefore, you don't receive payments of interest during the life of the bond – instead, you pay a much lower price for the bond initially than you will receive at maturity. Zero-coupon bonds are useful when you don't need a stream of interest payments, but just a lump sum at a future date. Remember, though, that you may have to pay tax on the interest you receive.

---

[1] Elroy Dimson, Paul Marsh and Mike Staunton, Credit Suisse Global Investment Returns Sourcebook 2010

The market for bonds

In most cases, you can sell a bond in the market any time before it matures. This is a useful characteristic, since it makes it a highly liquid asset, but it also carries a risk: because the coupon rate (interest rate) was fixed at the time the bond was originally issued, if interest rates have changed, the bond will change in value.

Although you can be quite certain of your total returns if you hold your bond to maturity, since your lender will repay you the par value at that time, you cannot be sure of the price of a bond in the market. If interest rates move higher than the coupon rate, the value of the bond will be lower, and if interest rates are dropping, the bond's value will rise.

At the time of writing, interest rates have been low for a long time but may start rising soon, which suggests that the market value for bonds could drop in the medium term. If you are buying bonds to hold until they mature, remember, this problem will not affect you.

How to use yields

The main way of assessing and comparing bonds is to calculate their yields. There are several types, as outlined below.

Nominal yield, or 'coupon rate'

The fixed interest rate given on the bond certificate. A bond with a coupon rate of 5 per cent will pay 5 per cent interest annually (often in staged payments every six months).

The current yield, or 'interest yield'

Suppose you buy a bond in the market; the price has changed from the par value, so how can you figure out the yield? The current yield, which is the coupon rate divided by the market price, gives you the figure.

Example

> For example, you buy a bond with a coupon of 20 per cent and a face value of £200, and you pay £180. What is the current yield?
>
> $20.00 \div 180 = 0.1010$
>
> The current yield is 10.1 per cent. Remember, the current yield varies according to changes in the market value of the bond, which are driven by interest rates.

The yield to maturity or 'redemption yield'

This is the total return you receive if you hold a bond to maturity, accounting for the market price, the coupon and the years remaining until the bond matures. It also makes the assumption that you are able to reinvest the interest you receive elsewhere at the same rate.

If you are buying bonds you will not need to calculate the yields yourself – they are widely published in the financial press and your broker or financial adviser will be able to give you the figures.

Avoid the highest yields?

❝bond investors are not aiming to make high returns❞

As mentioned earlier, bond investors are not aiming to make high returns; they are aiming to make highly predictable returns. Bonds will usually generate better returns than cash deposits at a bank or building society, but they are nevertheless not very exciting results. This makes some bond investors restless and dissatisfied, and leads them to search for higher yields. In essence, high yields carry higher risk, often much higher risk, so this is not generally a wise move for a private investor: high yielding bonds may carry a much higher risk of default.

Although bonds are well regulated internationally, there is still a risk of default – in 1998, for example the government of Russia defaulted on its bonds and did not repay the money to the bondholders. While most of the investors were institutional, and so were presumably more able to cope with this setback, private investors do not need this kind of problem, so stick to high-grade bonds.

How do you know if a bond is high grade? You use one of the rating systems (see the next section). These are rating systems which assess the risk that a bond issuer may be unable or unwilling to pay the debt or the interest, and investors should always check a bond's rating before purchasing. Although rating systems are generally good, there have occasionally been nasty surprises, especially in the area of corporate bonds, which are bonds issued by companies. You may recall the collapse of the corporate giants WorldCom and Enron a few years ago (for more details, see Chapter 8); in these cases, the bonds that the two companies had issued were rated as high grade right up until the moment that the companies collapsed amidst allegations of false accounting.

For the average UK investor, the moral of the story is probably either to stick to British government bonds, known as gilts, which have never defaulted, or to special investment funds that hold a broad portfolio of government and corporate bonds.

For more on the different kinds of risk associated with bonds, see page 81.

Rating bonds

A bond's rating is especially important if you are investing in corporate bonds or in government bonds issued by countries that have only recently entered the market, and if you may sell them before they reach maturity. The three main rating companies, Moody's, Standard & Poor's and Fitch, all make independent assessments of how creditworthy a bond issuer is and rate accordingly. In general, however, they agree with each other on the rating, and may change it if the issuer's situation changes. You should be aware, though, that in recent years the ratings agencies have come under a lot of criticism. It has been alleged that their relationships with certain major financial institutions and corporations have been overly cosy, and that they have sometimes not downgraded their ratings as quickly as they should have done. This is an issue for corporate bonds, but should not matter if you are concentrating on UK gilts. See Chapter 13 for more details.

Bond credit ratings (investment grade)

Standard & Poor's	Moody's	Fitch
AAA	Aaa	AAA
AA+	Aa1	AA+
AA	Aa2	AA
AA−	Aa3	AA−
A+	A1	A+
A	A2	A
A−	A3	A−
BBB+	Baa1	BBB+
BBB	Baa2	BBB
BBB−	Baa3	BBB−

In general, a private investor, even an adventurous one, should stick to bonds whose ratings appear in the table above – 'investment grade' means they probably won't default – and preferably to bonds higher than AA−. However, as mentioned earlier, bonds that have lower ratings than BBB− are to be avoided, although they may offer better yields.

Until 1980, most of the developing countries were not able to issue bonds internationally. Since then there has been an explosion in the number of countries that issue bonds and, as you might expect, there have been a number of defaults, particularly on interest payments.

Some Asia-Pacific government bonds are not investment grade. A bond fund may mitigate the risk through diversification, but a fund that only invests in the government bonds of a risky country will be fully exposed to the default potential. Although it is rare for a government to default on its bonds, it can and does happen occasionally. The risk is not only that the issuer may not repay the loan on maturity, but also that it may suspend interest payments. Most of these problems have been fairly minor – Peru failed to make its coupon payments for 30 days in 2000, for example – but as mentioned earlier, there have been one or two serious defaults, such as Russia, which is thought to have eventually settled its debts for less than 20p in the pound. According to Moody's, all the countries that have defaulted in any way since 1985 were rated at B1 or less for a year or more before they defaulted, which, for all but the specialist, is surely a good argument for staying with the best rated bonds.

At the time of writing (early 2011), there is talk of the possibility of some major government bond defaults. Strong economies who have their hands relatively free, like the USA and the UK (yes, the UK still has a strong economy compared with most countries in the world) are unlikely to do this for two reasons: first, they have the option to print money, which has the effect of inflating away their debt, and second, it would be very bad business to default, since people would not trust them enough to buy their bonds again. Nevertheless, we should never say 'never' when trying to forecast the future. As is discussed in Chapter 13, some of the EU member states that are members of the eurozone (i.e. they have the euro as their currency) are also in trouble, and since they are not in a position to print money because of euro-zone rules, there are fears that they could default on bond payments. In January 2011 the International Monetary Fund (IMF) warned that many other countries too, including Brazil and Japan, could be at risk of defaulting on their bonds. Perversely, the prospect of a worldwide sovereign debt crisis is a little reassuring, since it makes it more likely that the rich nations will work together to restructure the debts and avoid financial chaos. As always, time will tell; by the time you read this, the potential crisis may have been averted.

Gilts

For UK investors, playing safe usually means sticking to gilts. 'Gilts' or 'gilt-edged securities' are bonds issued by the British government. They get their name from their reputation for a very high degree of safety. It is thought, justifiably, that if you lend the British government

> **" for UK investors, playing safe usually means sticking to gilts "**

money by buying gilts, it is extremely unlikely that it will default on the loan. The British government has issued gilts for hundreds of years without ever having failed to meet payments on the due dates. About two-thirds of the British national debt is funded by the issuance of gilts; at times, it has been as high as 80 per cent.

Gilts are issued either for a fixed length of time, such as five years, or, more unusually, for an indefinite period. They pay interest half-yearly, and repay the capital at the end of the bond's life.

The return on gilts is generally lower than you can get by investing in more risky propositions, such as shares, but is often better than the interest rate you can get by simply keeping your money in a bank or building society. You can hold gilts in an ISA, thus sheltering them from tax. Most gilts are very liquid, meaning that they are easily bought and sold.

The best way to buy gilts?

You buy gilts through a stockbroker or directly from the government's Debt Management Office (DMO). The DMO has a 'purchase and sale service', which probably offers the cheapest means of buying gilts, but cannot give investment advice.

You can find out everything you ever wanted to know about gilts at the DMO's website at: **http://www.dmo.gov.uk.**

The other risks of bonds

The most important risk of investing in bonds is the risk of default, but there are some other risks that you should also be aware of, especially if you are not sure you are going to hold the bonds to maturity. In general these apply mainly to corporate and foreign bonds, so most UK investors need not be overly concerned if they are sticking to gilts. The risks are:

■ Foreign currency – if you buy a bond denominated in a foreign currency, the exchange rate may go against you. If, however, you have a known future expenditure in a foreign currency – let's say, you are going to put a new roof on your Spanish villa in seven years' time – then it could make sense to buy Spanish bonds, currently denominated in euros, with the money you have earmarked for the roof.

■ Inflation – don't forget that when inflation rises, the true value of the bond and its coupon payments will sink.

■ Interest rates – as we have already seen, when interest rates rise and fall, the market value of the bond changes, so if you are selling before maturity, you could make a gain or a loss.

■ Liquidity – sometimes there are financial crises and no one will buy your bonds at a fair price (this only applies to bonds being sold before maturity). Suppose there has been a banking disaster in the bond issuer's country, for instance, and all foreign investors have panicked. In such cases, you may have to wait a while before you can sell the bond in the market.

■ Sovereign risk – this is the risk that the government of the bond issuer's country suddenly moves the economic goalposts in a way that affects bondholders. For instance, it might suddenly introduce exchange controls to prevent you from bringing the money home when you sell the bond. This can cause heavy losses.

■ Intermediaries – some dishonest firms have, in the past, offered attractive package deals on bonds but have cheated their customers.

case study   **The Barlow Clowes scandal – how a certain kind of punter is exploited**

If you've ever heard of the Barlow Clowes affair in the 1980s, you may be wondering why gilts are said to be so safe, when thousands of people who invested in gilts through Barlow Clowes narrowly escaped losing their life-savings when the firm collapsed and two of its directors were jailed for theft. The point is that gilts are safe – it's the intermediaries who may not be. Many of the victims of Barlow Clowes had invested through financial intermediaries, creating two unnecessary layers between themselves and the dealers. It is a classic example of how investors can get caught by believing printed lies: it seemed so unlikely that a company would actually dare to make false statements in their literature and on consumer radio programmes on the BBC that investors assumed that it must be alright. The then Department of Trade and Industry's role in the affair was far from glorious – it knew about irregularities with Barlow Clowes for years before the collapse, and did nothing.

▶

▶

> Low-risk, low-return investments have a great appeal to inexperienced investors who are afraid of losing money and are paralysed by the apparent complexities of the investment world. This type of investor can be persuaded to purchase by emphasizing safety above all other qualities – but they may be paying too high a premium for this safety. Safety, like any other investment characteristic, has its fair price.
>
> Dishonest firms can sell 'scaredy-cat' investors overpriced products by disguising the charges. After a while, the investors start to itch for better returns. This is what Barlow Clowes exploited: the desire of people who want to have their cake and eat it by having a low-risk/ higher-return investment. There is rarely such a thing widely available in the markets, since risk is correlated to reward. In general, the more risk you take, the more chance you have of a better return. Bonds, being generally low-risk investments, do not often give high returns.
>
> To paraphrase Gertrude Stein, 'a bond is a bond is a bond'. In current market conditions, and in the long term generally, you are not going to make a better return on them than you can on equities without taking on more risk, such as buying very low-grade corporate bonds. There are going rates of return for bonds – if someone offers you a significantly better rate of return than is generally available elsewhere, be very, very sure that you understand exactly how they are able to achieve this. They may have no intention of keeping their promises!

The varieties of bonds

Bonds come in many different shapes and sizes, and it is worth getting to know the basic differences.

Index-linked gilts

These pay a rate of interest linked to the official inflation figures and the face value of the bond is adjusted for inflation when it is repaid. If you buy such a bond for its face value and keep it to redemption, you are therefore guaranteed to make a profit in real terms.

Undated bonds

Some gilts have no redemption date; the government simply goes on paying the interest for ever, unless it chooses to redeem. Others have a range of years (e.g. 2010–2015) within which the government can decide to redeem the gilt at any point. Others give a redemption date followed by the words 'or after' (e.g. '2010 or after'), meaning that the government can choose when it wants to redeem the gilt at any time after the redemption date.

Convertible bonds

Convertible bonds are usually issued by companies rather than governments, and offer the investor the chance to exchange bonds at some pre-agreed time for shares in the issuing company. Whether this is worth doing depends upon the market value of the shares when you convert. Obviously, if the shares have gone up you will make a capital gain by converting to shares and then selling them. The price of these bonds usually rises and falls with the share price, but at a lower rate. Usually the price at which you can convert to shares is set higher than the market price of the shares when the bonds are issued. Convertibles tend to be less sensitive to interest rate changes than normal bonds. Convertibles are usually sensitive to changes in the company's share price.

Debentures

Companies often issue debentures, which are an agreement to pay the interest – and repay the capital – out of the future earnings of the company. The bond is not secured on the fixed assets of the company, such as buildings, which are arguably less risky.

Asset-backed bonds

This is where the company offers the security of a specified asset it owns. If it cannot pay, the asset will be sold and the bondholders repaid.

Callable bonds

These bonds give the issuer the option to repay the bond early, and in return generally offer a higher rate of interest (the coupon rate). If the issuer does redeem the bond early, the chances are that it will be at a time when interest rates are lower and so the investors will have to buy bonds at a lower coupon rate.

Zero-coupon bonds

These pay none of the interest until the bond matures, and are usually priced at a discount to the value that will be paid at maturity to reflect this. In high-tax countries like the UK, they are generally thought to be unattractive, but can be useful if you have business in a low-tax jurisdiction.

Structured notes

These are not bonds, but look as if they are; a recent development, they are packaged products based on derivatives. Their benefits are generally for wealthy investors with plenty of cash to spare. See Chapter 7, page 161 for more details.

Ex dividend and cum dividend

Interest on bonds is usually paid every six months, so when you buy a bond in the market you will want to know if a dividend is just about to be paid. Approximately five weeks before the interest is paid the bond is declared to be 'ex dividend', meaning that if you buy it, the seller keeps the imminent dividend and the first dividend that you receive will be the subsequent one – this is indicated in the financial pages by 'xd'. Ex dividend bonds are cheaper than 'cum dividend' (meaning 'with dividend') bonds to compensate for the longer wait for the first dividend. Cum dividend bonds require the purchaser to pay for the 'accrued interest' since the last time the interest was paid.

So what kind of bond should you buy? It all depends on your individual circumstances, how much money you have in total, and your specific goals in holding the bond. Also, different bonds represent better or worse value at different times, so it is generally best to get advice from a broker or financial adviser just before you make a purchase.

Auctioning new issues

When a state body or a company wants to borrow money by selling bonds, it 'brings an issue'. In the USA, the government issues bonds to a regular timetable using the auction method. Individuals can obtain a tender form from a bank and apply for the bonds (usually Treasury bills which have a life of a year or less) at a set price, enclosing a cheque. Private individuals are classed as 'non-competitive bidders'. What happens is that institutions bid for large amounts of the bonds, at any price they choose, but usually quite close to the set price of $10,000 per bond. The US Treasury then accepts the highest bids to fulfil its quota and takes the average price of the accepted bids as the price to the non-competitive bidders, who are then refunded the difference between the average of the accepted bids and the price they paid when they applied for the bonds. In the UK, the practice of auctioning government securities has been adopted relatively recently, and purchasers don't know what kind of bond will be offered until about a week before the auction.

The price of bonds

The price of a bond varies according to macro-economic factors, of which inflation is the most important. If the interest rate in the market goes higher than the interest rate payable on a bond, the price you can get if you sell the bond goes down. Conversely, if the market interest rates go below a bond's interest rate, you can sell the bond for more than its face value.

Every day information on bonds is published in the *Financial Times* and elsewhere; you are given the current market price of the bond (which is usually different from its face value), the high and low of the market price in the current year (which gives you an idea of its volatility), and then two figures for 'yields'. Market prices quoted are the middle of the bid/offer spread, as with shares. The 'interest yield' simply tells you what percentage of your money you would get if you bought the bonds at the current market price. It is a simple calculation:

Example

> Suppose the bond in question is 'Treasury 7 ¼ pc 2014': the 7 ¼ pc is the coupon rate
> for the bond, '2014' is the year when the government pays back the capital invested.
> Since you must buy the gilt for a price different from its face value, the 7 ¼ pc coupon
> does not tell you the interest rate you are getting. Let's say the market price is 102.88.
> You divide the coupon by the market price and multiply the result by 100:
>
> $(7.25 \div 102.188) \times 100 = 7.1$ per cent
>
> 7.1 per cent is the interest rate, or interest yield, that you will get at the moment.
> Since the market price is higher than the face value of the bond, its interest yield is
> lower than its coupon, and if the market price rises, the yield will go even lower.

Understanding yields

ff the yield is the crux of bond investing JJ

The yield is the crux of bond investing, because it is the tool you use to measure the return of one bond against another. It enables you to make informed decisions about which bond to buy.

As we have seen, the interest yield, or 'current' yield is the rate of return on your bond investment but it is not fixed, like a bond's stated interest rate. It changes to reflect the price movements in a bond caused by fluctuating interest rates.

To pick the best deal available between comparable bonds (remember that company bonds are more risky than gilts, so you would expect a better rate on them in compensation), it is better to use the 'redemption yield', or 'yield to maturity', which is also given in the financial pages.

Redemption yield

The redemption yield tries to account for the difference between the price you pay for the bond and what you will get for it on redemption, plus any capital gain you will realize (if you purchase the bond below par) or minus any capital loss you will suffer (if you purchase the bond above par). It also includes all the interest you will earn. It's a complicated sum that in practice is not worth calculating yourself, so you can just look up the redemption yield in the *Financial Times*. In principle, it works as follows:

Example

Annie buys a 10 per cent bond with a face value of £100 in the year 2015 for £111.11 because the current interest rate is 9 per cent. The term of the bond ends in four years' time in 2019 for £100.

Annie will make a capital loss of £11.11 if she holds the bond to redemption, which results from the difference between the price she paid (£111.11) and the face value (£100).

Step 1. Dividing the loss by the number of years left to run:

11.11 ÷ 4 = 2.78

£2.78 is the amount of capital loss per year.

Step 2. Annie calculates what percentage £2.78 is of £111.11, the price she paid for the bond:

£2.78 ÷ 111.11 × 100 = 2.5 per cent

Step 3. At the time of purchase, interest rates were at 9 per cent, so the interest yield is:

Coupon ÷ market price × 100

10 ÷ 111.11 × 100 = 9

Step 4. Annie works out the approximate redemption yield by subtracting the annual percentage of capital loss (see Step 1) from the interest yield (see Step 3):

9 – 2.5 = 6.5

Annie now knows that the redemption yield is roughly 6.5 per cent. It is only approximate because it doesn't take compound interest into account, so Annie looks up the published redemption yield in the financial press to get an exact figure.

Redemption yields are useful for comparisons, but they don't remove all uncertainty, since the underlying market prices on which they are based will fluctuate, and the figures only tell you what return you would get if you held the bond to redemption, not what will happen if you sell before.

When comparing the redemption yields, say of different gilts, you will notice that some are higher than others. Usually, the longer that the gilt has to run, the higher the redemption yield because investors expect a reward for tying up their money for a longer time. Another reason is that different countries will have different economic outlooks, and market expectations will affect the yield. This effect is called the 'normal yield curve' and is usual when interest rates are relatively low (Figure 3.1).

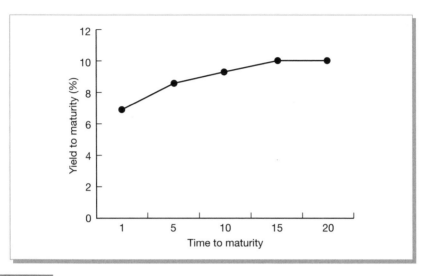

Figure 3.1   The normal yield curve

Since the price of bonds fluctuate in the market, the yields curves do too – they can vary by as much as 5 per cent during a typical year.

When there is uncertainty about interest rates, the market distorts the normal yield curve both by trying to guess what long-term interest rates will be and also by moving in and out of bonds in response to changes in interest rates elsewhere. Banks mainly buy short-term bonds ('shorts'), while the institutions tend to buy long-term ones ('longs'), leaving medium-term bonds (5–15 years) out in the cold, which can cause them to have a better yield than longs. When short-term interest rates are up, yields on short-term bonds improve. Uncertainty about interest rates can cause longs to have lower yields than the shorts, in which case the yield curve is inverted.

Figure 3.2 shows what can happen when there is uncertainty about interest rates. The hump in the curve over 10-year bonds indicates that they give a better yield than longs, reflecting their unpopularity. This can happen when interest rates are high but are expected to drop.

Sometimes the opposite happens and short-term interest rates are relatively higher than long-term rates. In this case, the yield curve changes to a 'downward-sloping' curve (Figure 3.3).

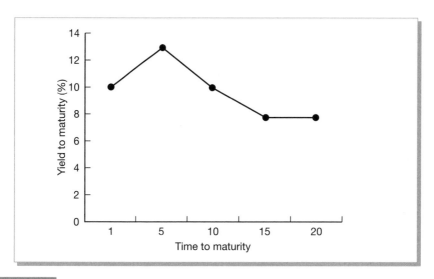

Figure 3.2   An inverted yield curve

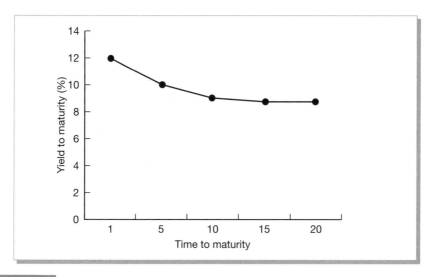

Figure 3.3   A downward-sloping yield curve

If you are a keen bond investor – as many retired people are – you can use yield curves to get a good sense of what market conditions are like for any type of bond you are interested in.

Bonds and ISAs

For UK taxpayers, interest on bonds is taxed at the rate of your tax band (see Chapter 12). In cases where you receive all the interest in one year (usually when the bond expires), this could affect your tax band, so it is worth doing some forward planning to take this into account. Is it worth using an ISA? It depends upon your tax status and your goals in purchasing bonds. The current ISA limit (for 2011–2012) is £10,340, so for instance if you are intending to use bonds to save for the purchase of an expensive new roof at a fixed time in the future, you might have to stagger your purchases to use up your annual ISA limits, or else not be able to keep all the bonds within the ISA.

Summary

The great thing about bonds is that they are predictable, and this, if you are reasonably affluent, allows you to manage your cashflow over the medium to long term. Like all other investments there are risks, and you can significantly increase these risks, either inadvertently or intentionally, by investing in certain types of bond. For example, you could choose to put all your money into, say, the bonds of a foreign government that is currently in default; you might make a profit if the government paid its debt, but this would be a big risk. Beware of investment schemes that seem to be based on bonds, but are really based on complicated derivatives (see Chapter 7) – they may not be as safe as they seem.

For private investors, the big danger is often the frustration they feel at the relatively low returns of bonds, which leads some people to invest in riskier fixed income schemes. Many people, especially when they are retired, see the interest they receive from bonds as something separate from the capital, to be creamed off as a nice little earner. By all means use investment income for daily expenses if you must, or if you can afford to, but don't imagine that this is going to make you richer – it could make you a lot poorer. At the end of a bond's term, the capital sum is returned, but its buying power will have shrunk through inflation. Perhaps the worst case of this in the twentieth century was in the 1920s, when respectable German widows literally starved to death as the value of their bonds were inflated away during the galloping Weimar hyper-inflation, when cash became virtually worthless. In such circumstances, you need to move your wealth into a different asset class fast to stop any further loss.

Perhaps such horrors couldn't happen here, but spending the interest from a bond is a way to use the law of compound *depreciation*, causing your assets to dissolve over the long term. Remember that the main financial characteristics of high quality bonds are:

- High liquidity – you can sell them very quickly, except for certain products.

- A fixed interest rate – useful in a world of fluctuating rates.

- Low risk – major governments pay their debts, mostly. The British government has never defaulted on gilts, although arguably it has pulled a few fast ones, like getting patriotic people to buy undated War Loans during the First World War. 'Undated' means 'I don't have to pay you back unless I feel like it, and if I ever do, it will be after inflation has made the bond worthless'.

- Low returns – you get the interest plus the chance of a small capital gain if you sell the bond in certain market conditions.

- Inflation risk – except for index-linked bonds, if you keep a bond to redemption, inflation may have reduced the value of the capital invested plus the interest earned. This risk is much greater on long-term bonds.

If you buy a bond just before market interest rates take a dive, you can make a substantial tax-free capital gain, as the market value of the bond will rise, but this doesn't happen very often. Buying bonds outside your own country in other currencies can be a good bet if you think the value of your own currency is falling. For those who don't want to become specialists in the field, bonds are basically safe and boring. You will have to keep a weather eye on the economy at all times if you hold long bonds unless you hold them to redemption, and even then you may find that inflation has taken a bite out of them.

The returns on safe, high-grade bonds are the best you can obtain at a low level of risk to maturity, and are probably best for most investors.

❛❛think of bonds as part of your asset allocation❜❜

Think of bonds as part of your asset allocation, functioning as ballast in your portfolio. Many advisers think that everyone should keep at least 30 per cent of their money in bonds, and much more if you are retired, but for younger people – say, under those 40 – there is a good argument for focusing exclusively on equities because they have a longer time horizon and therefore a better chance of seeing substantial capital growth.

In the next chapter we will turn to shares, which have very different investment characteristics from bonds, and examine the main issues and opportunities you should know about before entering the share markets.

4

Assessing companies – issues and opportunities

In this chapter we will look at some of the most important issues surrounding company accounts and management, and also at three points in the life of a company where the potential for profits or losses is especially high. Most new investors are not familiar with business, and it takes years of study and experience to really be able to read between the lines of company accounts, so this chapter will focus on the general principles and problems rather than going into great detail about financial analysis. (For a list of excellent books that provide this information see the further reading section at the end of this book).

This chapter covers:

- Financial statements

- Corporate governance

- Investment opportunities – new issues

- Investment opportunities – mergers and acquisitions

- When companies get into trouble

Why do companies issue shares?

As we saw in Chapter 2, large corporations have good access to the capital markets, and therefore have considerable freedom of choice in how they raise the money they need. Elaborate 'corporate finance' techniques have been developed in order to optimize the way in which a given company should raise capital, taking into account a very wide range of factors that could affect the decision, such as the cost of borrowing, the effect of taxation, and the effect on the ownership of the company. At its simplest, this problem can be described as a trade-off between borrowing (either by issuing bonds or by borrowing from an institution) and issuing shares to investors. However, in reality, the choices are much more complex.

When we, as investors, are examining a company that is coming to the stock market for the first time, or is already listed on a stock market but is now issuing more shares, we need to make a big effort to understand why it has chosen this method of raising capital rather than, say, borrowing the money from a bank. The company's stated reasons for the issue may not always give us the whole picture, so it is important to try to obtain independent expert opinions (for example, from analysts' reports).

As is argued throughout this book, most investors really are probably better off in the long term if they invest broadly in the market through funds, rather than trying to beat the market through dabbling in individual companies. A little knowledge is a dangerous thing, and some people can come badly unstuck by trying to outwit the market which, after all, contains tens of thousands of experienced professional investors who understand companies better than anyone else. Nevertheless, it is worth trying to gain some understanding of how companies present their financial information, and how they sometimes massage the figures to give a misleading impression.

Financial statements

The first thing to know about the financial statements that companies produce is that there is no single, generally accepted theory of how accounts should be reported. Financial statements produced in different industries and different countries may use very different accounting methods, and even two companies in the same industry may be very different in the way they approach their figures. This makes it very hard for investors and analysts to compare figures across firms and industries; you cannot just look at the profit and loss figures of, say, two mining companies, one in Canada and the other in Indonesia, and say, 'Aha! Company X is clearly more profitable than Company Y.' In order to make such a judgement, you need to know much more about the accounting rules in those countries and the methods by which the two firms arrived at their numbers.

Here are a few accounting principles that you should know about, that may sometimes give a hint of potential profits or problems:

- Historic cost – accountants usually prefer to value a company's fixed assets at the price that it originally paid for them, allowing for occasional revaluations. This can sometimes massively undervalue assets such as buildings and land.

- A conservative approach – managers tend to want to choose the most optimistic valuations in accounting, because they want to show that the company is growing. Accountants, on the other hand, tend to prefer the most pessimistic view. For example, when would you account for the sale of a product – when it was ordered by a customer, when it was invoiced, or when you received the money? These dates could be many months apart – or even years in some cases – so it could make a big difference to your profit figures. A manager might want to mark the sale as occurring as soon as the order was made, but an accountant might prefer to only call it a sale once the firm had received the money.

- Substance – there are lots of clever ways to hide company debts and profits, and some managers devote a lot of time to cooking up new schemes to do this. Basically, a firm wants to hide debts when it wants to look increasingly profitable, and it wants to hide profits when it wants to avoid tax. Accountants are supposed to see through all these clever tricks and prefer the 'substance' of such transactions over their 'form'.

- Accounting methods should be consistent – this is a very important issue. Companies that are constantly changing the dates of their accounting year, adopting new policies for the treatment of large items and so on may be doing so in order to hide something. They should explain the reasons for any major change carefully in the notes to the accounts, and these explanations should stand up to scrutiny. Consistent accounting policies are the only way outsiders can meaningfully compare one year's accounts with another's; sometimes a change is necessary, but a company that does this often may be attempting a fraud.

---

case study   **Recent accounting scandals: Satyam Computer Services**

Although accounting scandals in major listed firms are comparatively rare, they do occur, and it is unusual for two or three years to pass by without at least one major case of wrongdoing coming to light. Satyam is a large IT outsourcing firm (the fourth largest in India), which provides computer programming and similar services to many multinational corporations such as General Electric, Nestlé, and BP. It is listed on the New York Stock Exchange, and was widely regarded as one of the flagship companies for the rapidly modernizing Indian economy. In early 2009, Satyam's founder, Ramalinga Raju, suddenly announced to the board that the company had massively overstated its earnings and profits for several years, and had falsely claimed that it held some $1 billion in cash. The firm's share price crashed on the news, and Satyam was subsequently taken over by Mahindra Group. At the time of writing, investigations into what really happened are still continuing.

The moral of the story? Don't believe anyone who tells you that large companies never falsify their accounts!

A note on the 'Notes'

A company's financial statements usually come with extensive 'Notes' to explain them. Professional investors take the notes very seriously indeed, and often read them first. The notes should tell you about important matters such as what policies and practices the company uses in its accounts, what its tax liabilities are (these may be very complex for multinational companies) and details of share option schemes for employees and directors (which can affect profits significantly).

The auditor's report

The auditor's report is produced by an independent firm of accountants who check that the accounts have been properly produced and
that they are a fair and accurate report of the company's financial
performance. Every so often a huge firm is found to have managed to
obtain positive auditor's reports even though it was committing massive fraud (see Enron, page 174), but this is rare. The key thing to check
is whether the report is 'unqualified', which means that the auditors
are happy with the accounts, or if it is 'qualified' which means that the
auditors are worried about something. A qualified report is generally
a signal for the market to panic and for the firm's share price to drop
until some adequate explanation of what is going on emerges.

The balance sheet

A balance sheet provides a 'snapshot' of the liabilities and assets of a
company at a specified moment in time. In general, the company's
assets, which is what it owns, is listed on the left, and its liabilities, which includes its debts and the money that shareholders have
invested in the company, is listed on the right. The two totals must be
equal, or 'balance'.

One of the most important things to look out for in the balance sheet
is the firm's capitalization and depreciation policy:

- Capitalization is when you describe certain expenditures as investments (making them into assets) rather than just ordinary business
  expenses.

- Depreciation is how you account for the gradual reduction in value
  of assets in which you have invested – for example, if the firm buys
  a tractor for £100,000, it might knock £25,000 off its value as an
  asset over the next four years on the assumption that in four years'
  time it will need to be replaced.

An easy way to increase profit figures is to try to delay the recognition of capital investment for as long as possible, and then to try to
depreciate the value of the investment over as long a time period as
possible. The rules, of course, vary very widely between countries, and
it is genuinely astonishing what some countries allow their firms to
describe as 'assets'.

For analysts, the big issue is whether shareholders are really going to benefit from such investments that the company makes, and whether the company is trying to prop up its total value or its profitability by the capitalization and depreciation policies it uses.

The Profit and Loss statement

This should be the easiest statement to understand – it shows the profit or loss made by the firm during the period by subtracting what the company has spent from the income it has received. As always in accounting, things are not quite as they seem, and you will find that companies have very different definitions of what they regard as 'gross profit' or 'net income', for example, which makes it hard to compare the profitability of different companies.

The Profit and Loss account does not give you a detailed breakdown of the profitability of specific products and services, ostensibly because their competitors should not find this out. The best that can be said is that it provides some insight into the relative profitability of the company.

The cashflow statement

Some analysts like this statement the best because it tells you about how much cash is coming in and out of the company, and this is supposed to be harder to disguise. The aim is to check if the amount of cash the company holds is rising or falling. For instance, if the company's cash is falling and its stock holding is rising, this may indicate business problems that require explanation.

Newer companies often have negative cashflow, because they have to spend a lot of money before their customers pay them for the goods and services they are providing. Fast-growing companies also have problematic cashflows because they are selling more and more, and thus spending more and more, before they get paid for their increased sales. As with all financial analysis the aim is to strip out all the confusing definitions, which in this case entails trying to understand how much cash the company is generating that it can actually use to grow its business.

Accounting problems

The average investor doesn't get much of a look-in at shareholders' meetings, and it is difficult for the ordinary person to ask awkward questions about the accounts. This, you might think, is best left to the professionals, especially the large institutional investors, such as banks and investment funds, which own a lot of shares and have the expertise to investigate. These institutions have a lot of power over the firms they invest in and they are not afraid to use it, but this too can cause problems. In recent years, especially in the USA, there has been very strong pressure exerted by the institutions to force companies to improve their profitability; this, in some cases, has led to companies trying to massage the figures to produce the results that the institutions want.

Earnings management

In recent years, companies have been 'punished' for not meeting analysts' estimates of future profits by falling share prices. Firms that are worried about their share price have a strong incentive to 'manage' the earnings they report to give a good impression to the market. This may involve all kinds of techniques ranging from the slightly optimistic to the downright fraudulent. These often arise from 'problems' that aren't really the company's fault, such as a sudden one-off surge in sales which the company may try to smooth out into other accounting periods so that the market does not demand that it produces increased sales figures every time. The market likes stable growth, but the reality of business is that it often is not very stable, so many managers feel justified in manipulating the figures to some extent.

Corporate governance

Corporate governance refers to the process of ensuring that companies are managed honestly and in the best interests of their shareholders, customers, suppliers and the public at large. Financial deregulation across the world has increased interest in corporate governance, and everywhere you look efforts are being made to introduce codes of practice, legislation and supervision to ensure that companies behave more honestly than ever before. It is something of a pious dream, because businesspeople ultimately are in tough competition to make profits, and some of them will cut corners if they have the opportunity to do so.

The main worry for investors is whether a firm is really treating its shareholders fairly. Here are some typical contraventions of good corporate governance that have been occurring around the world during the last few years.

■ Keeping small shareholders out of the picture – this happens in subtle ways in the UK, but the really gross examples of this are in Japan, where many companies hold their annual meetings simultaneously, thus preventing shareholders from voting at more than one meeting.

■ Dilution of shareholding – this means issuing new shares that have the effect of reducing, or 'diluting', the value and voting power of the existing shares. In the USA in recent years this has been done by issuing massive amounts of new shares to executives as a bonus scheme, but it also occurs in other countries where insiders issue extra shares to themselves without anyone being able to stop them.

■ Creating new companies, sometimes registered charities, in other countries that are actually controlled by the firm. These entities have been used for 'off-balance sheet' transactions, for example to hide debts, by arranging deals that appear to be between unrelated parties but are in fact a smokescreen for fraud.

"properly run companies do tend to perform better in the long term" Investors should not worry too much, though, because there is evidence that properly run companies do tend to perform better in the long term; there is a lot to be said for being honest, even in business! Many large firms survive by operating honestly and focusing on stability – it is the newer firms, or the ones that have suddenly changed their fundamental strategies, that tend to be the ones that try to cut corners.

Since the banking crisis that began in 2007, a lot of attention has been given to the Basel Accords, a series of recommendations on banking governance and supervision that are produced by the Basel Committee on Banking Supervision (BCBS), an international group made up of central bankers from some 28 countries, including the USA, China,

Japan, UK, and other important economies. The latest version of its proposals, known as Basel III, aims to ensure that banks increase their capital reserves so that if they get into a mess again, they won't have to go to their governments to get help – in essence, it's an attempt to get rid of the 'too big to fail' ethos in the banking industry (see Chapter 13). A lot of bankers don't like Basel III because they believe that it will hit their potential profits, and are doing their best to get the measures watered down. But at a time when the public around the world are baying for bankers' blood, it seems likely that politicians will have to be a little tougher on the banking industry than they have been in the past.

Investment opportunities – new issues

When a privately-owned company is big enough, it has the option to offer some or all of its shares on the stock market in order to raise new money for expansion cheaply and, usually, so that the original investors can realize a big profit. The cost of making a 'new issue' is very high because the company must use specialized financial firms, such as investment banks, to conduct the process, and must spend a great deal on promoting and administering the issue process. There are several ways that companies can make new issues, but in this section we will focus on the one that private investors most often encounter, which is the 'offer for sale'.

If you remember the privatizations of nationalized industries in the UK during the 1980s and 1990s, you will recall that their initial share prices were pitched at a level that made it likely that investors would make a quick profit (and this was usually, but not always, successful). Not all new issues are like this: it all depends on market sentiment, and the share price may or may not rise in the months following the issue – there are usually no guarantees. The reason why the UK privatizations were different is that the government was making a political move; it wanted to take big industries such as British Rail out of the public sector in the belief that they would be more efficiently run if they were normal commercial organizations with shareholders that wanted to see a profit. As the 'owner' of these nationalized industries, the government was willing to sell them off relatively cheaply to encourage more investors to get involved in the stock market, and provided all kinds of incentives, like cheaper dealing fees, the ability to pay in instalments, and free shares to existing customers.

Now that the privatization boom is over, most new issues you encounter will be from commercial companies that do not offer such attractive deals. When considering investing in a new issue the first step is to obtain the new issue prospectus and read it carefully. You will then need to ask yourself the following questions:

1   What is the company going to do with the money it raises from selling off its shares? If more than 5 per cent is going to the original share-holders and another 5 per cent to the employees, it is probably not a good sign for new investors.

2   How much of the money raised will be spent on the costs of the new issue? These costs can be as high as 10 per cent – which, although staggering and excessive, is about the upper limit you should tolerate.

3   What will be the initial price of the new issue? The price is set in consultation between the company and its 'underwriters', which are financial institutions who promise the company to buy up all the unsold shares in the new issue. If no one buys the shares, the new issue is said to be a 'flop' and the underwriters are forced to buy the outstanding shares and dribble them onto the market slowly, usually selling at bad prices.

4   Do you understand the business and the accounts it provides in the prospectus? Does the business look as if it has a profitable future, given the initial share price?

5   What is the closing date for applications for shares? The closing date can be surprisingly short – sometimes only a few days – so you need to move quickly.

If you decide to invest and make your application on time, you have to wait to find out how many shares you will actually receive. This is because all the applications have to be totalled up, and if the demand is greater than the number of shares on offer (called 'oversubscrip-tion'), there are special rules on how the shares will be shared out. The way in which an oversubscribed issue is shared out varies from case to case, with some firms trying to make sure everyone gets a bit, and others trying to give all the shares to big institutions.

Oversubscription is fairly good news in the short term if you do manage to get some shares, because the share price is likely to rise for a while after market dealing starts. If an issue is undersubscribed, on the other hand, the price is likely to fall in the short term.

For guerrilla investors – the joys of stagging

'Stagging' is when you buy shares in a new issue with the intention of selling them, once market dealing begins, for a quick profit. It is one of the great sports of City professionals, and you often see long queues outside the application office (usually a bank in the City of London) on closing day of the application. The reason why 'stags' like to leave things to the last minute is because they have been watching the 'grey market' in the new shares to see how the price is likely to change once trading officially begins on the stock market. If they believe that the issue will do well and prices are likely to rise, they try to stag for a quick killing.

If you want to stag, you need to study the application form carefully to check the amount of shares you can apply for. For example, the rules may say you can apply for shares in amounts of 200 up to a limit of 1,000 shares, and then in amounts of 500 up to a limit of 5,000 shares, and finally in amounts of 1,000 shares above the 5,000 limit. If you apply for, say, 1,700 shares then you will get nothing, because you should have applied for either 1,500 or 1,000 shares to qualify.

Sometimes these cut-off points – the 1,000 and 5,000 limits – are used in deciding how shares are allocated in the case of an oversubscription. People who applied for large amounts of shares may be given proportionately more than people who applied for a small amount, but this does vary from issue to issue. Making multiple applications is cheating and you can be prosecuted for it, but you and your spouse and your children are all entitled to apply in their own names.

Stagging is fun if you like this kind of thing. The profits you make may not be very large, and you do risk being stuck with shares that don't rise for a long time after market dealing officially begins, so it is rarely, if ever, a sure thing. The main thing to watch out for is crazes; in the USA, for instance, there was a craze for 'Initial Public Offerings' (IPOs), which are a form of new issue, during the dotcom boom of the 1990s.

For a while every wacky internet company run out of someone's bed-room seemed to do well in its IPO, and lots of enthusiastic amateurs got involved in stagging. When the bottom fell out of the market, a lot of these overconfident stags lost a lot of money, so be careful and don't just assume every new issue will be a licence to print money.

At the time of writing (early 2011), the number of new issues has been relatively low for a number of years, owing to the financial crisis (most companies prefer to come to the market when it is booming, not drop-ping). For this reason, there haven't been many opportunities to stag. However, in 2010 a new China investment trust was launched by the well-known fund management group Fidelity, and attracted a lot of interest from stags. Shares opened at £1 when the fund was launched in April 2010, but wobbled down to 92p in late June. However, the price began to pick up again, and by late November 2010 it peaked at over 128p. So was it good for stags? Most stags want to sell immedi-ately, so the answer is no, but a stag with the patience to wait for a few months would have made a respectable profit.

Investment opportunities – mergers and acquisitions

❛❛acquisitions are generally good news for shareholders in the company that is being purchased❜❜

Companies have two ways to grow; either they can build their own existing businesses, or they can buy or merge with another com-pany. Acquisitions are generally good news for shareholders in the company that is being pur-chased because they are generally offered a price for their shares that is higher than the current market price. For this reason, it is worthwhile taking the trouble to understand as much as possible about this complex area.

'Mergers and acquisitions' (M&A) is a general term that covers quite a wide range of activities. These can be grouped as:

■ The acquisition of another company's assets – where a company buys some of the assets belonging to another company, which may include whole businesses, like a chain of newsagents, but does not buy the whole company.

■ Management buyouts (MBOs) – where the managers of a company buy the firm from its shareholders, and then, usually, take the company private. Leveraged buyouts (LBOs) are where such transactions are funded by debt; the purchasers in an LBO may be either managers or a group of other investors. The main problem with LBOs is often that the new company is burdened with a lot of new debt, because the purchasers have had to pay a high price; they are counting on being able to improve profits in order to pay this off, and they may not succeed.

■ Friendly mergers – where two companies merge into one new company with the full approval of the directors and a majority of the shareholders in both companies. This is generally done to rationalize their businesses and make them more profitable.

■ Unfriendly acquisitions – where a company buys enough shares in a target company to be able to force a takeover; this may involve the removal of the existing directors, and may be against their wishes and the wishes of the shareholders in the target company.

The word 'merger' is often used loosely as a euphemism for a takeover – in general, most mergers are really cases of one powerful company buying a less powerful one and taking it over.

Although shareholders in acquired companies generally do rather well out of the process, the same is not necessarily true for shareholders in the company that does the purchasing. This is because the new combined company has to find a way to 'add value' – essentially, to improve the value and profitability of its assets – over and above the premium price it has paid for the acquisition. This may take years, and there is considerable controversy over whether many of these deals work out in the long term. One of the reasons for controversy is that some interested parties – for example, a manager who is going to become the chief executive of the combined firm – stand to gain personally even if the merger is ultimately unprofitable for the shareholders, and may use doubtful arguments in pursuit of their private objectives. The main justifications for mergers, which may or may not be accurate, are:

■ The target company is cheap. In general, this is less likely to be true of public companies than private ones, because the share price of a public company tends to go up during the M&A process. The real bargains tend to be small, privately-held companies that are swallowed up by a large public company that is trying to dominate an industry. Sometimes, though, one public company may sell one of its businesses to another public company at a low price because it is trying to focus on other areas.

■ Diversification – investors diversify to reduce their overall risk, and sometimes companies claim to be doing the same by acquiring other firms. While this makes sense in less developed areas of the world, in the major stock markets this argument is not very convincing, because it is so expensive to buy another public company.

■ Synergy – this means that a company adds value by buying up its competitors or its suppliers and customers. In theory, this can make the new combined company more profitable by, for instance, keeping prices high and its costs low. Sometimes such synergies are purely financial, such as improving credit risk to enable the combined company to borrow more cheaply, or to gain tax benefits.

M&As are supposed to be about business growth, and tend to be associated with periods when stock markets are going up and rising share prices help an acquisitive firm finance its purchases of other firms. Looked at strictly from the point of view of good value, a 'bull market' (when the market is rising) is not going to be the time when companies are at their cheapest. There are also regulatory risks; the rules on M&A are both strict and complicated, and sometimes governments step in to block a merger, usually on the grounds that the combined company will achieve a monopoly position in an industry that could hurt customers by keeping prices high. If a merger is blocked, the would-be purchaser can lose a fortune in fees and other costs, and its share price may slump.

For guerrilla investors, the two main things to remember about M&A are:

1 Shareholders in a target company often receive a nice windfall profit if they sell their shares during a merger. Sometimes there is a bidding war which drives prices up far more than initially expected, and it is a good idea to get advice from your broker on the best moment to sell in order to maximize your gains.

2 If you own shares in a company that is buying others, you need to take a much more sceptical stance, asking yourself questions like: 'Is this transaction really going to result in a more valuable company, over and above the purchase cost?'; 'Why is the company really buying up other companies?'; 'Do the justifications make sense?' To see why M&A may not always be a good thing, think back to the dotcom boom of the 1990s, when new internet companies were being bought up at insanely high prices – when the bottom finally fell out of the market, many of the acquisitive companies went broke (see the story of WorldCom, page 176).

When companies get into trouble

Companies get into trouble for all kinds of reasons, and it is not always easy for outside investors to understand what is going on. In general, private companies and small companies listed on the 'over-the-counter' markets, such AIM, are more likely to go bust than companies that are listed on a major stock market, but sometimes even a big public company that is listed, say, in the FTSE 100 Index, can go broke. The laws on corporate bankruptcy vary across the world – for example, they are rather more lax in the USA than in the UK – but the process of winding up a company that has gone bankrupt is usually a long one, and shareholders must wait to find out if they will receive any money at all from the ruins. The first lesson, then, for guerrilla shareholders is:

If there are signs that a company is heading for serious trouble, it is often better to cut your losses and get out while you still can.

Some specialist investors focus on buying shares in companies in trouble, in the hope that the company will recover sufficiently for them to be able to sell their shares at a profit. This is a risky business and is probably best left to the experts. Bargain hunters of this kind usually have very sophisticated methods for assessing whether or not a company can recover that a beginner investor cannot hope to imitate successfully. The kinds of criteria they use include:

■ Does the firm have a good underlying business that can be revived?

■ How long will it take the firm to recover? (Usually, investors will not tolerate more than three years' recovery time.)

■ Is there a new management team that is capable of turning the company around?

■ Is the share price incredibly cheap?

Suspensions

Sometimes the shares of a company are 'suspended', which means that the stock market regulators have ordered that all trading in these shares should cease for the time being. Usually this is done when there is uncertainty about what is happening to the company, and the regulator suspends the shares until there is enough publicly available information about what is happening to give every investor a fair chance to decide whether or not to trade the shares. Suspensions aren't always a sign of trouble; for example, if one company is trying to buy another one, the shares in the target company may be suspended to give time for all the news to get to all investors. Often, though, a company is suspended because there are problems. If you are a shareholder, you will not be able to sell your shares until the suspension is lifted, which may take years and confront you with a much lower share price when you are finally able to sell.

Deciding whether a company is solvent

What kills a company? At the most basic level, it is the lack of cash to pay debts, which is called 'insolvency'. This is a bit like saying someone died because their heart stopped, though, and doesn't really explain all the circumstances leading up to the final moment. Nevertheless, there are often warning signs that a company is heading towards insolvency long before – often years before – the crunch finally happens. One of the most important tests is to look at the ratio of the company's borrowings to its assets – often called its 'gearing' or 'leverage'. To understand why this ratio is important, imagine you are a first-time buyer of a house, and although you only earn £20,000 a year, you somehow manage to take out a 100 per cent mortgage, borrowing £450,000 to buy the house. At the very least, you are going to be under a lot of pressure to make the monthly repayments – a sure warning sign of trouble ahead. Of course, in the UK property market there are all kinds of regulations and protections that are supposed to stop people borrowing too much and to save them if they get into trouble (although some people still get their houses repossessed), but in business there are no such protections. If a company finds a way to borrow much more than it can afford, it will have much more trouble wriggling out of its commitments than the average consumer.

The acceptable ratio of debt to equity varies across industries but in general, a debt to equity level of 1:1 or less is usually thought of as reasonable, and investors should treat any company with higher debt levels than this with some caution. If you want to be safer, a debt to equity ratio of 0.5:1 would be better, but you will find that many industries use much more debt as a matter of course. The essential issue here is the pattern of borrowing – is it increasing? If a company is steadily increasing its debt to equity ratio, it is also steadily increasing its risk of becoming insolvent.

If you have an interest in accounting, you can break debt-to-equity down in more sophisticated ways. For example, you can compare short-term debts with short-term assets, such as the money the company has in the bank, the stock in its warehouses, its invoices outstanding and so on. Here, the rule of thumb is that the ratio of current (i.e. short-term) debts to current assets should not be more than 2:3, although some giant companies have much worse ratios than this because they have the power to keep their suppliers waiting for their money.

The nice thing about these kinds of business ratios is that once you have learned how to use them properly (and this will take time and effort) they really do provide a lot of useful information about the financial health of a firm; companies may try to explain away problems, but the steely-eyed user of business ratios is not easily fooled. Ratios need to be taken as a whole – don't base your decisions on just one or two of them – so investors who do not have the interest or the patience to train themselves in their use will

❛❛the steely-eyed user of business ratios is not easily fooled❜❜

be none the wiser. As suggested earlier, if you really aren't numbers-minded, you are generally better off investing either in index funds or in funds where the managers do all this work for you.

Summary

There are lots of books that will teach you how to interpret company accounts, but the truth is that it takes years of experience to really become good at doing this. If you don't have the time or inclination, don't worry, because investing in a diversified portfolio of funds will probably give you adequate returns in the long term with much less heartache and potential for error. It is important, though, to recognize that company accounts really don't tell you what they appear to tell you, and that it is very, very hard indeed to compare figures across companies, industries and countries, even if you are a professional analyst.

Few investors, even ones that focus only on funds, can resist the thrills and spills of the occasional direct investment. To make a profit by stagging a new issue, or by selling shares in a company that is taken over, is a very satisfying activity when it is successful. Sometimes the signs are very clear that you can make a profit, and often the risks are quite low. Investors are more likely to come a cropper by holding on to failing companies until the bitter end; in general, it is best to avoid companies that get into serious trouble, especially small ones, and it is better to cut your losses early rather than to risk total loss by waiting in the hope of some improvement. In the next chapter we will look in more detail at some of the important theories and strategies that active investors use to try to improve their investment results.

5

Investment theories and strategies

On a theoretical level, a great deal of progress has been made in understanding the financial markets during the last few decades, but there are still many unanswered problems, such as the question of whether particular investment strategies really do produce better results than others. In this chapter we will look at some of the main theories that underlie the strategies that investors use; there is no all-encompassing model that completely explains how the markets work, but some models are considerably more convincing than others, and a number of principles have been well established – so new investors need to familiarize themselves with these. The financial markets are fluid and complex, and it is quite clear that some investors have followed very naive theories in the past without success – for example, it is unrealistic to expect to be able to pick fast-growing shares consistently over a long period of time.

For the private investor, the situation is confusing. There is a huge range of investment strategies offered by fund managers and other institutions, and each one seems to have a convincing story. This can be justified in part by the need to cater for different people's appetite for risk, but marketing techniques also play a part – just about any investment strategy will find a few interested punters if it is sold in the right way. There is also a great demand among investors for exciting stories,

ιat happen to be doing well may receive a
hat they may not really want. The net result
ɔr is faced with a barrage of success stories of
are at least superficially plausible. Plausibility,
ɛnough to convince us; the real test in invest-
find an appropriate strategy for our personal
long enough to see if it works. Many investors
chasᴇ ᴜ. other in the hope of outstanding returns and
eventually find that ᴜᴊey have performed worse than if they had followed a more conservative, but consistent and disciplined, strategy.

It is easy to get a false impression about how the most famously successful investors, such as Warren Buffett and George Soros, operate.
In general, it is not possible for non-professionals to imitate their
methods closely because they lack the expertise, access to markets
and access to money that these market veterans possess. Frequently,
successful professional investors operate in many financial markets
simultaneously and borrow heavily, using specialized knowledge to
spot unusual opportunities; as other professionals begin to catch on to
what they are doing, the profits begin to shrink until the activity is no
longer viable, and the investors have to move on. Guerrilla investors
should try to run before they can walk – unless, or until, you become
a real professional with a lot of money to invest, the chances are that
your investments will not perform well if you try to copy the methods
of the handful of high profile names that have produced extraordinary
investment returns over the years.

In this chapter we will look at:

- Fundamental analysis

- Discounted cash flow (DCF)

- The efficient market

- Index investing

- Understanding volatility

- Measuring risk-adjusted performance; the risk-free rate and
  expected return

■ Value investing

■ Growth investing

■ Small companies or large companies?

■ Market timing

■ Technical analysis – pure voodoo?

In this chapter it will be argued that private investors who want to achieve good returns over a long period of time are probably best advised not to attempt to pick individual shares, but to use funds (unit trusts and investment trusts) in a disciplined way within their asset allocation framework. To understand why this makes sense, we should first consider one of the bread-and-butter activities in the market: fundamental analysis.

Fundamental analysis

Fundamental analysis begins by studying a company to attempt to establish what its shares 'ought' to be worth, which may have little to do with the current share price. The prospects for the industry as a whole are examined, and then the accounts, records, economic prospects and management plans of the companies within that industry for comparison. Analysts then prepare detailed estimates of the company's future earnings, incorporating estimates of future sales, overheads, accounting policies and a host of other factors that might affect profits. The financial ratios, discussed in Chapter 4, are also used to make judgements about what a share is really worth.

Fundamental analysis, therefore, aims to produce a rational estimate of value based on a thorough examination of everything about a company that can be quantified in some way. A key assumption is that if the share price is found to be less than its 'true' worth – as estimated by the analysis – then eventually the market will discover this and the share price will tend to rise. Another important assumption is that past earnings may often be a guide to future earnings. Whether or not these assumptions really work in the real world – sensible though they may appear to be – remains open to question.

Discounted cash flow (DCF)

The essential idea of DCF is that the way to measure the value of any productive asset, whether it is a company, a bond, or anything else, is to add up all the cash it will produce in the future and adjust these figures for the 'present value' of the cash. For DCF purposes, 'cash' means the cash that is left over after all expenses, including reinvesting in the business (for example, to replace equipment).

Why do you have to adjust for 'present value'? Here's an example that explains this.

Example

Sally borrows £1,000 pounds from you interest-free, telling you that she'll either pay it back tomorrow, or in three years' time. When would you like the money back?

The correct answer, all other things being equal, is that you would like the money back tomorrow. This is because you can do other useful things with the money, like investing it in something that will produce a return during the next three years.

To work out what the present value of the money would be if Sally didn't pay you back for three years, you 'discount' it using this formula:

Present value (PV) = number of years until the money is paid ÷ $(1 + \text{interest rate})^n$ = number of years

So, if the interest rate on a high street savings account is 2.8 per cent, in this case the present value would be:

$PV = 3 \div [(1 + 0.028) \times (1 + 0.028) \times (1 + 0.028)]$

$PV = 3 \div 1.086$

$PV = 920$

If Sally doesn't pay you back for three years, the present value of the money she returns to you is £920, if the only other thing you could do with the money is to put it in a savings account.

Simple, isn't it? But it soon gets more complicated. At the time of writing, inflation seems to be rising. I might be able to get 2.8 per cent in a savings account now, but what is the real rate, adjusting for inflation, and will the real interest rate drop during the three years when I am waiting to get my money back from Sally? And what if I could get a better return by investing the money somewhere else – shouldn't I be using that interest rate in my calculations rather than the 2.8 per cent savings account rate?

When you apply DCF to companies, the calculations soon get even more complicated, especially for firms that are growing and changing rapidly. Can anyone really make an accurate estimate of how much Company X will be earning five years into the future? In many cases, the answer is 'no', but we still need to try, because estimates are useful in helping us to work out how much a company's shares might be worth in different scenarios. Here's an example of how to use DCF if a company is very stable and predictable.

Example

Suppose Ultrapredictable PLC has paid a dividend of £2 for some years, and that we expect this dividend to grow annually by 0.5 per cent in the future. Let's further suppose that bonds are currently giving us a 'risk-free' real rate of return of 1.3 per cent. What's a fair price to pay for the shares today?

Using the formula:

Fair share price = next year's dividend ÷ (required rate of return − expected dividend growth rate)

('required rate of return' is the real return you would get on bonds)

Fair share price = £2 ÷ (0.013 − 0.005)

Fair share price = £2 ÷ 0.008

Fair share price = £250

If the current share price is less than £250, then it is a 'buy', according to this method.

In reality, there are lots of ways to calculate DCF for companies, and some of them are staggeringly intricate. The accuracy of DCF depends a lot upon how good the analyst's judgement is, because DCF figures are always based on estimates and assumptions. Nevertheless, DCF is probably a sounder method of estimating value than the so-called 'relative value' methods, which depend upon comparing the characteristics of one company with those of a group of similar companies. Some people argue that DCF is too conservative, but others see this conservatism as a virtue in the overoptimistic world of investment. Some studies of how shares have performed in comparison to their DCF valuation at a given date suggest that firms that are undervalued on DCF calculations tend to perform better than overvalued shares in the medium term.

Calculating DCF yourself is too difficult for the non-specialist, but it is useful to understand how it works, and to recognize that one analyst's DCF figures may be completely different from another's. DCF figures are only estimates, but they can give a false impression of precision, so when you are considering these figures, take a good look at the analyst who has provided them, and the assumptions that have been used for the calculations.

DCF and other forms of fundamental analysis are a respectable activity that is widely used by professionals, but it is not really an exact science; remember, different analysts will come up with remarkably different estimates. In its efforts to predict future profits, fundamental analysis must make all kinds of assumptions which may or may not be valid, and only time will tell if they are correct. Many studies have shown that analysts' predictions overall are not very accurate, and it is often difficult for anyone, even other professionals, to judge whose analysis is most likely to be correct. This is disturbing. On the one hand, 'good' fundamental analysis – if one can ever determine what 'good' is – seems the most business-like approach to assessing real value; on the other hand, many of the plausible but spurious stories about hot shares and hot industries, such as the dotcom boom in the late 1990s, have mountains of apparently sound fundamental analysis to support them.

There are many factors that may contribute to the poor predictive ability of fundamental analysis, but one of the most important insights of the last 50 years is the way in which prices may sometimes move randomly – and, therefore, unpredictably.

The efficient market

In the 1960s an important study by Eugene Fama[1] introduced the notion that the small changes that are constantly occurring in share prices were randomly distributed. Note that Fama was referring to the small, frequent price changes that we see daily in the market, often a fraction of 1 per cent, and he was not arguing that violent share price

---

[1] Fama, 'Random walks in Stock Market Prices', *Financial Analysts Journal,* September/October 1965.

changes happen frequently. These random patterns, or 'random walks' are due, Fama thinks, to investors' reactions to every new piece of information about companies and industries as they are reported.

As Fama's work developed, he elaborated on this idea to hypothesize that the major stock markets, but probably not the small ones, have so many expert analysts and investors following every quoted company that the prices are constantly adjusted to account for everything that is currently known about the companies' prospects. Fama's 'efficient market' theory proposes that shares in the major markets are therefore correctly valued most of the time. What this is implies is that investors should not bother trying to achieve better performance than the market – if it is truly an efficient market.

This hypothesis was rejected at first, but over the years it has gained increasing acceptance in the financial community. Today there is great interest in the question of how 'efficient' particular sectors and countries are. With the massive growth of the financial markets across the world, there is considerable evidence that some are likely to be quite inefficient, because they are not as closely followed by market professionals and may rely heavily on foreign capital that can take fright at bad news. For example, when Indonesia had a financial crisis a few years ago, much of the foreign capital invested in Indonesian shares panicked and sold. This led to major quoted companies that owned enormously valuable assets being sold for a fraction of their intrinsic value. Anyone who bought at the low point saw extraordinary gains as the panic subsided and foreign investors began to move back in. Such market conditions are clearly not 'efficient' in Fama's sense, and many argue that inefficient markets of this kind do offer the opportunity for investors to gain superior returns through superior knowledge.

As it is currently understood, an efficient market has:

- a system of providing all the pertinent information about the market and its companies to all investors
- a system that ensures that this information reaches everyone at the same time
- a large number of sophisticated analysts studying all the shares with the aim of making profits.

This description applies to the major markets, such as the London and New York stock exchanges, but clearly does not apply to many of the smaller stock markets around the world, such as Zimbabwe. In addition, a major market like New York may still have some inefficiencies that are too difficult for most private investors to take advantage of, but can be exploited by professional organizations with more money, lower transaction costs and better information-gathering and analytical skills.

Academics now recognize that there may be three degrees of market efficiency:

1 Strong efficiency, where the current shares prices are fairly valued because all possible information has been taken into account. In such a market, the theory goes, no one can make excess returns consistently. Suppose you are a world expert on oil trading – you would still not be able to beat the market because other world experts would be spotting the same trends and opportunities as you, and quickly bid the prices up to a fair level.

2 Semi-strong efficiency, where current share prices are generally fairly valued because all that is publicly known has been taken into account, but not everything that is privately known. Some people and organizations with superior private knowledge may be able to beat the market.

3 Weak efficiency, where all the trends and patterns in the past price movements of a share have been taken into account. In this case, studying past price movements will not help, but analysing new information could do so.

The efficient market theory does not argue that it is impossible ever to earn superior returns, but that these returns, known as 'excess' returns, will be random, so that in a strongly efficient market no one will ever consistently earn excess returns, with the exception of a very few who do so only by chance.

Interest in market efficiency has helped spawn a new type of investing, called index investing, which is based on the idea that you are unlikely to outperform the average. Index investing simply tries to perform as well as a given market index, rather than trying to beat the market by, say, investing in a fund that claims to have a superior strategy. Index investing is discussed below. While most agree that the major markets probably are quite efficient, no one agrees on exactly how efficient they are – and indeed, their efficiency may be constantly changing – so index investing is not really the last word on investment strategy.

Index investing

Once available only to institutional investors, index investing has become an increasingly popular investment strategy, especially in the USA where hundreds of billions of dollars are now invested in index funds. Indexing is an investment approach that seeks to match the investment returns of a specified stock or bond market index. When indexing, an investment manager attempts to mimic the investment results of the target index by holding all the securities in the index. The manager does not vary from this strategy, and does not buy other shares in an attempt to get better returns. Indexing is therefore a 'passive' investment approach emphasizing broad diversification in a major market and low trading activity. Index funds hold shares in all the companies of a given index in the same proportion as they are weighted in that index. In the case of very large indices covering many hundreds of companies, an index fund may only hold a representative sample in its portfolio.

Although indexing derives from the unproven theory that the markets operate efficiently (see above), its rationale is based on the undeniable statistical fact that it is impossible for all investors together to outperform the overall stock market at the same time.

The costs of fund management and of share dealing are high for the private investor, and by contrast index funds charge low fees, reflecting the low cost of administration. Since there is no active investment management, in theory the fund's overheads ought to be lower, which may result in lower charges to you, the investor. Index tracking's main appeal is not to investors who want to make a 'killing'. It is attractive to long-term investors who seek a good long-term investment return through broadly diversified share investments.

When the overall stock market falls, you can expect the price of shares in an index fund to fall too. Indexing simply ensures that your returns will not stray far from the returns on the index that the fund tracks.

While the principle of index investing is simple, there are some points you should consider:

■ Funds offering very low charges may raise their charges in the future and may suffer from increased dealing costs, which could, over the long term, cause their performance to diverge from the index (this divergence is called 'tracking error').

■ Funds that track the large indices that cover most or all of the market, such as the FTSE All Share Index in the UK, may not all use the same representative samples. Only time will tell just how 'representative' these samples really are.

■ Funds with high charges may also suffer from tracking error because the charges reduce your returns.

■ If index tracking becomes a dominant force in the markets and a particular index, such as the FTSE 100 or the American S&P 500, becomes very popular with index funds, large sums of money could drive it up to an unnaturally high level, followed by a sudden crash. If you are interested in indexing, you should monitor how much of the total market capitalization of the companies in an index comes from investment by the index tracking funds so you don't fall asleep at the wheel. Read the financial press to keep up with index tracking developments.

■ Put some thought into which indices you pick. If you pick only the major UK and US indices, are you really diversifying properly? Consider putting some money into tracking an emerging markets index, like the FTSE World Asia Pacific (ex Japan) Index – but remember, the performance is likely to be more volatile in the emerging markets.

I am a fan of index tracking and am confident that this approach is a good idea for many, if not most, small investors at present. You can start with a small lump sum (as little as £500), you can drip feed more money in (say, £50 a month), and hold the fund through an ISA for tax benefits. Remember to reinvest any dividends you receive. If you want a bit of excitement, follow a volatile index, like one of the emerging market indices, and try to jump in at the bottom and out at the top; but if you do decide to do this, it is probably best to have a substantial proportion of your portfolio in UK and US index trackers as well, from the point of view of diversification.

Understanding volatility

Even the best companies that have enjoyed strong growth over many years see a lot of surprising fluctuations in their share price over shorter periods. These price fluctuations do not appear to relate to an intrinsic change in the value of the company, and are known as 'volatility'. When compared with, say the prices of bonds, shares clearly show much more volatility even though in the long term they tend, as a class, to generate much better returns. It is important to recognize that a major stock market that shows good long-term growth may still yield negative returns for shorter periods from time to time; for example, US shares had a long-term average real return of 6.2 per cent annually between 1900 and 2010, but had a negative average annual real return of −6.8 per cent between 2000 and 2003.

Volatility provides us with a way of looking at risk because high volatility is often, but not always, associated with higher returns in the long run. Shares as a class offer the best returns of all financial asset types in the long term, but have higher volatility, so investors need to allocate only their 'patient money' to shares because they need to be able to ride periods of poor performance. If you are saving for a deposit for a house that you hope to purchase in three years' time, for instance, it is inappropriate to invest your savings in shares because the market may be performing poorly when it is time for you to cash in and purchase the house.

> **❝investors need to allocate only their 'patient money' to shares❞**

This idea can be refined by distinguishing between the volatility of different kinds of shares. If you choose to invest in only the most volatile shares over, say, 10 or 20 years, you are likely to do significantly better or worse than the average performance of shares in that market. Over even longer periods these differences tend to iron out, so if you hold such shares for, say 70 years, their average performance is likely to be quite similar to the rest of the market. If, however, you sell at a high point, you could do very much better than average.

One way people attempt to exploit this phenomenon is by investing in shares with high volatility when they appear to be at a low point. In the example of the Indonesian shares crisis mentioned above, this is what the investor was doing: recognizing that the Indonesian stock market had high volatility, and investing at an apparent low point with the expectation that the shares would later lurch in the opposite direction, at which point the investor could sell out at a large profit. Like so many strategies, this looks easier than it is, for two main reasons:

1 You never really know when a low point is, because prices are unpredictable – they might just go on getting lower, as they did for years after the Wall Street Crash of 1929.

2 It is extremely hard psychologically to make a contrarian investment; when everyone, including all the experts, are certain that a given market or sector is going to get worse and worse, it takes a very cool-minded investor to ignore them and invest anyway.

One of the most important arguments for holding equities for as long as possible is that the longer you hold them, the more likely the portfolio will generate returns in line with the market overall, riding out all the short-term volatility – this is, of course, the argument for index tracking too. Holding for the long term is a prudent way to invest, but many investors are impatient for above-average gains, and do not have the patience to wait. Seeking above-average returns, however, is risky, because essentially you are seeking investments with high volatility, and when you want to sell out, the portfolio may be performing far below average.

Risk and risk-adjusted performance

Investment theory needs a quantifiable definition of risk in order to make judgements about how well investments have performed. One way to do this is to say that risk is the probability that the returns you make (called your 'actual' returns) are different from the returns you would expect from that kind of investment (called the 'expected' returns). 'Expected' returns are estimated against the benchmark of notionally risk-free investments, US and UK government bonds. As we have discussed earlier, no investment can really be said to be risk free, but for lack of something better we use these high-grade government bonds to represent it, assigning them a risk value of 0.

To estimate the expected return, we first look at what we can get on our risk-free investment:

> 12-month US or UK government bond yielding 4 per cent
>
> Risk = 0
>
> Expected return = 4 per cent
>
> Actual return = 4 per cent

The risk is said to be 0 because we believe that the government will definitely pay us the interest and return us the capital by the bond's maturity, so the expected return is no different from the actual return.

Let's say you have bought some shares in two companies, a very stable one and a very volatile one. You or your broker has calculated the expected return for each company. When you sell them, you may well find that your actual return is different from the expected return.

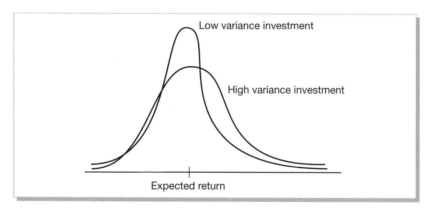

Low variance investment

High variance investment

Expected return

Figure 5.1   The random walk – how random movements build to look as if they might be a meaningful pattern

Figure 5.1 shows the range of possible returns, calculated from past performance and known as the 'variance' of the two companies. The stable company has had a low variance, meaning that it usually produces returns close to the expected return, while the volatile company produces much more widely distributed results. The volatile company is more 'risky' because it is more likely that the returns you make will be much higher or lower than the expected return.

When planning your portfolio, you can use this concept of risk, as variance, to decide what kinds of companies to invest in, and in what proportions; for example, you can weight it towards low variance companies that are likely to produce fairly predictable but unremarkable returns, or you can weight it towards exciting companies that might, or might not, do much better than expected. This method of assessing risk is quite useful, but it does have the same problem that so many other estimates suffer from: it is calculated using historical price movements, and as we know, future price movements may behave quite differently. After the 9/11 terrorist attack, for example, even the top US shares tumbled badly for a while, which would have put all their expected return calculations out of kilter.

If you want to estimate the variance of past returns yourself, you need to be familiar with basic statistics available in any standard textbook. Briefly, the way to calculate it is as follows:

1   Choose a period for analysis – for example, the preceding 10 years.

2   For each year, calculate total annual return (price plus dividends): [Price at beginning – (price at the end + dividends)] ÷ price at the end of the year.

3   Calculate the average annual return for the period (sum of returns divided by the number of years).

4   Now you have the mean average, but this does not tell you the variance.

5   Calculate the variance from the average for each year.

6   Square the results.

7   Add the squared results and divide by the number of years – 1.

8   Calculate the square root of the result to obtain the standard deviation.

The standard deviation number tells you how 'risky', or unpredictable, a company has been during the period, and can be used for comparisons with other companies.

Judging the performance of funds using the Sharpe ratio

Investment funds, unit trusts and other collective investment vehicles need ways of judging their performance, and the professionals use the concepts of expected return, actual return and risk adjustment to do this. You do not hear much about these ideas in the consumer press, but any professional will be able to discuss them with you if you wish. One commonly used test for funds is the Sharpe ratio, which calculates the risk-adjusted performance of an investment strategy against whole market:

> Sharpe ratio = (average return − risk free rate) ÷ standard deviation of returns

The Sharpe ratio is best applied to diversified funds rather than narrowly focused funds, and tells you whether a given fund has performed better than expected − the higher the number, the better it has performed, and can be used for comparisons with similar funds or the whole market. It is arguably a better test than just comparing the fund's results with, say, an index, but the search continues for even better tests.

Value investing

This approach was pioneered by Benjamin Graham, a New York investor who established the rational basis for fundamental analysis in his book *Security Analysis* in 1934.[2] Graham, who had suffered severe losses in the Wall Street Crash of 1929, advocated seeking out companies whose share prices were much lower than an intrinsic valuation of the assets they owned. Value investing, according to Graham, was a process like finding used cigar butts in the street that had one or two good puffs left in them. By and large these were unattractive companies that did not appear to have a bright future − they were bargains because they were worth more than the low valuation given them by the market.

---

[2] Graham, *Security Analysis*, McGraw-Hill, 1996.

Graham's criteria for selecting such companies were very stringent, and it is unlikely that any companies can be found today in the major markets that truly meet his standards. For example, a 'bargain' had to have very little debt (less than twice its current net assets), its price/earnings ration had to be less than 40 per cent of the average price/earnings ratio in the stock market over the preceding five years and its share price had to be less than 66 per cent of its book value, narrowly defined to include only tangible assets.

❝there is some evidence that value investing can produce above-average returns❞

Value investing, then, is a grim kind of bargain hunting, and there is some evidence that it can produce above-average returns. There are a few professional value investors operating in today's markets, but they tend to use their own idiosyncratic criteria for picking shares that are undervalued, which makes it difficult to compare the effectiveness of their methods.

For the private investor who lacks a burning passion for studying company accounts, value investing is probably not an advisable or sustainable strategy. Overly simplified value methods that you may see touted in investment magazines from time to time are unlikely to work at all – value investing is really a very detailed kind of analysis that cannot be reduced to one or two measures. For example, merely looking for shares with low price/earnings ratios does not seem to work in the short to medium term, although there is evidence that low price/earnings shares as a group do outperform those with higher price/earnings ratios over the long term.

Growth investing

Growth investing is essentially the opposite of value investing. Instead of looking for bargains among the lame ducks of the market, you search for dynamic companies that you believe are going to enjoy above-average business growth for many years in the future. Like value investing, the idea seems sound in principle, but in practice it is difficult to be sure that you are choosing companies that really are going to grow strongly for many years. Some companies have indeed grown strongly for decades until they have become giants of industry, such as IBM and Microsoft, but it does not follow that an investor would have been able to recognize this potential at the outset. In the early 1980s, for instance, Microsoft was just one of a handful of small software companies serving the very new, and very chaotic, personal computer business.

Growth investing depends in part on the study of past share price movements, which as we have seen, have been shown by Eugene Fama and others to be a very poor guide to future price movements. Another problem is that companies that appear to have a wonderful future ahead of them often have high stock market valuations because investors have already bid them up, and there is no way of knowing for sure that the companies will perform even better than the market already expects.

The classic example of growth investing becoming overly fashionable was during the US stock market boom in the 1960s. A number of large companies, dubbed the 'nifty fifty', were widely regarded as sure things which were destined to grow rapidly for many years to come. The nifty fifty included companies that today might be regarded as rather unexciting, like Xerox, DuPont and IBM, and were, during the 1960s, selling at valuations which later seemed far too high because they failed to perform as was hoped – the really impressive growth period for DuPont, for example, was from the 1920s to the early 1960s.

Small companies or large companies?

Small companies, often known as 'small caps', are firms whose stock market valuation, calculated as the share price × numbers of shares in issue, is relatively small, and large companies ('large caps') have big market valuations. While small caps have outperformed other kinds of companies for extended periods in the past in certain markets, there have also been periods when they significantly underperformed. Nevertheless, private investors may have some advantage in investing in small cap stocks because they are relatively illiquid; institutional investors, who like to invest large sums, find that they cannot always sell large chunks of a small company's shares without affecting the price. Private investors, on the other hand, can sell a few shares in a small company without having this problem.

Small companies are less well-studied than large ones, so the market may be inefficient. This implies that you might be able to outperform the average by superior knowledge, or superior analysis. On the other hand, small companies may be riskier and more volatile than they appear, so it may be that a more accurate risk-adjustment would explain any superior performance.

Small caps are attractive to amateurs who like the idea that a little business could suddenly make it big, but buying such shares on the basis of rumours or investment newsletters is not a good idea. If you really are attracted to small cap investment, you need to study them very thoroughly indeed and have a comprehensive understanding of their business and their industry.

Market timing

Market timing means trying to make profits by buying at low points and selling at high points – in other words, by trying to exploit volatility. It can take many forms, ranging from the very crude to the highly sophisticated, and carries extra costs, so to be effective it must make higher returns after these extra costs have been absorbed. The main extra cost, if done frequently, is the fees charged for buying and selling. These may be minuscule for the large institutions, but can become a very heavy drag on the performance of the private investor, who inevitably pays much higher transaction costs. The other main expense is an increase in capital gains tax on any profits you may make.

Although the efficient market theory tells us that market timing is unlikely to be an effective strategy over time, many investors do use it, often basing their rationale on external economic factors or market sentiment. Suppose, for instance, you hold some shares in a sector that has become wildly fashionable, and prices have been soaring for several years. You have made excellent paper gains, and you decide that market sentiment has just become too optimistic about this sector, so prices will crash. You sell, realizing your gains, and congratulate yourself on your market timing. Then the shares continue to rise for another three years before collapsing. This is the problem – it may be possible to judge that prices have risen far beyond all rational assessment of their true value, but it does not seem to be possible to predict when the market will 'correct' for this. It is extremely difficult to estimate the high and low points in the market.

Trying to read the runes of the wider economy can be an entertaining pastime, but there is not a lot of evidence that it helps to predict the market. For instance, some people think that if the returns on high grade government bonds (the 'risk-free' rate) are rising relative to returns on shares, some money is likely to move from shares to bonds, thus driving down prices. Studies have found no close correlation between share prices and returns on bonds, however.

Technical analysis – pure voodoo?

Once you become involved in investing you will almost certainly encounter 'technical analysis' which is a collection of techniques which aim to predict future price movements on the basis of repeating patterns that technical analysts claim to identify by studying historical price charts. Although it has a long history, academic study

❝technical analysis is not appropriate for private investors❞

of the effectiveness of technical analysis has found very little evidence that it ever works. The main exception to this is in the currency markets, where some specialists claim that repeating patterns do exist. For the stock market, however, the consensus is that technical analysis is not appropriate for private investors, largely on the grounds that it tends to require frequent trading, which pushes up transaction costs.

However, in the stock market there are two curious anomalies that appear to be consistent with the idea that price patterns may sometimes repeat themselves: 'the January effect' and the volume of shares traded.

The January effect

Nobody knows exactly why, but if you buy shares in the first two weeks of January, you will on average achieve a better return than if you had bought the same shares at another time of the year – or, at least, this has been a trend in the major markets for many years. If many investors tried to exploit the January effect, however, it would probably disappear.

Volume of shares traded

The shares of gigantic corporations like GE or Shell are bought and sold in very large numbers on every day that the market is open, and are said to have a high trading volume. Conversely, small companies, or those listed on very small stock exchanges, may not be sold at all on some days, or only in tiny quantities. There does seem to be some evidence that low-volume shares outperform high-volume shares, but this may simply be because low-volume shares are usually small, more risky companies, and the effect may be negligible after adjusting for risk.

Chartism

'Chartism' is often seen as the lunatic fringe of technical analysis, but it continues to have quite a wide following, mostly among investors who enjoy, or are addicted to, frequent trading. It is mentioned here really as an inoculation against it; private investors are bombarded with all kinds of investment schemes, and some promoters of chartism are known to target the unwary. There are two famous chartists whose work you are likely to encounter – Charles Dow and Ralph Elliott.

Charles Dow (founder of what is now the Dow Jones Industrial Average in the 1880s) was a financial journalist who thought that there was a three-stage pattern in price rises, followed by a three-stage drop, as in Figure 5.2.

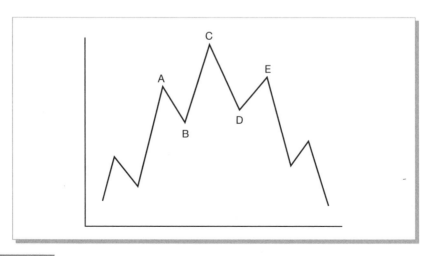

Figure 5.2   The 'head and shoulders reversal pattern'

The idea is that if you identify the top of the price rise ('C' in Figure 5.2), you should sell. The best that can be said about this is that academic studies of price patterns do not confirm that predictable patterns of this kind occur in the markets consistently.

Ralph Elliott was an American accountant who thought that there was a similar pattern to Dow's, this time three steps up and two steps down, which exists at every time period for share prices, from centuries to minutes. Figure 5.3 shows a schematic version of this.

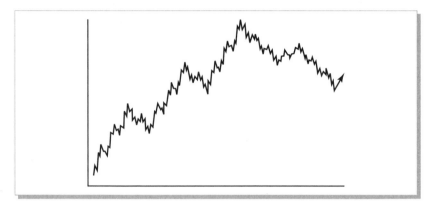

Figure 5.3   The Elliott wave

Elliott also used the Fibonacci numbers for price prediction. Fibonacci was a medieval mathematician who discovered a sequence that occurs frequently in nature. It is formed by adding the two preceding numbers in a sequence to get the next number, so it begins like this:

1, 1, 2, 3, 5, 8, 13, 21 …

Once again, there has been no independent corroboration that such patterns can be used to predict future price movements.

Summary

In the major markets, the arguments are strong that market efficiency makes it very hard for the amateur to select shares which will perform unusually well. The same is probably true for professional share-pickers.

For this reason, it seems sensible, if you decide to focus on the major markets, to adopt a risk-adjusted strategy and go either for an index fund or for broadly diversified funds that have the risk profile you want. As long as you do roughly as well as the market overall, and you continue to invest more from money than you save from your income, over the long term your results are likely to be satisfactory.

If, on the other hand, you get caught up in the fun and excitement of trying to select winners – and for many people it is fun – there are two main dangers:

1 You may buy and sell so frequently that high charges will eat up more than you gain.

2 You may inadvertently take the wrong kinds of risks, and substantially underperform the market overall.

Value investing, growth investing and the other methods discussed above are all interesting and attractive, but there is quite substantial evidence that they don't really work reliably. The main exception to this is in markets and sectors which are inefficient – say in China or South America. Here it may be possible, either by investing through specialist funds or else by actually taking the trouble to find yourself a broker in those locations, to produce outstanding results over time, but probably only if you have superior knowledge – in other words, that you actually understand why such a region is cheap when you buy, and why it is probable that prices will rise in due course. This is not necessarily unattainable knowledge; if, for instance, you work overseas occasionally, you may indeed discover such opportunities. In the next chapter we will turn to another very important area that affects investments abroad: foreign exchange.

6

Foreign exchange

Britain enjoys a relatively strong currency and, unlike many other countries, the regulatory framework discourages private individuals from trading in foreign currencies, so most private UK investors do not participate. However, it is important for all investors to understand the principles of foreign exchange, or 'forex', and to appreciate its importance when, for example, you are working overseas or own property abroad.

In recent years the worldwide market for forex has grown substantially because of the global trend towards financial deregulation; many countries now allow any currency to be freely held and exchanged in accounts within their borders. This makes investing in other countries and doing business with foreign companies much easier. Strictly from the point of view of the private investor in the UK, however, forex does not offer much scope for money making, unless you have commitments abroad – for example a home in a foreign country – in which case it is important to understand how to use forex to minimize currency risks. The forex market itself is very volatile, and is not a safe place for speculators, but it can be used to hedge (which means to reduce risk) if you make payments or receive money in foreign currencies.

In this chapter we will look at:

■   Avoiding the great travel money rip-off

■   The Bretton Woods System

■   The floating rate system

■   The balance of payments

■   Market sentiment

■   The foreign exchange market

■   Forward exchange

■   Predicting exchange rates

■   Currencies for guerrillas

Avoiding the great travel money rip-off

It costs money to change money, and at the retail end the total cost can be shockingly high. In the very worst cases you can lose around 20 per cent of the value of your money on the exchange, which means that if you spent £2,000 while on holiday abroad, you would have wasted £400 on just changing the money!

So, how do you avoid getting ripped off? The first rule has to be never use a credit card to withdraw money from a cash machine abroad (or at home, for that matter) because the charges for cash withdrawals are very high. Using a debit card abroad will be cheaper, depending on your bank, but watch out for a charge of 1.5–2 per cent on top of a not-so-good exchange rate. The virtue of using a card is that it is safer than cash if you are robbed, since you can cancel the card; some specialist currency companies are now offering a pre-paid card denominated in euros, which is a good, inexpensive way to carry money if you are travelling in the eurozone. Travellers' cheques, too, are a safe but expensive way to change money in most countries, although in more remote places, like Cambodia, they are still easier to use than cards or cash.

Money changers often disguise their charges by offering you worse than the market rate, combined with service charges and handling fees. The worst culprits for overcharging are the bureaux de change at airports and hotels because they have a captive market.

So, how do you get the best rates? In the UK, there are a number of specialist firms that do offer extremely good rates if you order your money in advance (you can find them via the internet). Make sure that you only deal with one that is fully authorized by the FSA. Although there should be no problems, you should be aware that none of these firms, not even the largest, fully authorized ones, operate a comprehensive compensation scheme in the event that they go bust; however, the better firms do offer a degree of protection by 'ring fencing' their clients' money, which is deposited with a third-party bank. In late 2010, however, Crown Currency Exchange, a firm based in Cornwall, went belly up, leaving thousands of customers out of pocket. Some customers had paid over very large sums to the firm in order to obtain foreign currency to purchase property abroad. At the time of writing, the firm is in administration and it appears unlikely that victims of the collapse will get much of their money back. So, be careful!

To understand the present forex environment and how it could change in the future, it is important to have a grasp of how we got here; it all goes back to the end of the Second World War, when the basic structure of the present system was established. At present (2011), the euro is under pressure because of global financial crisis, and some are predicting that it could collapse; for more detail on this, see Chapter 13.

The Bretton Woods system

As the Second World War drew to a close, the Allies (the USA, Britain, France, and others) held a conference at Bretton Woods in New Hampshire, USA, to plan a new international monetary system for the post-war era. Conscious of the currency problems that had occurred during the Depression of the 1930s, they were eager to found a better system that would promote much-needed stability. One of the architects of the system was the British economist JM Keynes, who was one of the first to point out that modern economies are essentially unstable, and that sophisticated methods of supervision are need to prevent them from spiralling out of control. At Bretton Woods it was decided to set up the World Bank to provide development loans and aid to weaker countries, and also the International Monetary Fund (IMF), to help provide liquidity within the world's monetary system. At this time, the USA had become the most powerful country economically, and it was agreed that the new global monetary system should be based on the US dollar, which was fixed at $33 per ounce of gold. The currencies of other countries were defined in terms of US dollars, so exchange rates were artificially fixed. When a country wanted to change its exchange rate, it was required to follow a procedure whereby it publicly gave warning that it was about to make the change, either by strengthening its buying power against foreign currencies (revaluation) or diminishing its buying power (devaluation). In 1949, when the new system was introduced, 28 countries promptly devalued their currencies against the dollar.

Bretton Woods helped set the stage for post-war socialism. Countries paid for the cost of establishing the centralized economies, which they felt were essential for social justice, and to rebuild their economies after the destruction of the war years, mainly by issuing bonds, which in turn encouraged inflation. As world trade recovered and the economies of many countries began to improve, huge funds of cash developed that were mobile and could be switched from one country to another and were difficult for governments to control. The demand for gold was high, and a secondary market for gold developed, where it sold for much higher prices than the official $33 per ounce rate. The relative economic strength of the USA lessened as other countries recovered, and in 1971 the USA decided unilaterally to abandon the original Bretton Woods system by devaluing the dollar and suspending the right to convert dollars to gold.

The floating rate system

Following the USA's decision, many countries decided to permit their currencies to 'float'. The floating exchange system is market-driven, and means that the rate at which you can exchange one currency for another is simply the best price that someone will give you at that moment. Rates change rapidly, even during a single day, and can fluctuate wildly; this is because the international market for foreign exchange pays close attention to economic conditions in individual countries, and will adjust rates every time there is a significant change in a country's economy. For example, back in the 1970s, when OPEC, the oil producing countries' cartel, dramatically raised the price of crude oil on two separate occasions, the floating rate system helped to reduce the ensuing economic chaos by making OPEC countries' currencies much more valuable – countries like Saudi Arabia found that they could buy many more dollars, pounds and yen with their riyals than before. In the view of many economists, this was a much better way of coping with a sudden crisis than would have occurred under the Bretton Woods fixed rate system, because under Bretton Woods if the exchange rates had not adjusted, the economic chaos would have been even worse. Under the floating rate system, then, if your country's economy is performing well in comparison to the economies of other countries, your currency will become stronger, and you will be able to buy more foreign currency with your money. If your country's economy is performing poorly, your currency will weaken and your money will buy less foreign currency. Remember, though, not to assume that all countries have embraced the floating rate system; Malaysia and South Korea, to name just two, still have various currency restrictions in place.

Abandoning Bretton Woods, however, did not mean that all the measures taken after the war were discarded. The World Bank is still in operation today, as is the IMF, which acts as a 'lender of last resort' to countries that suffer an economic crisis. The IMF is often criticized, perhaps unfairly, because when it bails out a country in crisis it has to impose very strict rules on how the economy is managed – so it looks as if some faceless international agency is telling a government what to do. The IMF has had to bail out numerous countries over the years (including the UK during the 1970s), and when it does so it tends to get the blame for the country's woes. But this is like blaming a doctor for a disease you have contracted; the IMF is there to try to help the country out of trouble. In recent years, the IMF has had to bail out Ireland, Greece, Latvia, Romania, Hungary, Russia, Indonesia and Argentina, among others, and although the measures it imposes are often harsh, its role is essential in helping to keep the world's monetary system stable and the international economy running. Without such an institution, the potential for global economic chaos would be greater.

The balance of payments

Economically speaking, countries are like companies; they have accounts, income, expenditure and assets to juggle. Each year, a country produces a 'balance of payments' statement which, like a company balance sheet, gives a 'snapshot' of the country's finances, showing the country's net earnings from abroad, its savings and debt, and the shortfall, which the government may have to cover by more borrowing. Broken down further, this consists of:

■ **Foreign currency income:**
 – money brought in by foreign investors, for example to buy factories or houses
 – money earned abroad from exports

■ **Foreign currency purchases:**
 – money spent abroad to import goods and services
 – money invested abroad by holders of the local currency.

The balance of payments distinguishes between the 'current account', which measures exports against imports, and the capital account, which measures investment into the country versus investment abroad. If a country exports more, in money terms, than it is importing, it is said to have a current account surplus, which tends to strengthen its currency against other currencies. If it imports more than it exports, it has a current account deficit, which will tend to weaken the currency. The capital account works in the same way: a 'net capital inflow', when more investment money is coming in than going out, tends to strengthen the currency, and a 'net capital outflow', when more investment money is going out than coming in, will tend to weaken the currency.

There are some factors affecting the capital account that are worth knowing about if you are interested in investing in other countries. The first is the level of interest rates available to investors (for example, bank deposit rates and bond coupon rates). If a country is offering lower rates than are available elsewhere, investors are likely to take their money abroad. Second, even if a government is running the economy sensibly, it may simply not be possible to prosper; investors will avoid countries where it is hard for businesses to make money. Third, investors tend to dislike bad economic policies, political unrest, civil war and the like, and will tend to keep their money away from countries experiencing these problems – this may occasionally produce good investment opportunities for bold – and properly informed – investors.

Much is made of the balance of payments by politicians, economists and commentators, but not all is quite as it seems. If you reconciled all the balance of payments statements they should, in theory, cancel each other out. They do not; there is a 'black hole' of many tens of billions of pounds that no one can account for. This tells us that at least some countries, and probably a lot of them, are not producing accurate balance of payment figures, so, as with company accounts, we should treat them with a degree of scepticism.

Market sentiment

Although it is the success or failure of countries in their import/export businesses (including importing and exporting capital) that is the basis for rates of exchange, this doesn't mean that if Country A does wonderfully well in its economy over a period that its exchange rate will just keep going up and up. Usually there are short-term fluctuations in the rates that have nothing to do with the underlying economic health of the country.

One factor that causes these short-term blips is the behaviour of the bigtime forex traders who are seeking to make short-term profits. The behaviour of the traders is often called 'market sentiment', and it is usually very hard to predict. Sometimes, though, you will see the exchange rate between two currencies fluctuating within an upper and lower limit, called a 'trading range' for a long time. If you believe that the trading range will continue to operate, you can try to make profits by buying near the bottom of the range and selling near the top, but you run the risk of one day finding that the trading range has disappeared, thus suffering losses. Forex traders, like other traders in the financial markets, are not averse to starting rumours to try to influence the market, and there are often strange price changes that have nothing to do with reality but seem to have been in response to a convincing, but spurious, rumour going round the forex market. It is not really possible to predict price fluctuations in exchange rates consistently, so beware of people who claim that they can do this.

❝it is not really possible to predict price fluctuations in exchange rates consistently❞

Another factor that can cause short-term rate changes is the action of the central banks. Every country has a central bank that is in charge of supervising and controlling the nation's monetary system – in the UK it is the Bank of England, and in the USA it is the Federal Reserve (known as the 'Fed'). Central banks often try to affect their currency's exchange rates by buying or selling on a massive scale in the forex market. They are not always successful; for instance, when the UK was trying to keep within certain target exchange rate limits for the European Exchange Rate Mechanism (ERM) in 1992, the Bank of England did this, but was foiled by a number of bigtime forex traders, including the famous fund manager George Soros, who bet the other way and won. Although these traders are blamed for being piratical, many professionals argue that they are doing a useful job by providing liquidity to the market and acting as a reality test for the actions of politicians. In the end, if the politicians are right and the traders are wrong, the traders will lose money.

When the situation is more stable, however, central banks tend to be more successful at keeping rates within an acceptable range. Another type of central bank intervention that can affect exchange rates is when they change the interest rates in their own country – in general, if interest rates go up, the currency may strengthen on the expectation that investors will move money into the country.

The foreign exchange market

When a company does business abroad, it takes on extra risks, the main one being that it cannot be sure how exchange rates will fluctuate. Usually a firm has to pay its supplier in local currency, so, for instance, a German firm will pay a Japanese supplier in yen, an American supplier in dollars and so on. To do this it will have to buy foreign currency in the market from banks, brokers and others. As rates change very quickly, the action is quite frantic in the major centres, which are New York, London, Tokyo, Zurich and Frankfurt, which turn over billions of dollars a day. The US dollar is the most frequently traded currency, and is known as a 'vehicle' currency – this means that many commodities, such as gold, coffee and oil, are priced exclusively in dollars in the international market. It is sometimes cheaper for, say, a Japanese dealer who wants to buy, say, Turkish liras, to use yen to buy dollars and then buy liras with dollars rather than to exchange yen directly for liras.

One way that the major currency dealers make money is by monitoring exchange rate quotes all over the world; every time they spot a difference, often very small, between exchange rates quoted in different places, they act quickly to buy in the cheaper place and sell in the more expensive one. This activity is known as arbitrage, and has the effect of keeping exchange rates all over the world in line with each other. It is only open to the very big-time players in the market, as the profits are tiny and requires the use of huge sums of money to be worthwhile.

Forward exchange

Companies that do business abroad regularly have some idea of their future expenditure – they know when the invoices will become due – but because exchange rates fluctuate, they do not know exactly how much it will cost. This can be very awkward, and can even make the difference between making a profit or a loss on their business. For this reason, companies are willing to buy foreign currency for delivery at a future date at a price agreed when they buy. This is known as 'forward exchange'. Usually the forward exchange rate will be different from the rate you can obtain for immediate delivery, which is known as the 'spot' rate. Suppose you run a German company that owes $100,000 to an American firm, due on 30 July. Depending on the rates, you can decide either to buy dollars at the spot rate for immediate delivery, and keep it in the bank earning interest until 30 July, or you can buy at the forward rate for delivery when the invoice is due. Depending on how rates change during the intervening period, one of the decisions may be more profitable than the other. In practice, though, most companies don't bother too much about trying to outwit the forex market; it is much better to have the certainty of knowing exactly what future expenditure is going to be, because it helps companies to plan their operations safely and enables them to use the money for other things in the meantime. Buying on the forward exchange market for this purpose is a form of insurance, and is called 'hedging'.

If you can buy more foreign currency at the spot rate than at the forward rate, the foreign currency is said to be at a 'forward discount', and if you can get more foreign currency at the forward rate than at the spot rate, the foreign currency is said to be at a 'forward premium'. The discount or premium of the forward rate is usually quoted as a percentage of the spot rate. The formula is:

Forward premium/discount = (F − S) / S × 100

where F is the forward rate and S is the spot rate. Thus, if the forward rate is £0.52:$1.00 and the spot rate is £0.50:$1.00, the premium is:

Premium = [(0.52 − 0.50) / 0.50] × 100

= 0.02 ÷ 0.50 × 100

= 4 per cent

Even when buying large sums of foreign currency there are still dealing costs involved, but these are generally quite small (fractions of 1 per cent), so as well as hedging there is also a lot of speculation in the forex market. With speculation, the risks are much higher, since you are trying to make a profit by guessing which way the market is going to go, rather than trying to protect profits that you are making in an underlying business.

Predicting exchange rates

As was mentioned earlier, it is the balance of payments that is the main force driving exchange rate movements in the long term, but other factors are thought to affect them too. Prediction of exchange rate movements is very far from being an exact science, and even the specialists are frequently wrong. Nevertheless, as a guerrilla investor it is a good idea to have a reasonably good knowledge of your home currency, the issues that might affect its exchange rate and the long-term trend. The two approaches that people use to try to make predictions are:

1 Trying to assess sentiment – this is done to try to anticipate short-term movements in exchange rates by studying the charts of past changes, trading volume (how much was traded), the rates of change and so on. This is termed 'technical analysis', and although, as is discussed in Chapter 5, many theorists believe that it is an ineffective method, technical analysts are sure that they can do it.

2 Studying factors such as economic change and political events – this is a form of 'fundamental analysis' (see Chapter 5), and while it is more credible, it still remains improbable that anyone can consistently make accurate predictions in the short to medium term. In the long term, however, it makes sense to consider such factors as:

- Inflation – countries that have high inflation have trouble exporting because their selling prices are going up, which implies that the currency is likely to weaken.

- Trade figures – although they are unreliable, they may give a clue to the direction of the economy over the next year or so. Looking at the trends in trade between two specific countries can give an indication of which currency is likely to get stronger against the other one.

- Capital flows – if investors are pouring money into a country when its economy is otherwise doing badly, this can prop up the exchange rate for a time.

- Savings rates – countries that save more tend to have strong currencies, all other things being equal.

■ One-off events – almost anything dramatic, from a terrorist outrage to an industrial disaster, can give the forex market the jitters.

■ Gross domestic product (GDP), productivity, unemployment and sales in the high street are all used as indicators – if the GDP rate has been increasing for a year or more, the currency should be getting stronger too.

Currencies for guerrillas

So far we have discussed how the international forex market works on a grand scale – we can think of it as the 'wholesale' market that is only open to the big players. It is frustrating to think, as you go on holiday and pay over the odds for your foreign cash, of how cheaply the professionals can buy and sell currencies. Ordinary investors, however, can benefit to some degree from trading in the forex markets if they have substantial assets, income or expenditure abroad. Suppose, for instance, that you are working in the Middle East for a few years and are being paid in, say, riyals. Suppose also that you have bought a holiday home in France which you are gradually renovating. This means that you have currency needs – pounds, euros and riyals – and that you have to do some forward planning and juggling. If you just trundle along blindly, converting currencies as the bills come in, you will often find that you converted currency at just the wrong moment, before a rate change in your favour, and if you use normal retail banking services to do it, you will probably be hit by all kinds of awkward delays and charges.

❝❝as long as you stick to currencies that you really use, you minimize the dangers❞❞

You can juggle your currencies better by holding them in multiple accounts in sophisticated banks based in low-tax financial centres such as Hong Kong. By doing this, you can, for example, exploit better interest rates on deposits of specific currencies and switch quickly, and relatively cheaply, from a weakening currency to one that is getting stronger. It is best not to try to speculate too wildly in currencies, because of the high risk, but as long as you stick to currencies that you really use, you minimize the dangers.

Some sophisticated banks in offshore centres are offering tailor-made currency services to this type of customer, such as currency accounts with embedded options enabling you to trade currencies at medium risk and relatively low cost. It works like this:

1 You open the account with a lump sum in the currency in which you are paid. In our example of the worker in the Middle East, this would be in riyals.

2 You make a deal with the bank that it can switch this money into another currency of your choice on an agreed day in the future at an agreed rate of exchange. The bank can choose not to do so if it wishes (normally this would be because exchange rates had moved against the bank's side of the bargain). This is essentially selling a 'call option' (see page 144), and the bank compensates you for the option by paying you a higher rate of interest in the meantime.

3 If the bank does decide to switch money to the other currency, then it does so at the pre-agreed exchange rate, not the spot rate. Sometimes both sides make a profit (a small one) when this happens.

This is quite an enjoyable way to dabble in forex trading in a small way, but remember to stick to the currencies you really use. That way, if one of your transactions goes against you, you can keep the money in that currency until you have spent it all. In our example of the British worker in the Middle East, for instance, the deal would be between riyals, euros and pounds, and if a trade went wrong and the account was stuck with euros, the money could be used for renovations on the house in France. The amount of money in such an account should be tailored to your levels of income and expenditure; if you were earning, say £60,000 a year in riyals and were planning to spend £30,000 over the next two years on renovations paid in euros, it would probably be a good idea to limit the initial deposit to, say, £10,000–£15,000. Of course, you could also hold other accounts and investments for your long-term savings and other projects. For example, you could also keep a sterling account in Hong Kong – possibly giving you a card that you could use at cash machines in the UK – to cover expenses in the UK when you come home for an annual holiday.

Summary

To sum up, UK investors should avoid trying to make 'serious' money in the forex markets because it is just too risky, but if you do have genuine foreign currency needs, you can use offshore accounts, perfectly legally, to reduce the costs of conversion, reduce the risk of converting at the wrong time, and possibly sometimes make modest profits too.

In the next chapter we will look at one of the most risky forms of investment – in many cases it is so speculative that it is more akin to gambling than investment: the strange world of derivatives.

7

Derivatives

Derivatives are financial instruments that are 'derived' from assets such as equities, bonds and commodities. They evolved from the commercial needs of the producers of basic goods to try to reduce their risks, which are essentially unpredictable fluctuations in supply (for example, bad harvests) and demand (for example, a market drying up because of new technology). Derivatives are used to 'hedge' against these risks, and can be seen as a type of insurance. However, they can also be used for speculation, and, as we will see in this chapter, many large organizations have incurred stupendous losses in operations that were supposed to hedge against risk, but in fact increased the risk exposure. The derivatives field has greatly expanded in recent years, but many potentially high-risk products are offered to private investors who neither need them nor possess the skills to use them effectively. As a guerrilla investor, it is quite unlikely that you will really need to hedge by using derivatives, although the industry may tell you that you should. The temptation to speculate using derivatives may be strong for those with gambling instincts, but the probability is high that speculation will lead eventually to substantial losses.

In this chapter we will look at:

■ Commodities

■ Futures

■ Financial futures

■   Options

■   Spread betting – tax-free investing?

■   Derivatives – the casualties

■   Hedge funds

■   Structured products

Commodities

Commodities are the basic raw materials that the world needs in order to function – they are the fruits of the earth. They include wheat, coffee, oil, sugar, livestock, and precious metals such as gold and platinum. People who are in the business of producing or processing these commodities are performing a vital function for which we should all be grateful. Many of these businesses trade in their commodities on a cash basis; prices fluctuate according to supply and demand, often in seasonal cycles. For instance, the cash price for wheat is lowest at harvest time, when there is plenty of it about. Precious metals have seasonal cycles too: prices usually increase in the autumn as jewellers begin to prepare their products for sale at Christmas and need more raw materials.

> **"commodity prices are unpredictable – all kinds of events can affect prices"**

Commodity prices are unpredictable – all kinds of events can affect prices, including wars, political unrest, strikes, extremes of weather, changes in consumer buying patterns, plagues of insects, plant and animal diseases, and the activities of financial interests who wish to influence the market. This has been the case for hundreds, if not thousands, of years. It makes life difficult for producers and users alike, since it is very hard to run a business if you don't know how much you can buy and sell your goods for. For this reason, a market has evolved for 'commodity futures'.

Futures

Buyers and sellers of commodities can make a contract to deliver a product at some time in the future at an agreed price, thus taking the uncertainty out of their operations. They can agree on the amounts, quality and date of delivery, and both parties will put down deposits to protect each other from one side defaulting on the deal. This is known as a 'futures contract'. Futures are a kind of insurance policy, or 'hedge', against the risks of price volatility, because businesses can simultaneously trade in futures and in the cash market. In fact, most futures contracts are cancelled before the delivery period.

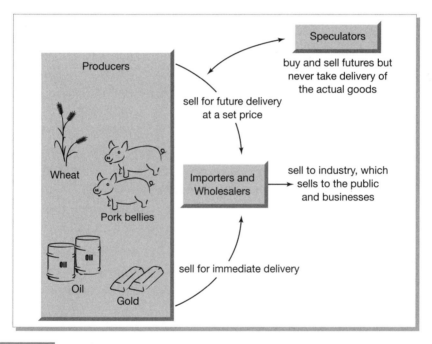

Figure 7.1   The players in commodities

This is where the speculators come in (see Figure 7.1). It is argued that speculators are a vital part of the futures market, because they provide it with greatly improved liquidity. Speculators aren't interested in using the commodities themselves; they are gambling on the difference between the price of a futures contract and the actual delivery price. Thus the commodities businesses, or 'hedgers', and the specula-tors behave differently in the market. The hedgers are able to offset, roughly, gains or losses in the cash market by an opposite effect in the futures market, and are thus able to run their businesses more stead-ily. The speculators have to watch the fluctuations of futures contracts every day, and get out on top when they can.

Commodity swaps

Suppose you are an aluminium company who agrees to protect a customer against a rise in price over a fixed amount. In return, the customer agrees to compensate the company if the price falls below a certain level. This is known as a 'swap', though it is related to options (see page 143). Swaps generally last for 2 or 3 years, though some can be for as long as 15. Oil is the most actively swapped commodity, and there are even bonds available with redemption values stated in terms of an amount of oil, thus tying themselves to future oil prices.

Buying on margin

Hedgers have never liked to pay the full price for their purchases long before the goods are delivered. Traditionally, when you purchase a futures contract, you only pay a small percentage of its value as a deposit. This is the main attraction for speculators, since it means that you trade futures 'on margin', enabling you to bet more money than you have.

Example

If you buy $200,000's worth of a futures contract, you only have to pay, say $20,000 as an upfront deposit. If the gamble pays off and the value of the con-tract goes up to $280,000, you can sell, making a profit of $80,000 on a deposit of $20,000, an increase of 400 per cent rather than the 40 per cent increase you would have made if you had paid out $200,000. If the deal goes against you, you could end up owing much more money than you originally deposited.

It is the fact you buy on margin that makes futures risky for the specu-lators, since the margin means that prices are around 10 times more volatile for speculators than they are for the hedgers, who actually trade in commodities themselves and do not use the margin to buy more than they otherwise would. The futures markets have grown massively as more and more speculators have become involved, and this has increased short-term volatility.

Financial futures

Shares, bonds, currencies and other financial instruments can be treated as commodities and futures contracts can be made on them. There is a wide range of financial futures and new ones are being invented all the time. Most futures are tied to important currencies or widely followed indices, such as the FTSE 100, the Standard & Poor's 500, sterling, yen, US treasury issues and so on. They are also tied to interest rates and bonds. Margins on financial futures can be considerably less than the 10 per cent or so required as a deposit on commodity futures, and this increases the risk unless you are using financial futures to hedge against charges to large liquid investments you have elsewhere, in which case you are behaving in the same way that a hedger in the commodities business does.

Example

Suppose you are dealing in futures based on 'long gilts' (e.g. long-term gilts). In this case, the contract size is $50,000. Suppose that the price when you buy is 100-28 (this means 100 $^{28}/_{32}$). Gilts move in 32nds of 1 per cent; each 32nd is called a 'tick'. The margin you must deposit is $500. If you are certain that gilts are going to go up and you want to buy gilts at a future date when money becomes available, you might buy the futures contract now to hedge against the expected higher cost of the gilts when you have the cash to buy them. If you are wrong, all is not lost, because the lower cost of gilts will roughly balance the loss you make on the futures contract. You can close out a futures contract either by delivering the gilts on the due date or by selling an identical contract. Most people do the latter.

If you are speculating, however, the situation is different.

Example

Suppose the underlying value of your gilts contract dropped by 50 per cent; you would not have lost $250 but $25,000, all on your $500 initial deposit. The rules of the system say that investors' contracts have to be checked daily for losses and profits; if you are losing, you will get a 'margin call' for more money to cover the losses, and you can close out the contract to stop any further losses.

Players in financial futures

Owners of very large share portfolios, such as brokers, unit and investment fund managers, pension funds and other institutions, trade in financial futures to hedge against the chance that share prices will fall. Anyone can speculate by taking a buy or sell position on a futures contract, betting that shares will either rise or fall. Futures used to be traded on exchanges using the 'open outcry' system, where traders shouted at each other over the din of the 'pit' where they trade, communicating using a system of hand signals; today this is generally done using linked computers (known as 'electronic trading'). Futures prices generally keep in step with cash prices, but are adjusted to account for interest rate differences. Occasionally futures prices can become much more expensive due to activity in the market; then the arbitrageurs step in to profit from the difference, pulling futures prices back to normality in the process.

Electronic trading has been welcomed by many because it is thought to be fairer; an outside investor can see real-time prices and buy and sell over the internet by joining a high-priced subscription service. This is seen as an improvement because in the days of open outcry, the traders could 'barge the queue' and trade ahead of outside customers.

The financial institutions can arrange their hedges through private contracts or else use one of the big futures exchanges such as:

■ The Chicago Board of Trade (CBOT), a major market for financial futures, now merged with the Chicago Mercantile Exchange (CME) and owned by the CME group.

■ Chicago Board Options Exchange (CBOE) – the main market for options (see page 143) on equities, indexes and interest rates.

■ The London International Financial Futures and Options Exchange (LIFFE, pronounced 'life') – the major market outside the USA, and is now part of the NYSE Euronext group which is owned by the New York Stock Exchange.

■ The Tokyo and Osaka stock exchanges in Japan offer futures tied to the Nikkei Index.

- The Singapore Mercantile Exchange (SMX).

- The Hong Kong Futures Exchange – offers financial futures, mainly based on Far East indices.

Trading in futures for guerrillas

The majority of players in commodity futures are speculators. Each year, they leave billions of pounds' worth of commissions with the brokers. It's a casino with the odds firmly rigged against the smaller investor. It may seem exciting, but it's not a good investment – almost everyone gets wiped out within a few years. To win as a speculator, you have to possess an enormous amount of knowledge and huge amounts of cash to get any kind of an edge. The only people who really know what is going on are the commodities businesses themselves – so don't expect your broker to have any special expertise. Stay out of commodities. The same goes for financial futures, unless you are hedging.

Options

Share options give you the right to buy or sell a share at a certain price within a fixed time period. You pay for the option buy you don't have to exercise it. You can also buy options on futures contracts, interest rates and currencies in the same way. The price you pay for the option is called the 'premium', and the price at which it is agreed that you may buy or sell the shares or futures contract is called the 'strike price' in the USA and the 'exercise price' in the UK.

The price that you pay for an option depends upon the period of time allowed until the option expires (the longer it is, the more expensive the option – see Figure 7.2), and also upon the difference between the strike price and the current market price of the share or futures contract.

Options give you leverage. All you have to pay is the price of the premium to make a bet that the exercise price will be better than the market price at some point before the option runs out (in the case of traded options) or at the point that the option runs out (in the case of 'European-style' options. You don't have to come up with any more money unless you already know you have won your bet.

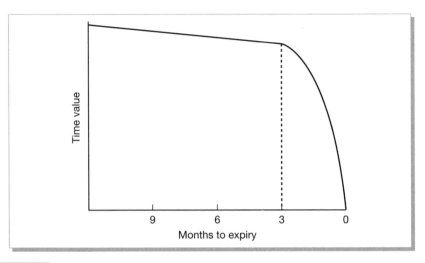

Months to expiry

Figure 7.2 **The time value of an option**

There are two kinds of options, 'puts' and 'calls'. A call option gives you the right to buy, and a put option gives you the right to sell. Traded options enable you to buy or sell your option if you win the bet, instead of buying the shares or other securities themselves.

❝all you can lose on an option is the premium❞

As we have seen, unlike paying the margin when you buy a futures contract, all you can lose on an option is the premium, while the possible gain can be as high as you could get in futures. Options on shares can usually be bought for between 8 and 15 per cent of the share's market price. Except for 'traded options' you cannot buy or sell an option after the initial purchase.

Call options

Here is an example of how a call option works.

Example

Suppose you think that shares in Company X are going to go up in the next three months. You can buy a three-month call option on 1,000 shares at, say, 184p; the premium will be 18p per share, so you will pay £180 plus dealing costs for 1,000 shares. If the share price is at 187p after three months, you could exercise the option to buy in the hope that the share price will continue to rise; you will have spent £180 + £1,840 = £2,020, so, not counting dealing costs, the shares will have to rise above 202p for you to make a profit.

Put options

Here is an example of how a put option works.

Example

> Suppose that you think Company X's shares are going to go down in the next three months. You can buy a put option for 18p per share for 1,000 shares at 184p. If the shares go down to, say, 150p, you can exercise your option by 'putting' it on to an option dealer, forcing him/her to buy your shares for £1,840, which you now exercise your right to buy for £1,500, and pass them on to the dealer. The cost to you, not including dealing charges, is £1,500 + £180 = £1,680, so your profit is £1,840 – £1,680 = £160. Since your broker can conduct both transactions quickly, you won't have to come up with all the money to buy the shares. (This applies to exercising call options as well.)

Double options

Double options are combined put and call options, with a premium which is nearly double a normal premium. You are betting that the share price will move out of the range represented by the premium cost.

Hedging

Suppose you own some shares which you don't want to sell, but you expect them to fall in the short term. You can buy a put option in the share to protect them against a fall in value. In general, this kind of hedging is costly and unnecessary for the smaller investor.

Writing options

It is possible to 'write' options on shares that you own through your broker, who will try to find an option buyer. You get the premiums, less dealing charges, and you buy the shares when puts are exercised or sell you shares if a call is exercised. It is also possible to be a 'naked writer', which means writing options on shares you don't own – an absurdly dangerous activity if you have no money to back up the risk of loss.

Traded options

Traded options exist only in certain shares and their form is fixed by the options market. You can buy puts and calls at certain prices fixed around the share's market price for periods of three, six or nine months. As the share price moves, the option prices move with it. The big difference between traded options and ordinary ones is that you can buy and sell a traded option as often as you like during its life. As well as the market in shares, you can also buy traded options based on the FTSE 100 Share Index and other indices.

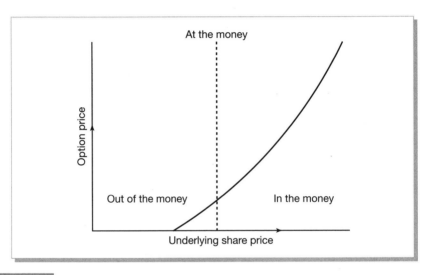

Figure 7.3   **How option prices relate to share prices**

Example

Suppose you want to buy an option in Company X's shares, currently trading at 330p; put and call options may be available at 300p, 320p, 340p and 360p. The 300p and 320p prices are called 'in the money' if you are buying a call, because they are lower than the share's market price, and the 340p and 360p prices are called 'out of the money' because they are higher. Conversely, if you are buying a put, the 340p and 360p prices are 'in the money' and the 300p and 320p prices are 'out of the money'. If you bought a call at 300p, the premium might be 50p, so if you sold it immediately you would make a loss of 20p per share, even though the option is 'in the money', since you would buy the shares for 300p + 50p = 350p and only be able to sell them for 330p.

The way that the price of the option is calculated is complicated. Essentially, it is split up into two parts, the 'time value' and the 'intrinsic value'. The time value is set according to the time that an option has left to run – the longer the time left, the higher the time value – and at the moment that the option expires there will be no time value left. Time values are worked out on computer and are based on an estimate of the chances of an investor being able to exercise an option. Factors that influence time values are the time left, how near the option is to being in the money, and the volatility of the underlying share or commodity.

Intrinsic values are simply the amount by which an option is in the money, so if you had bought a call at 300p in shares selling at 330p, your option is in the money by 30p, which is its intrinsic value. The sale value of the option will vary throughout its lifetime. With a nine-month option the time value reduces fairly slowly for about six months before dropping at an increasingly rapid rate. In-the-money options tend to move in parallel with the share price, while out-of-the-money options are less responsive.

As with shares, options have a 'spread' – you pay the higher price when you buy and get the lower price when you sell – and you pay dealer's charges on top of this.

How to trade in options

First, find a broker who will take you on. As with investing in shares, options brokers will offer different levels of service, such as execution only or advisory and discretionary services, which carry different levels of commission. Your broker will want you to deposit money with him/her, from which s/he will take the premiums as you deal. When you contact your broker with instructions to deal, the broker will try to get the price you ask for; if s/he can't, you can place a limit order for a fee. S/he will then do the deal for you later that day if prices make it possible to do so.

The rationale for private investors' interest in traded options is essentially the attraction of leverage combined with the limited risk of loss. If you buy an out-of-the-money call and the share price rises, you make around 10 times what you would have made if you had simply bought the shares, and the most you can lose is the premium, part of which you may be able to get back by re-selling the option before the expiry date. The longer the options, the more expensive it is because there is more chance of you making a profit. In-the-money options give you lower profits, but a bigger chance of making one, so they are a safer bet. Investors tend to buy puts less often than calls, perhaps because it is easier to imagine that a share is going to go up than it is to believe that it is going to go down.

For guerrillas – who really benefits from options?

The dealers certainly do. They make a profit on the transactions irrespective of whether the purchaser wins or loses. There may occasionally be moments when you are sure that a price is moving in a certain direction and can buy options at a price that will give a profit, but regularly buying traded options can be an expensive gamble, especially if you are inexperienced.

---

case study   **Traded options – a private investor's view**

A reader of the first edition of this book, Peter Hicks, has a slightly different view of the benefits of traded options; he writes that:

> I have found writing naked puts to be most rewarding: a way of making money without actually holding stocks and using up the annual tax-free capital gains allowance of around £12,000 for a married couple while leaving one's capital safely on deposit… In the traded options market, buyers far outweigh the sellers. Many interested institutions are forbidden to be sellers by the terms of their constitutions. Loosely, there are too many 'punters' (buyers) and too few 'bookies' (sellers). Hence traded options tend to be a sellers' market, and prices favour sellers, I believe – particularly put sellers.

> In April [1996] I fancied Lucas. My hunch was reinforced by [an analyst's newsletter]. I toyed with the idea of buying 4,000 at about 213p – but I would much prefer to buy 4,000 at 200p! So, I 'put' myself at risk to have to buy 4,000 Lucas at 200p at any time up to November. For taking this so-called risk (I would be quite happy at 200p) I received a check for £420, net of all expenses – a nice tax-free bonus to add to the interest on uninvested capital. I will only have

▶

to purchase the stock if the price falls below 200p but will only lose
if the price falls below 1991/2 whereas if I had bought the stock at
213p I would have lost £940...

Mr Hicks, an experienced private investor, keeps funds outside the
market in order to back up his speculation, which, strictly speaking,
does not count as 'naked writing'. He makes the following points:

▨ Buyers – no margin is required. The potential loss is restricted to the
size of your initial check, just like placing a bet with a bookie!

▨ Writers and sellers – you are the bookie! Margin is required, but the
amount depends to a large extent on the relationship between you
and your broker. If you have a significant portfolio of shares lodged
in a nominee account with your longstanding, friendly broker, he
might not require any further margin.

▨ Taxation – option gains are subject to capital gains tax (CGT),
so you should restrict your potential gains to the annual tax-free
allowance. For buyers, the tax point is the date when the gain
occurs – when you sell your option for a price above that which you
paid. For sellers the tax point is the expiry date of the option. This
can result in a worthwhile tax holiday. In July, it is possible to sell
options with an expiry date in the following April (the next tax year).
The CGT 'will not have to be paid until the following year – a two-
year tax holiday'.

Spread betting – tax-free investing?

'The gambling known as business looks with austere disfavour upon
the business known as gambling', wrote Ambrose Bierce more than
a century ago, and this certainly seems to be true of financial spread
betting today. Unlike derivatives trading, spread betting is incontro-
vertibly gambling, as defined by UK law, and for UK tax payers it offers
the attraction that all gains are free of capital gains tax and transaction
duties. A lot of professional traders in the City of London enjoy spread
betting on their own account.

Financial spread betting offers similar opportunities to futures trading
for hedging and speculating, but generally in smaller amounts, which
allows the amateur with a few pounds to spend to join the game. The

'bookie' (one a of a number of authorized spread betting firms) offers a 'spread', which is the range between a price at which it will sell and the price at which it will buy, on specific companies, indices, currencies and so on. You make a bet that, say, the FTSE 100 will drop over the next few months, so you buy at the firm's buying price (the 'bid price'), which is the lower end of the spread. You agree a figure for each percentage point or penny of the share price – let's say, £1 per point – and wait to see what happens. You can pre-agree a limit for any losses and for gains, or you can follow the market and close the contract when you wish. There is no commission, as this is contained within the spread that the company quotes you. Remember, though, that like most futures contracts these are geared transactions, so you could lose more than your original deposit.

As well as the tax advantages, spread betting offers another benefit – you can sell short easily. 'Short selling' means speculating that a security is going to drop in price. It has long had a bad reputation, and short sellers have been blamed for everything from the Wall Street Crash of 1929 to Britain falling out of the European Exchange Rate Mechanism (ERM) in 1992, and it can be difficult for a small investor to find a way to sell short safely in the conventional markets (for instance, it can be hard to sell put options when you want). With spread betting, going short is as easy as going long.

The main disadvantages are that the spread can often be quite high and that, like options, contracts do have an expiry date that you don't choose (the company tells you which expiry dates are available). Spread betting tends to offer a smaller range of expiry dates than options. Also, spread betting firms don't offer a very wide range of companies and indices to bet on, which limits the opportunities for really sophisticated hedging or speculating strategies.

The details of the mechanisms of spread betting are seductive to amateur investors who have never come across them before; it is easy to get sucked in to fantasies of how much money you are going to make, when you really don't have a clue whether Company X or Index Y is going to go up or down. Since the amounts at risk are small, it is easy to think that you won't lose much, but if you trade frequently and hit a losing streak, you could easily lose a few thousand pounds even if you are only betting a pound a point.

Don't forget, though, that you can use spread betting as a hedge; if you own shares in a large UK company, or in funds that aim to mimic a major index, you could bet that the price of your real investment will drop, the idea being that you don't mind losing the spread bet if the real investment goes up. If you do this, though, you will still need to consider whether the cost of this exercise is justified, and calculate carefully the size of your bet to match the risk of the drop of the main investment.

Personally, I don't believe that many non-professionals really use spread betting to hedge. Hedging takes discipline, is boring, and doesn't offer big profits. Speculating, on the other hand, is fun, encourages wild behaviour and offers the promise of large gains – all very natural and human, but unlikely to make you rich in the long run. Guerrilla investors will rarely need to make a spread bet, but there may occasionally be opportunities when it is worth-

❝❝guerrilla investors will rarely need to make a spread bet❞❞

while – for instance, when you are absolutely certain that Company X's share price is going to go through the floor – but until then, it is best to stay away.

Derivatives – the casualties

As we have seen, derivatives can be used either for hedging or for speculating; unfortunately, many people try to use them for both at the same time. Suppose, for instance, that you have a substantial investment in the FTSE 100 companies, and you are convinced that in the long term they will perform outstandingly well. In the short, however, you are concerned that their value may fall. You can buy a derivatives contract that will guarantee a specified return for a period if the market value of your shares falls below a specified level; this gives you 'insurance' at a price that may or may not be acceptable. If you go on to purchase other derivatives contracts based around your holdings in the hope of increasing your returns, you are almost certainly increasing your risks, which is the opposite of your original intention. You might think that no one would be crazy enough to do this, but a large number of organizations have suffered serious losses by acting along these lines.

Derivatives traders tend to dismiss criticism as ill-informed, and while it is true that many derivatives contracts are genuine hedges, the fact remains that those in the business of providing such contracts have no great incentive to prevent their clients from losing money. Many of the critics, moreover, are actually extremely well informed; for example, Warren Buffett, the famous investor and one of the world's richest men, has called derivatives 'time bombs', not only for the participants but also for the economic system as a whole. Buffett's main objections are that:

■ Derivatives contracts depend upon the creditworthiness of the parties involved, and since the sums are so large, the collapse of one party can have serious knock-on effects.

■ These knock-on effects could lead to a chain reaction of collapse across whole industries.

■ The value of open contracts are reported in the accounts, but may give a very misleading impression of their final value or loss. Cases of deliberate misreporting do occur.

■ The growth of derivatives has led to the concentration of large amounts of risk in a relatively small group of firms which in itself increases the risks.

■ Regulators cannot supervise derivatives adequately because of their complexity, and are not able to assess the level of risk exposure of specific firms.

As discussed in previous editions of this book, Buffett and other distinguished commentators, such as George Soros, have long warned that derivatives could destabilize the world's financial system, and indeed financial derivatives did play a major role in the financial crisis that began in 2007. Nevertheless, these exotic instruments remain very attractive to financial institutions and major corporations, and there has been considerable resistance to attempts to reform the derivatives system. To understand why financial derivatives have become a major worry to the regulators, we need to look back at the last few decades to see how they have grown and developed to the point where, as Soros puts it, 'derivatives and synthetic securities have been used to create imaginary value out of thin air'[1] on a vast scale.

The kinds of derivatives that Buffett and Soros have been warning about are not the standardized contracts traded on the futures exchanges, which were set up to ensure that all their transactions were transparent, properly regulated and backed up by adequate capital, but the 'over-the-counter' (OTC) arrangements that are negotiated privately between financial institutions. Most OTC contracts are varieties of forward rate agreements (see page 153) or 'swaps'. Of these, swaps have become the most problematic. In essence, they are the exchange of two streams of cash flow (i.e. a series of cash payments, known as 'legs') that are based on separate instruments. For example, two banks may hold two different bonds, and agree to 'swap' the stream of coupon payments. During the 1980s, banks began to do OTC swap deals extensively, and the regulators agreed not to regulate these deals on the condition that they were not offered to the public, or in any system similar to an exchange, where a contract might be offered to many others simultaneously. As many swap deals were worth tens of millions of dollars, it seemed, in the 1980s, that these arcane arrangements would remain the preserve of institutions that possessed the necessary expertise to use them sensibly.

During the 1990s, however, there were a number of well-publicized derivatives disasters. In 1995, Britain's oldest investment bank, Barings, went bust because its head derivatives trader in Singapore, Nick Leeson, had secretly run up losses of an estimated £827 million in unauthorized risky derivatives trades. The previous year the municipality of Orange County, California, went bankrupt after losing $1.6 billion on interest rate swaps. In 1995, Procter & Gamble and Gibson Greetings successfully sued Bankers Trust for misrepresenting derivatives the bank had sold them that resulted in large losses. Then, in 1998, a hedge fund, LTCM, made such large losses that it potentially threatened the international financial system:

---

[1] 'America must face up to the dangers of derivatives', George Soros *Financial Times*, 22 April 2010.

LTCM – even the 'rocket scientists' can get it wrong

In 1998, Long Term Capital Management (LTCM), a so-called hedge fund, suffered such large losses trading in derivatives that it had to be rescued by a consortium of 14 major US securities firms and commercial banks. At the time of the collapse, LTCM was said to have a potential loss of some $80 billion, a staggering sum that might have sparked off a worldwide financial panic had it not been for prompt action by Alan Greenspan, the then Chairman of the Federal Reserve Board.

Prior to the collapse, LTCM had been regarded as one of the top American hedge funds. The term 'hedge fund', incidentally, is misleading. Hedge funds are not generally conservative operations intended to reduce their clients' risks – they are intended to achieve good returns, and are designed to avoid regulation, only admitting financial institutions and rich, financially sophisticated people as customers.

LTCM was started in 1994 with $1 billion of its investors' money. It was the creation of John Meriwether, former vice chairman of Salomon Brothers, who was immortalized in the excellent book about Salomon Brothers in the 1980s, *Liar's Poker* by Michael Lewis. LTCM boasted two Nobel Prize-winning economists, Robert Merton and Myron Scholes, among its employees.

LTCM had a lot of prestige because of its talented team and the large amount of money it had raised as its initial capital stake. In its first few years, it achieved above-average for its investors. In 1995 and 1996 it produced net annual profits of over 40 per cent. In 1997, the profit fell to 17 per cent.

The main way LTCM made profits was by exploiting temporary differences in valuation between similar types of financial securities, increasing the potential profit or loss by highly geared bets in the futures markets. The idea is that varieties of, say, foreign bonds, are similar enough to be comparable, so you buy a bond that looks cheap and simultaneously sell an equal amount of another bond that looks expensive.

To get a clearer idea of the complexities involved, imagine that a fund manager thinks, before the days of the euro, that the European Community is moving ever closer towards a common currency. The fund manager decides that this implies that yields on European government bonds will move more closely together than before and

▶

notices that, say, Spanish government bonds are yielding a lot more than German government bonds, so buys Spanish bonds while selling an equal amount of German bonds short in the futures markets.

This type of activity is supposed to be a kind of arbitrage and is often claimed to be 'market neutral', meaning that the fund wins a profit whether or not interest rates go up or down, since it is long on one bond and short on the other one. That's the theory – but the fund is still relying on the assumption that the yield 'spread' between the two bonds will get closer together.

So, how do you get from a measly 1 per cent or 2 per cent profit on a transaction like this to the lofty 40 per cent annual return that LTCM was making early on? You do that by doing lots and lots of deals across the world's derivatives markets, using as much margin as possible. LTCM relied on sophisticated mathematical models of price behaviour to decide exactly how to construct their deals. These models were based, by definition, on assumptions about the market, but they used vast amounts of historical data, so they were quite good at predicting the future under 'normal' market conditions. LTCM could use the models to detect short-term price anomalies and pounce on them.

One thing is certain about the stock market. If someone comes up with a good wheeze that makes money, a crowd of other people will start copying the technique. Once everyone is doing it, the opportunity for profit vanishes. By 1997, LTCM saw that the opportunities were drying up, and started to take more risks.

It was bad timing. Around the world, financial uncertainly was increasing. The Asian currency crisis of 1997 was succeeded by the Russian government's decision to default on its bonds (yes, governments do default) and to devalue its currency. A large number of foreign institutional investors who had charged into Russia earlier got badly burned. LTCM's sophisticated financial models were suddenly all wrong, because the markets were behaving in a different way from how they 'normally' behave.

Fear drives professionals to make unprofessional mistakes, and good assets get dumped indiscriminately. The market overall stops being the marvellous, rational place that eminent economists can develop mathematical models for – it starts behaving like a drunken sailor on shore leave. LTCM couldn't just dump all its contracts because they were too complex and doing so would have caused even more losses.

▶

> LTCM's problem was taken seriously enough in the USA for the Federal Reserve Bank of New York to approach some institutional creditors to suggest that they did not force the firm into bankruptcy. A group of creditors agreed to inject some $3.65 billion into LTCM to stave off the problem and give it time to unwind its positions, in return for acquiring control of the firm.
>
> The saving of LTCM evoked a lot of criticism. While it was not technically a government bailout, the authorities had been involved. Critics argued that it set a dangerous precedent, since other, even larger, hedge funds might be tempted to take crazy risks, confident that if something went wrong in the future, they would be excused from their obligations – this is known as a 'moral hazard'. According to the free market economics that dominated US thinking at the time, firms that make mistakes should be allowed to fail, or else the world's economy will become increasingly fragile. It is hypocrisy, they said, to save Wall Street firms while lecturing other countries on the evils of protecting their own troubled financial institutions.

High-profile derivatives catastrophes, like the collapse of Barings Bank and the bankruptcy of Orange County in California, allegedly occurred when employees who were told to use derivatives to hedge, or to speculate within carefully defined risk levels, actually took on much more risk. In many cases these 'open positions', as active contracts are called, were not properly explained in the accounts, and the top executives may not have understood the extent of the risks to which their organizations were exposed. Following these upsets, it was claimed that derivatives were now better understood and such events would not occur again. The LTCM case was more worrying, because it exposed the extent of the potential danger of 'counterparty risk' in the little-regulated OTC market. A 'counterparty' is simply one of the parties (i.e. participants) to a contract; in the burgeoning swaps market, there were many series of interconnected contracts, worth very large sums, that depended upon all the counterparties fulfilling their contractual obligations. The near-failure of LTCM demonstrated that there was a real risk that the collapse of one firm could set off a domino effect of counterparty failures in the OTC market that could cause the collapse of many financial institutions around the world.

After the LTCM crisis, a number of major banks formed the Counterparty Risk Management Policy Group (CRMPG), which made a number of recommendations on how to deal with the problem. One of the issues it highlighted was that many of the swaps contracts were being improperly documented, making it difficult for the institution itself, or its regulatory body, to know the full extent of the risks it was taking. In keeping with the mood of the times, the group stressed the importance of self-regulation by market players, although it did also propose that major players in the OTC market meet periodically with regulatory bodies to monitor developments.

In late 1999, however, a report by the President's Working Group on Financial Markets recommended that 'bilateral transactions between sophisticated counterparties' should be excluded from any regulatory measures, which led to the USA's Commodity Futures Modernization Act of 2000, which essentially gave major financial institutions free rein to self-regulate in the OTC market. The rationale for this *laissez-faire* policy was that it would give the US institutions a competitive advantage in the booming derivatives markets. With the collapse of Enron in 2001 (see Chapter 7), calls for regulation of derivatives began to increase, and at the time of writing (2011), regulatory legislation is in train; it remains to be seen whether this will be sufficient.

Derivatives and the financial crisis (2007–ongoing)

Between 2000 and 2007, when the financial crisis began, the OTC derivatives market continued to grow; by late 2008 the total notional value of the global OTC derivatives market was over $600 trillion, a staggering figure ($600,000,000,000,000). However, this notional figure is misleading. As several academics have pointed out, it's like adding up all the tickets that have been sold in a lottery and multiplying them by the value of the prize; so, for instance, if the prize is £10 million and you sell 10 million tickets for £5 each, it's like saying that the notional value of the lottery is £100 trillion, when the total money that changes hands is only the ticket money, which is £50 million. It is estimated that only about 3 per cent of the notional value of most derivatives as actually at risk. However, credit default swaps, which were used extensively in financing the US housing boom during the noughties, had quasi-insurance characteristics which meant that the whole sum, estimated to have been $35–$65 trillion in 2007, was at risk, and could have been as high as the GDP for the entire world (estimated to have been $65.61 trillion in 2007).

The financial crisis that began in 2007 is discussed in detail in Chapter 13. In the present section, we will just focus on the issue of the massive explosion in the use of derivatives since the LTCM crisis. Although many institutions were making fortunes in derivatives, high-profile failures continued, including:

■ China Aviation – in late 2004, a subsidiary of China Aviation, China Aviation Oil (Singapore), suddenly announced that it had lost $550 million trading oil derivatives. It soon emerged that the company had been aware for weeks that it had lost over $390 million on the contracts, but illegally hid the losses while it tried to find investors to save the company. The losses occurred because the company had gambled that oil prices would fall during late 2004, when in fact they rose steeply. Several of the company's top executives were arrested on charges of forgery, insider trading and failure to disclose losses. An investigation by PriceWaterhouseCoopers, the accountancy firm, found poor corporate governance 'at every level in the company' and claimed that the firm had not understood the risks of derivatives trading.

■ Deutsche Bank – in 2006 a young trader at Deutsche Bank, Anshul Ristagi, was sacked after losing an estimated £30 million over a two-month period while trading 'collateralized debt obligations' (CDOs) and allegedly covering up the losses. CDOs are packaged bundles of debt contracts, similar to structured notes (see page 161) that are difficult to value because of the complexities of the risks to which they are exposed.

■ Amaranth Advisors – this US firm managed a number of hedge funds and collapsed in 2006 when it lost $6 billion on natural gas futures. In 2010 the Federal Energy Regulatory Commission found that Amaranth traders had manipulated prices of natural gas futures – the case continues.

Such failures were often dismissed as being healthy; after all, if you really believe in unbridled remarket economics, as many in the US did during the Bush era, you expect some businesses to fail when they make mistakes. What is now coming to light is that many of the 'strong' institutions that were making fortunes in OTC swaps were also making mistakes and committing abuses, including predatory lending practices in the US 'sub-prime' mortgage market (see Chapter 13), misrepresenting the risks of derivatives products to their customers, and, in some cases, actually constructing derivatives-based products that were intended to fail. Under President Bush (who took office in 2001), regulators were discouraged from interfering; now, under President Obama, the mood in the USA has completely changed in the wake of the financial crisis. For instance, in March 2010 Gary Gensler, the current chairman of the US Commodity Futures Trading Commission, told an audience at Chatham House, the distinguished UK think-tank, that:

the financial regulatory system failed the test. So many people in Europe and in the United States who never had any connection to derivatives or exotic financial contracts had their lives hurt by the risks taken by financial actors. OTC derivatives were at the centre of the 2008 financial crisis. They added leverage to the financial system with more risk being backed up by less capital. US taxpayers bailed out AIG [see Chapter 13] with $180 billion when that company's ineffectively regulated $2 trillion derivatives portfolio, managed from London and cancerously interconnected to other financial institutions, nearly brought down the financial system. As we later learned, much of the bailout money flowed through AIG to US and European banks. These events demonstrate how over-the-counter derivatives – initially developed to help manage and lower risk – can actually concentrate and heighten risk in the economy and to the public.'[2]

These sentiments are quite a sea-change from the days of the President's Working Group on Financial Markets, which advised President Bill Clinton in 1999 to remove many restrictions on the OTC market. Bill Clinton said in an interview in 2010 that he had been wrong to take this advice, but blamed the Bush administration for reducing regulation even further, saying, 'I think what happened was the SEC and the whole regulatory apparatus after I left office was just let go.'[3]

---

[2] Remarks of Chairman Gary Gensler, OTC Derivatives Reform, Chatham House, London 18 March 2010, Commodity Futures Trading Commission Washington DC.

[3] 'Political Punch Power', ABC News, 17, 2010 7:20 PM.

Hedge funds

Although it is abundantly clear that the growth of derivatives has led to their misuse, either intentionally or by accident, it is also true that genuine progress has been made in the understanding of how they ought to be valued – in fact, these advances are the main factor that led to the boom in derivatives trading among market professionals. 'Hedge funds' are part of this phenomenon; they started out as highly specialized funds that only accepted investments from financial institutions and very wealthy and sophisticated investors (many of whom were senior executives in financial institutions) who were, in theory at least, able to understand the risks that the hedge funds were taking. In recent years new hedge funds have appeared to serve the retail market, and it is now possible for the ordinary person to invest in some of these funds. Hedge funds were originally supposed to be strictly focused on hedging certain complex risks, but today the term encompasses many different kinds of investment, usually involving the use of derivatives. The risk exposure of any fund depends on what investments it makes, and often fluctuates from day to day, or even hour to hour. Some hedge funds do not appear to be in the business of hedging at all, except in the sense that they are trying to reduce the risks of speculation. Even the hedge funds that genuinely try to hedge probably do not manage to completely cancel out the risks they take.

Most hedge funds are out to make high returns and are only suitable for investors who really do have a high appetite for risk. Generally you are required to commit your investment in the fund for a specified period, often three years or more, after which time you may not be able sell on any business day, but only on days specified by the fund. People who want to invest in a hedge fund should investigate its policies and prospectus in great detail; hedge funds are not as transparent as other funds, in part because they need to keep the finer details of their investment strategies secret from the competition, so investors need to be careful. Common strategies include:

> **❝people who want to invest in a hedge fund should investigate its policies and prospectus in great detail❞**

■ Aiming for high returns by building up a portfolio of long and short derivatives positions based on shares and bonds, with the hope of making gains from rising prices while protecting against volatility.

■ Trying to reduce exposure to market volatility by buying under-valued shares and selling overvalued shares to achieve a 'market neutral' effect.

■ Finding 'special situations', such as mergers, and using derivatives to increase the potential gains.

■ Betting on political and economic trends by heavy speculation in derivatives. George Soros, the famous trader celebrated for his massive currency speculations that have temporarily affected the economies of whole countries, including Britain, was one of the first to apply this high-risk approach.

One could call George Soros a guerrilla investor, but we should remember that he has been in the business for many decades and is one of the leaders in the field; the rest of us should probably stay away from this, unless we want to dedicate our professional lives to derivatives! There is a somewhat dubious case for using hedge funds to reduce the risks of the rest of your portfolio, but this is generally only worthwhile if you have really substantial investments – say £1 million or more.

Structured products

Despite the growth of derivatives markets and the contracts they offer, derivatives fiends have an appetite for ever more complex deals, dismissing the standardized contracts available on futures exchanges as 'plain vanilla'. To meet this new demand, financial institutions are offering tailor-made contracts designed to suit the exact needs of individual investors. These are known as 'structured products' and usually take the form of a number of different risk contracts that are combined into one agreement. In general, they are intended to protect investors from short- to medium-term risks. For example, suppose you are concerned that European Community policies are about to wreak havoc on the economy; you can purchase a structured note that allows you to bet on the US dollar against the euro. Or suppose that you think London property prices are about to collapse, so you buy a structured note to protect the value of your Kensington mansion falling below a specified value. Completely unrelated risks, upon which you have a firm view, may be combined together in one contract, using the values and time periods that you want. The aim is usually to allow your other investments to increase if the markets go up, but to limit any potential losses if the markets go the wrong way.

You probably need to invest at least £25,000 to purchase a tailor-made contract of this kind, which suggests that normally you will have a much larger portfolio invested in the relevant markets. The note has to be held to maturity – you can't sell it in the meantime – but you can, and must, get a guarantee that the principal is protected. This guarantee will usually be from a high grade institution such as a bank.

The problem with this kind of hedging is the assumption that your views on the risks to your portfolio are well-judged; you may, for instance, be obsessed with the fear that a certain market may crash, but this fear may be completely unrealistic. Some other undesirable event – that you haven't even thought of – may occur instead. The company providing you with the contract may be valuing the risks rather better than you are, and making money out of your poor judgement, but they are unlikely to tell you that your fears are unjustified if they want your business. The correct evaluation of risk is the name of the game, and unless you are a whiz at derivatives mathematics and can work out a fair price for the contract yourself, the chances are that you will pay over the odds. Unless you really are under pressure to smooth out short- to medium-term volatility in your portfolio – as many companies are – then you should really ask yourself whether you do need to hedge, and whether the consequences of not hedging will be serious in the long term.

Finally, the criticisms of the growth of derivatives apply to structured products too; it is not impossible for a major bank to go broke and be unable to fulfil guarantees on structured notes already issued.

Summary

Guerrilla investors need to be well-informed, so it is important to familiarize yourself with the field of derivatives, even if you will only use them very rarely and carefully. Their growth has been looked upon with concern by many of the most respected professional investors because of the difficulty of regulating them properly; all the financial markets depend upon careful supervision to prevent them from collapsing. The appearance of derivatives as a 'wild beast', as one senior banker puts it, charging uncontrolled through the world's financial system is an issue that needs to be resolved if we are to avoid a destructive economic meltdown.

For individual guerillas who want to build their wealth over the long term, derivatives may very occasionally offer a chance to protect a portfolio or to take a quick speculative profit, but they should not be the main focus of investment activity. The key questions, remember, are:

- Do I really need to hedge?
- Is this really a true hedge? (Usually it won't be).
- What are all the risks?
- How much will it really cost?

Most of the time guerilla investors who do their homework thoroughly will find that they can happily avoid this dangerously seductive field. In the next chapter, we will examine the problems of financial fraud and sharp practice, and how you can avoid becoming a victim of such wrongdoing.

8

Fraud and sharp practice

Most of the world's financial regulators do their best to prevent outright fraud, but fail to control endemic sharp practices in the financial services industry. For instance, for the investor who loses money, it may be small consolation that the loss was due to sharp practice such as 'misselling' rather than outright fraud. This chapter explores the problems and offers guidance on how to avoid such losses, and looks at the following:

■ Grand fraud versus petty fraud

■ What regulators can and can't do

■ 25 years of misdeeds: from Milken to Madoff

■ Sharp practice – pensions misselling

■ False accounting on a grand scale – Enron and WorldCom

■ The naughty noughties

Grand fraud versus petty fraud

Financial regulation is very important to all the financial markets because without it investors would lose confidence and withdraw their money. In centres where the markets are very active indeed, such as London, New York and Hong Kong, regulation is quite strict, and rightly so. In some of the newer and smaller markets, however, regulation may be less effective.

Before looking at the two main regulators that affect UK investors – the UK's Financial Services Authority (FSA) and the USA's Securities and Exchange Commission (SEC) we should consider the main types of risk from fraud that investors may encounter:

Grand corporate frauds

These are a familiar feature of business life, especially during boom times when companies are trying to grow fast and are under pressure to produce rapidly growing performance figures. Often the problems start innocently enough – a large company battles its way to a dominant position in a new industry, say, and its bosses genuinely believe that they have the Midas touch. Some time later the opportunities for growth start to wane and market analysts start to ask awkward questions. The temptation then becomes very strong to begin massaging the books to make it look as if the company is still doing well. Some time later – often years later – it emerges that fraud has been committed, there is a flurry of court cases and the government introduces new legislation to prevent such a thing from ever happening again. Nevertheless, frauds continue to happen in spite of tighter regulations, often when the next boom comes along and supervision becomes more lax. There is really very little private investors can do about this risk except for diversifying their assets widely – the chances are that when such frauds are being committed, the market analysts are optimistic about the firm, so the private investor has no way of knowing for certain that something is wrong until it is too late.

> **frauds continue to happen in spite of tighter regulations**

Petty frauds and sharp practice

This covers a wide variety of problems. Some are systemic within in an industry – for example, when the deregulation of pensions led to pensions 'misselling' in the UK during the late 1980s (see page 172). Others may be due to the actions of one financial services company that does not perform its obligations (in the 1980s, for instance, a firm called Barlow Clowes offered packaged bond investments but did not use investors' money to purchase the bonds). Others can be very petty indeed – for example, the brokers who get you to write a cheque made out to them personally and steal the money, or the firm that over-charges you or encourages you to trade just a little bit too much in order to earn extra commissions. There are also scams – often very old ones, but dressed up in new clothing – that target the greedy or the uninformed. There are hundreds of ways to cheat people, and despite relatively good regulation in the UK there will always be some people who get tricked.

Market insider fraud

Professionals working in the financial markets sometimes have access to privileged information. Sometimes such individuals abuse this trust by, for example, trying to make money by trading in shares that they know are going to go up, or by suppressing information that they know will hurt a share price.

Compared with blue-collar crime, the punishments for white-collar crimes such as these are relatively mild, especially for those who try to stay within the grey area where it is not entirely clear whether a certain practice is illegal or not. Although, as we will see below, there are a number of compensation schemes in effect to protect investors against total loss, claiming your money may be a very long proc-ess, and you may only get a proportion of your money back. For this reason it is very important that guerrilla investors keep proper records and take all the precautions they can; doing simple things like actually checking that a firm is registered with the Financial Services Authority and that it is covered by a compensation scheme for the type of busi-ness you have in mind can go a long way towards preventing yourself from being victimized.

Here are some of the basic precautions you can take to avoid becoming the victim of fraud:

■ As mentioned earlier, always check that the firms with which you do business are registered with the FSA, are permitted to do that type of business and are covered by a compensation scheme – you can do this at: **http://www.fsa.gov.uk**. You can also check the FSA's list of unauthorized companies and obtain up-to-date information on current issues.

- Never buy shares or other securities from people who cold-call you. They are not allowed to do this, and it is probably a scam – typically it is done by a company that is based abroad to avoid the regulators.

- Beware of any deals offered to you (usually by phone) that require you to pay some money as security against the deal. This is usually an advance fee fraud, where the fraudster makes off with the money you give.

- Never take anything for granted – always check share prices, company information and so on from other sources, such as the press and annual reports.

- Never do anything in a rush. Ever. In the unlikely event that you miss a fabulous deal, there will be another one along eventually – almost always, rushing means that you don't do the proper checks, which can lead to serious mistakes.

- Keep all records and put everything in writing. It may be boring but it will help you prove a claim if anything goes wrong.

- Never make out a cheque to anyone personally, but always to an authorized firm.

- Be very careful about share tips ('tips' are when someone tells you Company X's shares are going to go up). Sometimes they are well-meant, and sometimes they are given by professionals who have had success in the past – but that doesn't mean that this tip will be correct. If the tip amounts to insider dealing (see page 171) you could be committing an offence by acting on it. Some of the soundest tips require you to invest and wait for many years to see if they work – e.g. 'Country Z is in a mess, so buy its best companies and wait for them to go up when the country recovers.' That's fine if you know about Country Z and have the patience.

What the regulators can and can't do

Most countries have regulatory authorities to oversee how financial services firms operate. It has to be said that their task is quite difficult, because in many situations of potential malpractice it is difficult to decide whether anyone has done anything wrong. To take a simple example, suppose a wealthy 35-year-old single woman who has been speculating in commodities for six years comes to a broker and wants to place £500,000 on some very risky positions; it might be argued that while that person might be unwise to take such a risk, she is sufficiently experienced and sophisticated to understand what she is doing, and the broker does nothing wrong in placing her bets for her. In contrast, if a recently bereaved 60-year-old man whose entire nest egg is £500,000 and who has no experience of commodities trading does the same thing, the broker might be said to be negligent in allowing such an inappropriate person to take huge risks that he doesn't understand. Regulators have to wrestle with these kinds of questions – and many much more difficult ones – as part of their job of supervision. They are also ultimately answerable to the investing public, so often much of their work involves closing the stable door after the horse has bolted. In other words, when a major scandal occurs and many investors feel they have been cheated, the regulators have to be seen to be doing something to make sure such a thing will never happen again, even though the chances are that some other different kind of malpractice is much more likely to occur.

One of the main benefits that regulators offer the public are compensation schemes, usually funded by contributions that approved firms make each year as a cost of doing business. These compensation schemes generally cover not only deliberate frauds, but also inadvertent bankruptcies and other disasters where the investing public loses money. Although compensation schemes provide a useful safety net, as mentioned earlier they often take a very long time to pay over money to investors, and they may only cover a proportion of the losses; from the investor's point of view, it is much better not to get caught out in the first place.

The Financial Services Authority

In the UK the main financial regulator has been, since 2000, the Financial Services Authority (the FSA). It was set up by the government to oversee fairness in the markets and to regulate a very wide variety of firms offering financial services. It appoints the directors of the Financial Services Compensation Scheme (FSCS) which operates independently and may pay out on claims against firms authorized by the FSA, and covers problems with such things as:

- bank deposits
- insurance policies
- stockbrokers
- mortgage lending and arranging.

Currently the FSCS's maximum compensation limits are as follows:

- £85,000 per person for losses relating to deposits made with authorized firms (such as banks)
- £50,000 per person for losses from investments made with authorized firms.
- £50,000 per person for losses relating to mortgages
- 90 per cent of losses relating to insurance, with no upper limit.

Clearly, it is really important to check with the FSA that any firm you are dealing with is officially approved for the services and products you are considering purchasing from it, and to establish the level of compensation available if things go wrong. If you deal with an unauthorized firm, you may not get any compensation at all, so don't do it! Even so, do not rely on FSA authorization as a cast-iron guarantee, and make the effort to investigate firms in other ways, such as by talking to other customers.

The FSA has not covered itself in glory during the financial crisis that began in 2007, but this has not been entirely its own fault. The understandable public outcry against the bank bailouts (see Chapter 13) affected the FSA, and it has clearly been under difficult and conflicting political pressures from successive governments during the crisis. At the time of writing it is reorganizing itself for the umpteenth time, apparently to the deep indifference of most people in the City, who tend to have a low opinion of regulators. Perhaps that's just a case of poachers hating game-keepers; the fact is that the FSA is a lot better than nothing at all, and it does try to keep the public (that's you and me) informed about what is going on through its website, which is a considerable improvement on the bad old pre-FSA days when it was very much harder to find out what was going on.

The Securities and Exchange Commission

As you might expect, the Securities and Exchange Commission (SEC), the main US regulatory body, is much more gung-ho than the FSA, which takes a gentler approach (although the FSA has imposed some staggeringly large fines in recent years). The SEC, in contrast, regularly uses covert surveillance, plea-bargains (where one wrong-doer promises to help catch another in return for a reduced sentence) and other aggressive investigative methods in order to catch the rule-breakers. In the past, the SEC has been criticized for pursuing the innocent, and for failing to distinguish between inadvertent infringements of highly technical minor regulations and out-and-out fraud. The US corporate and financial culture is, of course, very different from the UK's, and it is often hard to interpret the issues properly when a scandal erupts across the pond. In general, UK investors are not usually immediately affected by problems in the US, but it is worth following the news of US market activity and what the SEC is up to, because sooner or later, in this globalized world, changes in the US economy and markets are likely to affect the UK's economy and financial markets, as occurred during the sub-prime scandal that began in 2007 (see Chapter 13).

Set up in 1934 in the middle of the Great Depression, the SEC's main job is to regulate US stock markets. One of the main ways it does this is to require companies to produce not only annual reports but also quarterly reports (i.e., every three months), and it takes a very severe attitude towards any misinformation contained within them. One very useful service the SEC provides is its online database, EDGAR, which provides a massive amount of material including statutory company filings, records of investigations, and so on. Information on many large UK companies can be found here because of their connection with the US markets. You can access EDGAR at: http://www.sec.gov/edgar.shtml.

25 years of misdeeds – from Milken to Madoff

The first edition of this book was written in 1994, when the UK was only beginning to recover from the major financial scandals of the 1980s, and covered the most prominent, which was that of Michael Milken, the 'junk bond king' and his associate, the stockbroker Ivan Boesky. There has been no difficulty in finding more recent scandals to replace them in each subsequent edition; every few years, more episodes of colossal financial chicanery have come to light. It's worth noting, though that these scandals have tended to be quite different in their nature. For instance, Milken, a financial genius who developed a market in 'junk bonds' (corporate bonds which had low credit ratings) that funded an orgy of corporate takeovers during the 1980s, was convicted of insider trading (illegally dealing in shares using privileged insider information). This was quite different from, say, the pensions misselling episode, the false accounting practices of Enron and WorldCom, the collapse of the Icesave bank, or the Ponzi scheme operated by Bernard Madoff (all discussed below). Each time, after the scandal has come to light, the regulators have acted to prevent it happening again. And each time, within a few years, a different kind of financial misdeed has been perpetrated.

So, what is the private investor to do? Well, it's not all completely bad news. Many of the scandals only affected wealthy people who were taking more risk than normal. As for the rest, consumer protection has improved in the UK: victims of the Icesave collapse received their compensation relatively quickly, and it now appears that even the policyholders (nearly 1 million of them) with Equitable Life, which ran into serious trouble in 2000, may eventually receive some compensation. Even so, the sheer variety and enormous scale of the things that can go wrong should prompt us to stay alert at all times. As a guerrilla investor, you need to cultivate your ability to smell a rat, and not just rely on the authorities to bail you out; it's always better to avoid the problem in the first place.

Sharp practice – pensions misselling

In the UK one of main dangers investors face is not out-and-out fraud but what might be called systemic sharp practice, often following a change in regulations that opens up a new market for a set of financial products that are sold in the wrong way, or to the wrong set of people. Suppose, for instance, that a single 21-year-old student with no dependants is persuaded by an agent to buy life insurance: it's not exactly fraud – or at least, it would be very hard to prove fraud – but unless there are exceptional circumstances, it is not appropriate for such a person to buy life insurance because they simply don't need it (see Chapter 10).

In the 1980s many people who did not have access to an employer's pension scheme had a very limited range of options for how they could save for retirement. A change in the regulations introduced personal pension schemes to improve their situation, and many financial services firms jumped aggressively into this new market, and between 1988 and 1994, many ordinary people were sold personal pensions even though they would have been better off remaining in, or joining employers' pension schemes to which they had access. Although this problem was foreseen by many commentators, little was done until the end of 1994, when a review was ordered.

The investigation found that some firms had 'missold' personal pensions and, in some cases, endowment policies, to many thousands of people for whom the products were not intended. Companies were ordered to contact everyone who had taken out a personal pension during the period who might have been affected, and to put things right if the customer had suffered a loss. The process was a massive one, taking many years. At first, older people's schemes were checked because they were about to retire or had already retired, and then, some five years later, the focus turned to checking younger people's schemes.

The law says that if you suffer a loss of this kind, you must do everything you can to reduce it if you are seeking redress; during the long wait after the pensions misselling scandal, people were told to join or rejoin their employer's scheme in order to reduce the potential loss to the value of their pensions. To add insult to injury, a number of insurance companies were found not have compensated customers after their cases had been reviewed and the misselling had been identified. For example, in 2002, Royal & Sun Alliance was fined £1.35 million for failing to compensate more than 13,000 such customers who had suffered losses of over £32 million (earlier, the company had been fined for not conducting its review of missold pensions properly).

Although at the time of writing this shameful episode has largely been resolved, the possibility remains that various forthcoming changes to the pensions system may trigger new bouts of misselling. Part of the problem is that customers really don't understand the range of options open to them, nor the complexities of pension schemes, and rely on poorly trained salespeople to explain the issues to them. Guerilla investors should not make this kind of mistake – if you are going to purchase any kind of financial product, make sure you understand it thoroughly before you invest, and don't rely solely on the information that salespeople provide. As with other scandals, it is worth noting how long the process of redress took – some people had to wait more than seven years to have their pensions sorted out.

> **❝don't rely solely on the information that salespeople provide❞**

False accounting on a grand scale – Enron and WorldCom

Massive financial scandals do happen, even in the best-regulated countries, and it is worth trying to understand how they occur. One way of looking at it is to think of the urge to make money by rule-breaking as like water – it will seep into any cracks that open up in the system as they appear. That's why the really big scandals in each decade tend to be different in character – it is because the opportunities for doing wrong are different at different times. For example, the major scandals in the 1980s were about insider trading, because the regulators had not instituted rigorous enough controls at that time, but the scandals of the late 1990s were based mainly on false accounting, arising from unrealistic market expectations about rapid growth in the dotcom and telecommunications industries. In this section we will look at two of the biggest scandals that followed in the wake of the dotcom boom: the collapse of the US giants Enron and WorldCom.

The Enron scandal

One of the biggest scandals of recent years was that of Enron, an energy company that grew rapidly to become the seventh biggest company in the US from its formation in 1985 when InterNorth, a natural gas company from Nebraska, took over Houston Natural Gas. At its peak, it was employing 21,000 people in offices around the world. Although it had started out as an energy company, during the boom years it had entered other businesses, including selling internet bandwidth and dealing in complex derivatives based on the weather. The company was considered a 'blue chip' – in other words, large, stable and reliable – and had AAA rated bonds; its rapid expansion was explained by the period of deregulation of many gas and electricity markets around the world, that enabled it to become an international intermediary to national power companies, offering them a wide range of services, including derivatives contracts against adverse weather and interest rate changes. In the four years up to 2000, Enron's earnings jumped from $13.3 billion a year to over $100 billion, and it embarked on a wildly ambitious programme of investments in power plants and pipelines around the globe. Some of these investments began to go wrong quite quickly; for example, Enron purchased Wessex Water in the UK, only to find that UK regulators imposed unexpected price limits on it, and an Indian power plant that was unable to obtain payment from its largest customer. As one of the great success stories of its day, Enron was under enormous pressure from Wall Street to produce figures every three months that were in line with analysts' predictions.

Unknown to the outside world, Enron reacted to these problems by becoming involved in 'optimistic' accounting methods; by the third quarter of 2001, for instance, its financial report did not include a balance sheet, and marked more than $1 billion in expenses as non-recurring. Much later it also emerged that Enron was not reporting its derivatives deals on their net value, which is the normal method, but on their gross value, which increased its sales figures. It also transpired that Enron had been using offshore companies called SPEs (Special Purpose Entities) to adjust the quarter in which income was received, to hide losses and to inflate sales figures.

▶

▶

The first sign that anything was wrong with the company was when Enron's chief executive, Jeffrey Skilling, announced in August 2001 that he was resigning. In the previous few months he had sold some 450,000 shares in the company for $33 million, but still owned more than 1 million shares. In response to questions by Wall Street analysts, Enron's chairman Kenneth Lay gave assurances that there was nothing untoward about Skilling's departure. The market had its doubts, and Enron's share price continued to fall. As analysts began to look more closely at Enron's figures, more doubts began to emerge about Enron's accounting practices, but after the terrorist attack of 9/11, attention was diverted elsewhere.

In October 2001 Enron started selling off some of its assets, including Portland General Electric and Northwest Natural Gas. Soon after, it announced the $1 billion loss mentioned above. The American market regulator, the SEC, announced that it was investigating Enron, and in November Enron announced that it had overstated its earnings by nearly $600 million and that it had $3 billion in debts to the SPEs. Its AAA bonds were downgraded to 'junk' status overnight and the scandal began in earnest. Enron's accountants, the massive firm Arthur Andersen, was found to have deliberately destroyed evidence to do with its Enron business, and promptly collapsed. Enron's share price fell from $85 to 30 cents during the year as a wave of litigation began.

The moral of the story for investors, perhaps, is that during boom times regulatory controls and corporate governance (the methods of over-seeing company processes such as accurate financial reporting) tend to get lax; when things begin to go wrong, everyone starts baying for blood. As Warren Buffett, the famous investor, puts it, 'It is only when the tide goes out that you see who isn't wearing any swimming pants.' This is a problem for outside investors because during the good times we are always assured that everything is fine and that any obscurities in company accounts are to do with the firm's innovative, cutting-edge practices. When problems emerge, there is a massive tightening of regulation and public assurances by the government that such a thing will never be allowed to happen again (in the case of Enron and other scandals that happened during the same period, new legislation, the Sarbanes–Oxley Act, was introduced which is discussed below). For this reason, investors should not have supreme confidence even in 'blue chip companies'; while it may be possible to smell a rat sometimes, the chances are that you will occasionally have an investment in a company that goes badly wrong. For this reason, good diversification across many companies and industries – usually done by investing in funds – is arguably the best strategy for survival.

The dust had not long settled from Enron when a new scandal erupted over another massive company, WorldCom. WorldCom had started out as a tiny business offering cheaper long distance telephone calls in 1983; by 1999 it was a large public company and its founder, Bernie Ebbers was still in control of the firm and a billionaire.

---

case study   **WorldCom**

WorldCom had grown so fast because of the boom in telecommunications, particularly with the internet and mobile phones; in the 1990s it had been able to buy no less than 65 companies in these industries, mostly with borrowed money and was regarded by market analysts as a prescient firm that had spotted the true potential of telecoms.

The serious problems facing a company that grows very quickly by buying lots of other ones are well known – for example, that it is very difficult to meld these purchases into a streamlined system – but during booms nobody seems to care. In WorldCom's case, later criticism alleged that there was a massive amount of inefficiency, redundant computer systems and duplication of work because of the lack of integration between all the newly acquired companies. Another problem was that WorldCom had adopted 'optimistic' accounting practices, for example by massaging figures to make it look as if profits were increasing steadily.

Things began to go wrong in 2000 when the US government banned WorldCom's bid to acquire Sprint; this had the effect of focusing attention on the profitability of the company's existing businesses and the share price began to drop. Ebbers had purchased a large number of WorldCom's shares 'on margin' (i.e. with leverage) and was being forced to produce cash for margin calls – in October he took a personal loan of $400 million from the company to do this, but with the share price

▶

▶

continuing to fall he faced the prospect of total ruin. In a subsequent court case, it was alleged that during this period the company began deliberately to run two sets of books – the real accounts and a set that allowed the company to declare increasing sales and profitability. For the financial year 2000, the company reported $7.6 billion in earnings, and in 2001, $2.4 billion. These figures were adjusted after WorldCom went bankrupt in 2002 as losses of $49.9 billion and $14.5 billion respectively, and even these staggering losses were later found to be underestimates.

WorldCom's curious accounting practices were uncovered by an employee, Cynthia Cooper, who was working as an internal auditor. Finding some anomalies, Cooper worked for months to uncover evidence of fraud totalling billions of dollars. In 2003, a report found that the firm had exaggerated earnings and understated its expenses by a total of $74.5 billion during its last two years of business – this was claimed to be the largest accounting fraud in corporate history. During the trials and media frenzy surrounding the scandal, much of the fury was directed at investment banks and analysts who were alleged to have helped the company prop up its share price. One of the analysts implicated, Jack Grubman, was fined $15 million and banned from securities transactions for life at the end of 2002. Anger was also directed at Arthur Andersen, the company's auditors and one of the largest accountancy firms in the world. The basis of accounting depends on the idea that such firms are independent and have total integrity, and when the SEC finally banned the firm from auditing altogether, the whole system of accounting in public companies was called into question.

The Sarbanes–Oxley Act

All investors in the stock market, great and small, have to consider the most basic risk of all – do the executives of the companies they are investing in manage their companies honestly in the best interests of the shareholders? Top executives in large companies wield a great deal of power even if they are not themselves important shareholders, and this may offer them the opportunity to act in their own best interests rather than in the interests of the shareholders as a group. As well as shareholders, of course, there are other groups, the 'stakeholders', such as employees, customers and the public at large, who want the company to be managed properly – in other words, ethically, within the law, and without actively doing harm to others. The scandals that erupted in the USA in the early 2000s were not unlike many that occurred in the aftermath of earlier booms, but the stakes were arguably bigger; in an era of globalization and financial deregulation, the importance of high standards of behaviour in corporations are as, if not more, important than they have ever been. The problems at Enron, WorldCom and other large firms led to the introduction of the Sarbanes–Oxley Act in the USA that set out high standards for executives of publicly quoted firms, with heavy penalties for infringements. Already there are signs that international firms may be seeking to get around some of these restrictions by relocating some of their operations in countries with less stringent laws. Herein lies the problem; if

❛❛if regulation is too heavy, businesses will tend to look for other places in which they can operate❜❜

regulation is too heavy, businesses will tend to look for other places in which they can operate more efficiently, even if they have no intention of doing anything illegal. Heavy regulation does nothing to help the efficient running and profitability of business. Clearly, there needs to be a balance between lax regulation, which is good for business but encourages crooks to misbehave, and tight regulation, which is bad for business but prevents a lot of fraud. There can be no absolute answer to where to set the regulatory bar, which is why we see it moving up and down the severity scale over time. This is an uncomfortable fact of investment life, but it is one that successful investors have always been able to live with. As investors, we would like absolute protection, but we can't expect any government agency to provide it; self-reliance and a healthy scepticism are important too!

The naughty noughties

One of the unintended consequences of Sarbanes–Oxley was to boost the London Stock Exchange, as high-paid market professionals relocated from the USA to the UK and many international firms chose to be listed in London, where regulations were less onerous. While corporate America remained under a tight leash, however, a new problem was appearing elsewhere in the financial system.

In 2000 OTC derivatives were almost completely deregulated in the USA (see Chapter 7), and the derivatives market grew massively over the next seven years. Financial institutions, not only in the USA but elsewhere, increased their gearing to unheard-of levels as they traded frantically in derivatives contracts, many of which were based on the overvalued US property market. As a consequence, a financial crisis began in 2007; this is discussed in more detail in Chapter 13. In this section we will focus on two of the scandals that emerged from the financial crisis: Icesave and Bernard Madoff.

case study   **Icesave**

In late 2006 Landsbanki, an Icelandic bank, introduced an attractive online savings account in the UK called 'Icesave'. Easy to use, and offering good interest rates (over 6 per cent), Icesave gave British savers a choice between a cash ISA, a savings account with immediate access, and various fixed-rate deposits. It was a great success in the UK, drawing in 300,000 customers, and in 2008 it launched in the Netherlands, where 125,000 customers opened accounts in the first five months. Many local authorities in the UK, along with other institutions such as the universities of Oxford and Cambridge, had deposits with Icesave. 2008 was the year of the 'credit crunch' in the banking system, and it was common knowledge that many banks around the world were under pressure. Nevertheless, the UK press was not overly concerned about Icesave, since it appeared that deposits were covered by compensation schemes. A story in *Guardian*[1] in March 2008 even referred to the 'irony' of a nervous saver who had withdrawn his money from Icesave but had then deposited it with Northern Rock just before that bank got into trouble.

Then, in October 2008, Icesave suddenly closed and its owner, Landsbanki, went into receivership. A row quickly developed when it emerged that the Icelandic government did not intend to guarantee the deposits of bank branches outside Iceland, which included the Icesave accounts. Alistair Darling, the then UK Chancellor of the Exchequer, froze Landsbanki assets in the UK using anti-terrorism laws. As the wrangling

---

[1] *Guardian*, 'Icelandic banks feel the chill as credit crunch stretches north', 30 March 2008.

▶

▶

between the Icelandic, British and Dutch governments rumbled on (it's still a live issue at the time of writing in early 2011), UK savers were relieved when the Financial Services Compensation Scheme announced that it would cover their losses, and start paying out compensation quickly. Most UK victims got off lightly, getting their money back within a few months; customers of Landsbanki in Guernsey, the Isle of Man and the Netherlands, however, have suffered losses.

UK investors, then, had a lucky escape; this was largely due to the UK government's wish to reassure the public at a time when all the banks were in trouble, and we cannot be certain that the government will act so generously every time a bank collapses and it is unclear, as it was in the case of Icesave, whether depositors are fully covered by the UK compensation scheme. Was the saga just a case of a small country trying to punch over its weight in international finance, or was fraud involved? We still don't know for sure, but the UK's Serious Fraud Office is working with the Icelandic authorities to investigate.

So, could the guerrilla investor have foreseen the problems with Icesave without being an expert on the banking sector? I think so. A foreign bank comes out of nowhere and suddenly starts offering the best savings rates available – that's a red flag for a guerrilla. Nobody offers a great rate out of the goodness of their hearts, and it is usually a sign that you are taking on extra risk – that's why, for instance, corporate bonds produce higher yields than gilts. Nevertheless, suppose you felt reassured that your deposits would be protected, and that you opened an Icesave account in 2006. Would you have ignored the collapse of Northern Rock in late 2007, or the stories of a credit crunch in the banking system that then emerged? The fact is, there was plenty of time in which to switch your account back to a safer and more boring account with a UK bank to endure a lower interest rate. As it turned out, Icesave investors in the UK were compensated quickly (this may actually be a record!) so you might argue that you were better off keeping the money with Icesave until it collapsed; personally, I don't think it was worth the risk.

Bernard Madoff

Out of all the cases of chicanery, short-sightedness, greed and folly that occurred during the boom of the noughties, one individual stands out as the most blatant exemplar of outright criminality at the top of the financial profession: Bernie Madoff. Madoff was a New York stockbroker and investment adviser who had once been the chairman of NASDAQ, the US stock exchange. He was a senior figure on Wall Street, serving on various industry boards, making substantial political contributions and charitable donations, and was active in high society in New York and Florida. He was widely regarded as an authority on financial matters; at a roundtable discussion in New York in October 2007 on 'The Future of the Stock Market' he assured the audience that:

> by and large in today's regulatory environment, it's virtually impossible to violate rules. This is something that the public really doesn't understand. If you read things in the newspaper and you see somebody violate a rule, you say well, they're always doing this. But it's impossible for a violation to go undetected, certainly not for a considerable period of time.[2]

Just over a year later, in December 2008, Bernie Madoff was arrested for a massive investment fraud that he had, in fact, been operating for 'a considerable period of time' before it was detected.

Although often described as a hedge fund, Bernie Madoff's investment arm actually managed investments within his own firm on behalf of clients rather than, as is the case with most hedge funds, depositing the investments with another bank or broker where they can be independently inspected. Although the full story has yet to be uncovered, the basic method of his fraud is thought to have been simply to produce false account statements for clients and to pay them out of a pool of cash held at a bank when they wanted to make a withdrawal, rather than out of a fund invested in the stock market as would normally be the case. This is a classic 'Ponzi scheme', named after Carlo Ponzi, a fraudster who ran such a scheme just after the First World War. Ponzi schemes are doomed to failure because eventually there will be no cash left to pay off all the investors, but this rather obvious drawback has not deterred generations of fraudsters from setting up such schemes.

[2] http://philoctetes.org/Past_Programs/The_Future_of_the_Stock_Market.

▶

▶

Limiting his client base to the wealthy, and cultivating an image of exclusivity and secrecy, Madoff described his investment strategy in vague terms, saying that it involved the use of options based on blue chip shares. His clients included many wealthy individuals and foundations in the USA and Europe, who often invested through 'feeder funds' (independently controlled funds that invested most of their assets with Madoff). When investors questioned him, he was unwilling to provide much detail on how he was able to achieve his results. The main attraction seems to have been his unusually consistent results – for one 14 and a half year period, one of his many feeder funds, Fairfield Sentry,[3] only reported negative returns for 7 months, or 4 per cent of the period, a rather unlikely result.

The total size of the fraud is not yet clear, but it seems to have been somewhere between $20 billion and $60 billion, making it the largest swindle ever. About half of his investors lost no money, but others were not so lucky. A number of individuals lost their entire fortunes, and several charitable foundations, educational establishments and hedge funds had to close down because of losses. Banco Santander, from Spain, and Bank Medici, from Austria, are thought to have lost more than $2 billion each. And there were several suicides, including that of Rene-Thierry Magon de la Villehuchet, a French aristocrat who had invested in Madoff on behalf of wealthy European clients, including royalty. In 2010 one of Madoff's own sons, Mark, committed suicide.

[3] 'The World's Largest Hedge Fund is a Fraud', November 7, 2005 Submission to the SEC, Harry Markopolos, p. 14.

One of the most discussed aspects of the Madoff case was the fact that the SEC had been receiving complaints about his activities for many years. As early as 1992, there had been a complaint that an associate of Madoff was operating a fund with unusually consistent returns; the SEC investigated and discovered that the money was invested with Madoff, but did not investigate Madoff's own fund. There were several other complaints, including one from a respected hedge fund manager, and an article appeared in *Barron's* magazine in 2001 questioning how Madoff could achieve such consistent returns. The most persistent complainer, however, was Harry Markopolos, a forensic accountant who approached the SEC on several occasions from 2000 onwards with evidence, based on his analysis of Madoff's investment performance, that his fund was likely to be a fraud.

Harry Markopolos was celebrated in the media as a whistleblower, and wrote a book about his experiences, *No One Would Listen: A True Financial Thriller*. The book, his submissions to the SEC, and his evidence to various investigative bodies, have been criticized for a rather self-righteous and overly certain tone. Certainly his 2005 submission to the SEC seems poorly written and polemical.[4] Such eccentricities may help to explain why his arguments, which were mathematically sophisticated, did not attract the attention they deserved before the fraud was finally unmasked. The SEC conducted an internal inquiry into why it had not acted sooner, and found that on the first occasion that Markopolos had approached them, in 2000 at its regional office in Boston, the office's director had simply not understood what Markopolos was talking about.[5] His second approach, in the following year, was also not acted upon. However, when the complaint from the hedge fund manager, mentioned earlier, arrived in 2003, an investigation was begun, but was put on the 'back-burner' after a few months.[6] A separate investigation was begun by another office, which uncovered some significant evidence, but was also closed down after a few months.[7] When Markopolos approached the SEC again in 2005 his allegations were taken seriously, but again were not fully investigated. It's an extraordinary story of regulatory failure, and one that is yet to be fully explained. Markopolos himself has put it down to simple bureaucratic incompetence, reportedly saying that the SEC is 'too dumb to be crooked; the FBI told me that', and calling the UK's FSA 'a total joke'.[8]

---

[4] The World's Largest Hedge Fund is a Fraud', 7 November 2005. Submission to the SEC, Harry Markopolos.

[5] Report of Investigation, United States Securities and Exchange Commission Office of Inspector General, Case No. OIG-509, 'Investigation of Failure of the SEC To Uncover Bernard Madoff's Ponzi Scheme', p.8.

[6] Ibid., pp. 9–11

[7] Ibid., p. 15.

[8] *The Sunday Times*, 'Harry Markopolos: I carried a gun in case Bernard Madoff came after me', 21 March 2010.

Could guerrilla investors have avoided losing all their money in the Madoff scandal? Yes! First of all, guerrilla investors do not ever put all their money into one investment, whatever it is, and however safe it appears to be; guerrilla investors who were convinced by Madoff might have put only a half, or a quarter, of their total financial assets into his fund. Second, guerrilla investors are not impressed by exclusivity and secrecy, especially when it is not possible to understand how a fund manager is achieving unusually consistent returns. Third, since guerrilla investors monitor the press for stories that could affect their investments. a guerrilla investor would have come across the *Barron's* magazine article of 2001, or a similar article published in the same year in *MAR/Hedge*, a financial newsletter, at some point between 2001 and 2008, which would have raised the question of how Madoff was achieving his abnormally consistent returns.

Nevertheless, it is true that Ponzi schemes are particularly hard to spot, especially when the perpetrators are ultra-respectable, as Madoff appeared to be. In any case, some of his feeder funds did not tell their clients that their money would be invested through Madoff. It is very hard to believe that someone as knowledgeable and successful as Madoff would start such a scheme, which by its nature must eventually fail. Perhaps he thought he could keep it going until he died (he wouldn't have been the first to evade the consequences of fraud that way). So it is possible that guerrilla investors might have lost some, but not all, of their financial assets in the fraud. Fraudsters who run Ponzi schemes are generally extremely plausible, as Madoff was, and are really skilful at playing on the weaknesses of their target market. People trusted Madoff. It's no good thinking, 'well, I wouldn't have trusted him'; somewhere out there, there is a fraudster who would be able to win your trust, so don't rely on your gut instinct alone. But for the record, here are the main warning signs to watch out for:

■ steady returns on a volatile asset – share prices are volatile!

■ some form of exclusivity – this may not be in the form of a rich investors' club, as it was with Madoff; it could be something as seemingly innocuous as a scheme that claims to exploit tax advantages available to people in your profession

■ hiccups in the paperwork, and delays in making withdrawals

- unregistered or unauthorized investments, or ones that are in poorly regulated countries

- guaranteed returns on asset types that do not produce guaranteed returns

- unorthodox marketing techniques, such as recommendations made by people you know socially. Watch out for 'affinity fraud', which targets groups with close religious, ethnic, professional or cultural ties and exploits their tendency to trust each other.

Summary

Beginner investors often become overly concerned about the dangers of fraud; but by and large, a much bigger danger is either overpaying, in terms of charges, or investing in something that doesn't match your real needs and appetite for risk. The best way to defend yourself is to become as much of an expert as you can in the types of investment you are contemplating; that means reading everything you can find about them, talking to a wide range of investors and professionals, and looking not just at the recent past but also at issues that affected such investments 10, 20 or even 50 years ago. Many mistakes are made when gullible investors accept the 'all the cool kids are doing it' argument – in other words, that the latest craze is sure to work well because lots of other people are supporting it. Experience teaches otherwise – it is far better to decide very specifically on the goals you want to achieve, and work from there to find investments that are likely to enable you to do this.

In the next chapter we examine some of the opportunities and pitfalls of getting involved financially in other countries, both in investment and for saving tax.

9

Overseas investment

Overseas investment has come of age; the globalization of finance and cheap air travel has encouraged thousands of ordinary people to take an interest in foreign investment, principally by purchasing a home abroad. Although the golden age of the luxury expatriate lifestyle has gone, many people work in other countries with lower taxes and are able, legally, to accumulate wealth more quickly than they could at home, while stock market investors have better direct access to foreign exchanges than ever before. Nevertheless, overseas investment remains complex, and it is important to take a methodical approach; the risks are often greater, and many of the consumer protections that we enjoy in the UK are absent overseas.

This chapter discusses the following central issues:

- Achieving global diversification

- No-tax and low-tax territories

- Working abroad

- Banking offshore

- Offshore trusts and companies – expensive to feed?

- Dual nationality for guerrillas

Achieving global diversification

Once you are lucky enough to be in possession of a large amount of capital, your thoughts inevitably turn to how to keep it safe from all the unrelenting forces that are continually trying to take bites out of it. The world looks different to the wealthy; they are much more interested in international political and economic patterns than most people, since these have a bearing on the future of their own money. Obviously, it is vital to be as well-informed as possible, but before we look at the benefits of moving money around the world, we should consider the reservations that many people have about taking a step outside the conventions of their own country. People often think that there is something wrong with investing abroad, but there is nothing necessarily odd or improper about doing so – in fact, it is an essential part of the global economy.

Unlike many countries where centuries of wars, revolutions and expropriations have made people wary of their own governments, in the UK and the USA the popular view is that one is better off keeping one's money at home. This perception is sustained by a variety of commercial and political lobbies in whose interests it is that the public continue to think this. Most countries want to keep their citizens' money where they can control it – inside their own borders. Sometimes laws have been passed that prescribe dire penalties, even death, for individuals holding investments outside their own borders.

During the last two decades financial deregulation has changed all this, but countries such as South Korea and Malaysia are still making it very difficult for their citizens to hold foreign investments, or even to send money abroad. When the situation is that bad, citizens are often not allowed to leave their own countries, except with the greatest difficulty; they must resort to drastic measures to remove themselves and their money to freer places, often running the risk of reprisals against their relatives and friends whom they leave behind. Many attractive countries will only let a few people in, often basing their immigration policy on the amount of money the immigrant has. Latin America, Asia and the Middle East abound in regimes that limit the amount of money their nationals can take abroad, and the wealthy rack their brains to find ways of getting money out. Even clean, civilized Sweden is the enemy of the rich, with its draconian tax laws, and many wealthy Swedes have found it necessary to leave permanently.

❝the reason why people take their money abroad is generally to protect it❞

Most people, perhaps, would like to keep their money at home, all things being equal. The reason why people take their money abroad is generally to protect it, rather than out of greed for more; having all your assets in one place makes them vulnerable, as history has shown over and over again.

Looked at from the point of view of asset allocation, the argument for diversifying abroad is strong; by spreading your assets across the world, you may be able protect them from localized negative economic effects. While this is relatively easy to do with your financial assets, such as shares and bonds, by investing in a globally diversified portfolio of funds without ever having to go abroad, it is harder to diversify your non-financial assets if, like many people, they consist mainly of a house or a flat.

Foreign homes

More than a quarter of a million UK nationals now own property abroad. Most of these people are middle-aged or older, and tend to choose familiar areas of Western Europe, such as the south of Spain, rural France, Tuscany and the Algarve, served by budget airlines and with the potential for rental income. More recently, interest has increased in rather more exotic locations, such as Thailand, Croatia and Turkey, where property is often considerably cheaper. As a lifestyle choice this may work out well; some people find it possible to return to Britain regularly to work and do business while basing themselves in their foreign home, while others use their overseas property to provide holiday accommodation for themselves and their friends and relatives, and many people find it possible to retire comfortably abroad (see Chapter 11).

From the point of view of investment, however, there are a number of obvious risks which, to judge by the plethora of optimistic television programmes on buying a home abroad, many people do not consider. Looked at from the point of view of optimizing your returns at a given level of risk, foreign property in holiday areas are not necessarily a great investment. Although certain areas go through booms – for example, the south of Spain, or the Luberon valley in Provence, the setting for the famous change-of-lifestyle book *A Year in Provence* by Peter Mayall – others do not, and investors are faced with the same kinds of problems with market timing as they do in the stock market. Foreign property owners can easily become trapped in a cycle of escalating local costs and falling capital values – property, unlike financial instruments, is highly illiquid, so it is not easy to pull out if things start to go wrong. Furthermore, much of the potential return may be from rental income, which must be managed as a business and will be subject to market forces. The risk, then, is relatively high and the question remains of how to estimate your potential returns and whether these returns are likely to be adequate compensation for the risk.

Strictly speaking, from the point of view of asset allocation, buying one foreign home will not give you better diversification at the same level of risk since you will increase your exposure to currency fluctuations, taxes, problematic local building regulations and so on. This is not to say that it is inadvisable to buy a foreign home, but rather that for many people it may turn out to generate disappointing returns in the long run.

So, why do it? The answer is usually lifestyle. Cheap booze, fabulous food, a lovely climate, nice people, beautiful architecture and a change of pace are just a few of the draws. But it really helps to know the country well, and to learn the language. If you have long-standing connections with a country, you speak the language, and you have many good friends there, you are much more likely to make sensible decisions about any property you purchase in that country. You'll know about the downsides of living in that country, and you'll already have developed good coping strategies. The people who make a long-term success of owning a property abroad generally fit this description. Their main reason for doing it is not to make money, but to have an enjoyable life that involves spending quite a lot of time in that country. They know the risks, and they make contingency plans to deal with them. In effect, they are investing in their well-being, which is perfectly sensible.

Some UK citizens certainly have made a quick profit on buying and developing properties in other countries during boom periods, but if you are in it purely for the money it's a much trickier proposition, even if you speak the language and have really good local knowledge. Rural France, for instance, is full of gloomy middle-aged 'Anglais' who are huddled together in expat ghetto villages, completely failing to learn French and finding it difficult to survive when the pound has dropped against the euro (as it has at the time of writing) and nobody wants to buy their house. Some people sell everything and go out to Spain with completely unrealistic expectations of finding work or starting a business. Others have run into serious legal problems in places like northern Cyprus, Morocco and the Balkan countries because they have not obtained a cast-iron legal title to their properties.

The conclusion? Buying overseas property is not for starry-eyed amateurs, and even if you do know what you are doing, the chances are that the investment returns won't be particularly good; that's fine if you get the life you want out of it, but make sure that you are not kidding yourself about the investment potential.

No-tax and low-tax territories

We have all heard about them – the piratical tax havens where millionaires hide their ill-gotten gains – and in the UK there are a lot of strident voices calling for their abolition. The reality, however, is somewhat different. A tax haven is simply a country or territory which has low taxes. Some countries have made being a tax haven their main business, going out of their way to attract companies and private investors from other countries by developing sophisticated financial services combined with taxes that are deliberately set at rates well below those in the investors' countries of origin. Many of the world's largest companies and banks use tax havens as a matter of course, often basing their headquarters there. As well as saving tax, this can also give the advantage of having part, or all, of the business outside the jurisdiction of bigger, more tax-hungry governments.

So, how do investors use tax havens? There are several ways:

■ As a place to bank. The better tax havens provide sophisticated banking facilities and international cash-machine (ATM) cards that can save you money and time if you travel a lot.

■ As a place to save cash. If you do not have to pay tax on your world-wide assets in your home country – for example, because you are working abroad – you will earn a little bit more interest. It will generally be easier to move money to other countries from a tax haven, and you will often be able to keep accounts in several currencies.

■ As a place to base your financial investments. You can use, say, a bank in a tax haven to purchase funds, bonds and shares all over the world in the normal way, enabling you to keep your portfolio offshore. Assuming that you are not liable to tax at home, your money will grow faster because of the tax savings and you may be able to participate more easily in foreign markets than you could at home.

■ As a place to retire. This has become less attractive for the middling rich, but still may make sense for the superwealthy as a way of avoiding inheritance tax.

■ As a way to do international business. Big business has the financial and legal muscle to make this work – small businesses generally don't.

The important thing to remember about tax havens is that they are vulnerable to change. Simply putting your money in a tax haven and forgetting about it is unwise; you have to keep on top of developments that may affect your investments. Each tax haven has different laws and different prospects, and all are vulnerable to pressure from foreign governments. Some tax havens have very unsatisfactory banking laws that do not protect outside investors. To make a tax haven work for you, you may sometimes have to be resident there, or to form a company based there. This doesn't mean that you have to live there all the time – you can usually qualify by simply renting a property on a long lease. Holding an investment portfolio through a bank or trustee in a tax haven, and keeping the physical securities in another country, gives you the benefit of low or no taxes, freedom from any future currency controls and protects you from the dangers of expropriation. Thus, since your deal-making and income-earning abilities are likely to be confined to a higher tax country, the best time to make the move is when you can afford to live off your investment income indefinitely – hence the large numbers of retired people in tax havens. Tax havens offer some opportunities,

> **❝simply putting your money in a tax haven and forgetting about it is unwise❞**

mentioned above, to people who are still trying to accumulate capital, but it is expensive and can be difficult legally, especially if you find that you have to return home permanently at some point.

If you are intrigued by tax havens and want to investigate them further, it is worth visiting them in person. Detailed information is easier and cheaper to get on the spot rather than going to consultants in other countries, and many schemes and wrinkles cannot be advertised in the countries where they are of most interest. Remember that many countries, including the UK, don't tax money held abroad unless it is 'repatriated', so if you spend income from your overseas assets abroad you may not need to move to a tax haven.

The tax havens of Europe

You may wonder why it is that the EU countries allow such a variety of tax havens to exist on their doorsteps. When I put this question to an eminent international tax lawyer, he replied that, 'the politicians and big businessmen of Europe are corrupt and they have to have somewhere to put their money'. While this may be so, it would seem wiser for anyone resident in Europe to take their money farther afield to the havens of the Americas or the Far East, well away from any possible EU legislation in the future, and to regard the European tax havens as halfway houses for specific operations. In the same way, North American investors may be wiser to keep their money in the European tax havens rather than in the Caribbean.

The UK

Curiously, the UK is technically a tax haven – but not if you're British. Because of the arcane distinctions between 'residence' and 'domicile' (see page 241), someone who was born in another country, or whose father was domiciled in another country at the time of birth, can live in the UK for many years without having to pay tax on investments held outside the UK, as long as the income is not brought into the country. The rules allow such a person to hold property and businesses in the UK via a company incorporated abroad, so capital gains tax and inheritance tax may also be legally avoided.

Why does the government allow this? Simply because it wishes to attract wealthy foreigners into Britain. The UK has an advantage over many tax havens in that it is relatively large and well-regulated, and offers a wide range of business and professional opportunities.

Switzerland

Switzerland is a small country with good natural borders. For centuries it has survived by playing complex economic games with its more powerful neighbours and since the Second World War has acquired a worldwide reputation as a haven for capital. An ultra-conservative society with a world-class financial sector, Switzerland does not, in fact, let people settle within its borders easily. If you are a millionaire you can probably get citizenship, at a cost of several hundred thousand pounds, as long as no objections about your morality or other civil virtues are made, although cheaper schemes appear occasionally. The main attraction is the famous 'secret' banking system which hitherto has enabled third-world dictators and other notorious types to hide their money. Since the collapse of the USSR, Switzerland has allied itself much more closely with the rest of Europe. While it is true that a lot of money is hidden in Switzerland, it is by no means completely safe since Swiss banks with branches in other countries have been known to succumb to pressure from foreign governments, particularly from the USA. At the time of writing, there are stories that Switzerland has frozen the assets of the recently deposed president of Egypt, Hosni Mubarak, so it seems that even third-world dictators can't be sure of protecting their money in Switzerland anymore. Also, since taxes are relatively high, while Switzerland may still be a haven for capital, it is not really a tax haven.

Monaco

Monaco is a tiny principality on the Côte D'Azur, surrounded by France but very close to Italy. The French do their best to tax assets in Monaco. It's relatively easy to acquire residence there, but it is probably wise to keep your assets elsewhere. Monaco is an eyesore of skyscrapers – its fin de siècle romance is long gone and even the casinos are just for tourists.

The Channel Islands

By an accident of history, these islands are subject to the British Crown but have their own governments; in theory, the British government cannot tell them what to do. The larger islands, such as Jersey and Guernsey, are awash with millionaire lawyers and accountants. Income tax is low on money brought into the country, there is no capital gains tax or VAT, and the cost of living is delightfully low. For wealthy Britons, making a permanent move to the Channel Islands gives immediate benefits, and is close enough to the UK for it to be easy to make short trips home, but it costs a lot of money. The tiny island of Sark allows you to become domiciled there if you rent a property for more than a year, which is a cheap option. Jersey and Guernsey have highly sophisticated banking and financial facilities. Running a Channel Islands-based company costs about £6,000 a year, which is on the high side.

Other euro tax havens

Territories such as Andorra and Gibraltar offer similar advantages to the Channel Islands: cheap living, expensive property and low taxes. Gibraltar is popular as a base for offshore companies, but its close ties to the UK make it undesirable for British nationals. Luxembourg and Liechtenstein are not really tax havens, but they are excellent places to keep money and to trade from, probably better than Switzerland in most cases.

Tax havens in the Americas

These are mostly in or near the Carribean – the Cayman Islands, the Bahamas, Bermuda, the Dutch Antilles and Panama are the best known. The big international banks all have a presence there, as do thousands of corporations. They are more vulnerable politically than European tax havens but you can often obtain residency cheaply, and Europeans are generally more welcome than Americans, owing to the pressures applied by the US bureaucracy.

The Far East

Banking in the major financial centres of the Far East, such as Hong Kong, offers many of the advantages of tax havens while often being perceived as more respectable. The Far East is generally a low-tax area, and expatriates who are temporarily – and legally – not paying tax at home have the opportunity to build up substantial sums in a short time.

Example

Jim was a happy-go-lucky student when he first went out to Asia travelling. Ten years went past and he was still there, and still penniless. Then he met Anne, and they decided to settle down. The problem was that they didn't have enough money to come home to the UK and get on the housing ladder. Jim bit the bullet and went out and got a job. After a couple of years of struggle in Hong Kong, the couple moved to Australia, where Jim took a Masters degree and got a better job – but Australia is a high-tax country, and there was no way they were going to make it back to England on Jim's take-home pay. Then Jim got lucky, and got a corporate job in a major bank, working all across Asia. The work was tough, but the pay was high and the tax was very low; within four years he was able to save £80,000 in cash, enough for him to request a transfer home to the UK, where he was able to buy a house, get a mortgage and settle down to a conventional life.

Working abroad

If you have the chance of working abroad in a low-tax country for a few years, don't disregard it – it might be the best chance you ever have of building savings fast. Many expatriates are paid more than they are at home, pay less tax and have lower living expenses. While you are abroad, you can avoid paying UK tax, subject to certain restrictions, by making deposits in tax haven banks or investing in offshore funds. The gains you make will accumulate tax free, which is like having an ISA, but better.

Example

> Elaine works for five years in one of the Gulf states. She is paid £7,000 a month, more than double what she gets at home, and is not liable for local tax. Life is dull and expensive, but she is still able to save £3,000 a month. She puts this in respectable investments based in a tax haven.
>
> When Elaine decides to return to the UK, her investments have grown to £250,000. Since she already has a home and assets in the UK, she decides to leave the fund where it is rather than repatriating the money.
>
> A few years later, Elaine gets married to a US citizen and decides to move to America permanently. Her fund has grown even bigger, and provides an excellent nest egg with which to start a new life. Once the money is in America it will be subject to US tax, but until that point it has grown faster than normally because it has been tax free.

It is important to learn languages

❝the best opportunities are for the multilingual investor❞

People who want to be internationally active in business and investment and don't speak another language are shooting themselves in the foot. The best opportunities are for the multilingual investor, so take the trouble to learn a language or two and don't be afraid to go to countries where they don't speak your native tongue.

Banking offshore

Most respectable offshore jurisdictions are swarming with the branches of well-known banks. Remember, there is nothing illegal about having an offshore bank account, so long as you declare it to the relevant tax authorities and pay any tax for which you are liable

The main reason for a private person to have an offshore account is so that you can transfer money between countries easily and cheaply when, for instance, you are doing business abroad or paying bills on a foreign property.

It isn't very difficult to open an offshore account, as long as you can show that you are a respectable, law-abiding person:

1 Draw up a shortlist of banks in the tax haven of your choice. You can research these via the internet and also from bank directories available in large public libraries.

2 Write a letter to each of the banks you have shortlisted, telling them how much money you will deposit initially and an estimate of roughly how much money will be going through the account annually. Some banks don't accept small accounts, so you need to give this information. Ask for information about the bank, such as its annual report.

3 Look up the finance ministry, chamber of commerce and similar bodies based in the relevant tax haven on the internet. If the information is inadequate, write to them asking about guarantee schemes in case of a bank's failure, and details of the tax system.

4 You will find that banks vary a lot. Some banks are very snooty and don't want you unless you are rich, but won't say so openly. Others leave you with the impression that they are run by cutlass-brandishing buccaneers with parrots on their shoulders. Now that globalization is respectable, you should find banks that offer you the services you want and will take your business. If you don't, look at another tax haven.

Example

Rob works in England but has a villa in Italy, and finds it best to keep money to pay the domestic bills in another currency in an offshore account. He doesn't like keeping a lot of cash in Italy because a few years ago the Italian government, without any warning, took a large sum of money from his Italian account as part of an emergency measure during one of Italy's frequent economic crises.

Rob has a card from his offshore bank that lets him withdraw cash from cash machines in Italy in euros at a lower rate than if he changed the money at a bank, so he pays for most of his costs in Italy this way. If he has to pay an Italian bill while he is in the UK, he instructs his offshore bank to transfer the money direct to the payee.

Offshore trusts and companies – expensive to feed?

There are hordes of parasitical professionals who are only too keen to set you up with any number of paper entities which have a curious tendency to be expensive to run. Usually you must appoint company officials and trustees who are resident in the tax haven concerned, and while you can make every effort to ensure that such individuals are honest, they may be vulnerable to outside pressure in a crisis. If your objective is principally to protect your capital and you are prepared to live a fairly mobile life, it is generally cheaper and safer to keep control of your assets as far as possible by gaining domicile in a low-tax area, understanding the tax regimes of the countries where you spend your time, and carefully diversifying your portfolio, trading through banks and brokers situated in tax havens other than your own. Trusts are examined in more detail in Chapter 12; if you are committed to remaining in your own country there is a case for having a trust in a tax haven in favour of dependants in order to avoid inheritance tax.

People who are trying illegally to evade tax in their own countries are the prime targets of sharks. The reason is simple; if someone steals their money, the tax evaders can do nothing about it without inviting the attention of their tax authorities. Some people are always trying to be too clever and are 'suckers' for complicated schemes that they don't really understand. Changing your domicile is a far cheaper, safer and, above all, legal move than setting up overcomplex schemes that may not be accepted by the tax collectors.

Dual nationality for guerrillas

While governments and passport officers don't particularly like dual nationality, having two passports gives the wealthy private investor enormous scope for 'arbitrage', in the sense that it is possible to exploit differences in the tax and other regulations between different countries. The USA is one of the few countries where it is difficult to hold dual nationality.

There are many ways to obtain a second passport. The cheapest methods are through marriage, ancestry or religion. Specialist immigration lawyers can advise on your particular needs and opportunities. Clearly, some passports are worth more than others – try travelling around the world on an Israeli, Lebanese or Syrian passport, or on one from an African country, if you want to experience how the less-advantaged half of the world lives! Many people are eager to get US nationality but, while it may be better than being, say, from Paraguay, my view is that most other first-world passports are an infinitely better bet. Most countries are hypocritical enough to give passports to people who are able to pay for them, often by 'investing' in the country concerned, and this may be worthwhile as a last resort.

Dual nationality does not give you '007' status, but it does give you options, not only for yourself but also for your children, and can be invaluable in protecting your assets over the long term. Even if you only use the advantage once in your life – for example, by helping a son gain exemption from military service in a troubled country, or substantially reducing inheritance tax – it could prove to be one of the best investments you ever make in a world where the rules are always changing.

Summary

As we have seen, there are many strong arguments for becoming more involved in international investment, and in our increasingly globalized world the process for doing this is becoming easier and cheaper. The really important thing is not to get too bound up in trying to save, legally, every last penny of tax – often life is a lot easier if you do pay some tax; nevertheless, if you do aspire to build substantial wealth as a guerrilla investor, you should definitely consider the possibility of working abroad for a few years at least, because it can give you a great advantage in asset building.

In the next chapter we will look at some of the main non-financial asset types – such as property – and discuss what role, if any, they should play in your overall portfolio.

10

Investing in other asset classes

Although 'asset allocation' is often taken to refer to a portfolio of shares and bonds, it is worth considering non-financial assets such as property, which may offer better returns in certain circumstances and should, in any case, form a part of most investors' total wealth. This chapter examines the most commonly available assets outside the financial markets, but argues that, for UK residents at least, only property should be an essential element in most people's portfolios. If, on the other hand, you live and earn your money in a low-tax region where gold can be easily traded, and it is difficult to obtain good title to property, such as much of the Far East, then it may well make sense to hold assets such as gold instead of property – in fact, in Vietnam, house prices are quoted in terms of gold rather than currency!

In this chapter we look at:

- Property

- A word on gold

- Collectibles

- Wine

- Your own business

- Pensions

- Insurance-linked investments

Property

Property, or 'real estate', has to be a good investment for most people who live in the UK. In fact, it is often argued that you should acquire your own property before you start investing in the stock market, since the chances are that within a few years the value of your home will have increased, and this is a firm long-term basis on which to build your other assets. Property is something that gives you a lot of control; you can see it, live in it and let it. Even if you are not naturally good at DIY, there is a lot you can do to improve the value of a property simply through physical work, and you might improve your health in the process. As a UK property owner you are well protected by the law (this is not the case in many other countries) and you can participate in a market in which the powerful in the land have a big stake themselves. In most cases, your primary residence – the house that you actually live in – is free of capital gains tax (CGT), which means you can keep the profits you make on selling your house and use them to make more profits. Some people think that the freedom from CGT is an artificial distortion of the housing market; it is certainly true that if CGT was suddenly applied to your main home, or if CGT was completely lifted from other investments such as shares, we would see some very dramatic changes in the entire UK investment landscape, including property.

In Chapter 5 we looked at market efficiency. The property market is an 'inefficient market', which means, among other things, that it is possible to achieve better than average returns through superior knowledge. In property superior knowledge usually means having good local knowledge, and, perhaps, a good knowledge of how to add value to certain types of houses, or how appealing to certain types of buyer, can actually increase your profits.

When looked at in this way, property is a kind of business. As in all businesses, to succeed you must avoid the consumer mentality. Many home buyers are unsophisticated; they are willing to pay the market price for a property without considering the direction of the market or whether they can let it for sufficient rent to cover the mortgage. They will tell you that gains you make in equity (equity is your share in the value of the house, the rest being the money you have borrowed to buy it) are cancelled out because you will have to pay an equivalent price for any other house you move to. This is misleading, since you can, for instance, move to a cheaper house, renovate it, and increase the value of the equity further. Not everybody enjoys all the hard work, but many people are willing to make the effort and have enjoyed substantial rewards by adding value to their homes. From an investment point of view, the work that people do to add value to a property makes it quite different from financial assets like shares and bonds. You can't add value to your shares by your own efforts, unless you believe that you have an uncanny ability to select the right shares, and you call that 'work'; but as we saw in Chapter 5, page 108, the evidence suggests that investors cannot really add value consistently by selecting shares that they believe will perform outstandingly. Buying and renovating a home, selling it at a profit, and repeating the process is one of the great British hobbies, and for the last two or three generations it has worked extremely well.

Although the UK's property market is structured in such a way that, over time, most people are likely to see the value of the property grow, this is not the case in many other parts of the world. Also, although the performance of UK property has been good since the end of the Second World War, it is not impossible that the market could undergo some kind of structural change in the future that makes it perform poorly in the future. This may seem unlikely, because home owners are voters and would be likely to vote out any government that allowed the property market to be damaged, but we have to accept that, however unlikely it may be, it is still possible that property could become a bad investment in the future. To see how this could happen, let's consider two unlikely worst-case scenarios:

■ Scenario 1 – London ceases to be a magnet for overseas business-people and visitors. Property prices in London plummet, and this has a ripple effect on the regions as Londoners are no longer able to use their equity to buy second homes in the country, or to move back to the provinces to buy a bigger house.

■ Scenario 2 – a government decides to remove all taxes on shares. Investors start to move money out of property into shares because of shares' liquidity. Property prices begin to sink, and as more people catch on, the trend continues.

These are unlikely scenarios, but they illustrate the point that there are a number of structural factors, such as the role of overseas investors and the tax-free profits you make on the sale of your primary residence, that prop up the market. If one or more of these factors was removed, the market could change permanently for the worse.

Most of us assume, though, that the present structure of the market will continue, so we worry more about the cyclical nature of UK house prices. Every few years – about every decade or so since the Second World War – there is a boom in prices, often driven by generous lending policies, and this is followed by a crash in prices or a stagnant period when prices don't seem to move at all. At the time of writing, the general worry is that, following several years of increasing prices, there may be a long slump in prices. Much of the debate is centred on whether we are in for a 'soft landing', with prices slowing or stabilizing for a while before drifting upwards again, or whether we will have a 'hard landing' with drastically reduced mortgage lending, falling prices and a big rise in home repossessions.

The main thing to know about such booms and busts is that they have occurred repeatedly since 1945 in the UK, and are likely to continue to do so unless there is a structural change of the kind mentioned earlier. To understand how they work, let's look at the boom and bust of the late 1980s and early 1990s, which many people have forgotten.

In the late 1980s house prices had risen massively and borrowing was easy. Many young people felt that if they didn't get on the housing ladder at once, prices would go on rising and they would never be able to afford a home. The industry professionals, including estate agents, solicitors and lenders, seemed to encourage this view, and people were able to borrow more than they could afford because controls were lax and it was easy to exaggerate how much money you earned. Interest rates rose and there was a crash in 1989; the effects were devastating, especially for new home buyers. Young people had paid what were then large sums for renovated slum dwellings in some of the grimmest parts of London – typically £60,000 or more – but by 1994 these properties were selling for around £25,000 at auction. Repossessions soared and lenders sold houses for less than the outstanding mortgage, leaving large numbers of people homeless and still in debt. Some people were prosecuted for fraud for having exaggerated their incomes when they took out their mortgages. A much larger group of people were stuck making high monthly repayments in homes that were worth less than they had bought them for, and had to soldier on grimly.

Eventually the government had to act, and the situation slowly improved. People were allowed to reduce their payments for a while, and by the late 1990s the market was beginning to pick up again, as interest rates dropped and borrowing rules became looser once again. Those who had borrowed too much and had been repossessed faced a long road back to home ownership, while those who had managed to tighten their belts and keep paying their mortgages had endured a long period of waiting, but saw the values of the properties start to recover. In the opinion of many, the Conservative government eventually fell because of the trauma people had experienced in the house market, which is one reason why it is thought that governments will work hard to soften the pain of any future house price crash. At the time of writing (early 2011), mortgages are hard to obtain, but during the current financial crisis the government has kept interest rates artificially low, which has substantially reduced monthly mortgage payments for many borrowers. It remains to be seen whether this intervention can be sustained long enough to prevent a repossession crisis like the one that occurred in the early 1990s.

The characteristics of property

The main characteristics of property as an asset class are poor liquidity, high transaction costs, and risks from adverse legislation, as well as the cyclical nature of the market discussed above. Let's look at these in a little more detail.

Illiquidity

If you suddenly need cash, you cannot simply ring up a broker and sell your house to raise the money. It may take months, or even years to sell a house. Interest rates, maintenance costs and taxes can go up suddenly. For these reasons, property owners need to have cash or liquid investments such as shares that they can sell in an emergency.

High transaction costs

Compared with the cost of selling bonds or shares, the cost of buying and selling property is high. In fact, transaction costs in the UK are lower than in many other countries, which can come as a shock if you buy a property abroad. Solicitors' fees, estate agents' commissions, taxes, survey fees and other costs will usually amount to thousands of pounds by the time you have completed the deal. Remember to factor these costs in when you are deciding how big a property you can afford. Don't skimp on property surveys, because these provide you with some assurance that there are no hidden problems that could prove costly later.

Adverse legislation

Property is a political issue, and because it cannot be physically picked up and taken away, it is vulnerable to new laws and regulations that can affect it adversely. Although the UK has been generally favourable towards property owners during the last few decades, after the Second World War there were a number of changes made, particularly to the law relating to landlords and tenants, which affected property owners very badly. As in other Western countries, the UK still has some sitting tenants and rent-controlled properties that cannot be sold by the owners, who receive a fraction of the market rent. In other countries, there have been times when new regimes have simply taken away large houses from their owners permanently, have suddenly raised local property taxes by 2,000 per cent or more to soak foreign home-owners in resort areas, or have introduced rules preventing property owners from obtaining the permanent freehold of the land on which their property is built.

In spite of these problems, property in the UK has been a good investment for a long time, largely because of the effects of gearing. Unlike other types of investment, borrowing against property is relatively cheap and you can borrow long term, which enables property owners to 'gear' their investments and greatly increase their gains if prices rise, as discussed in Chapter 7. If you buy a house for 100 per cent cash and the price increases by 10 per cent, you have only made a 10 per cent gain, but if you buy a house using, say, a 90 per cent mortgage, you make a 100 per cent gain because your deposit has only been 10 per cent of the value of the house. Naturally, the effect works the other way if prices fall, but inflation helps to mitigate this and in the UK market, most people believe that so long as you ensure that you can always make the monthly repayments, gearing is a good way to increase your returns.

Location, location, location

The most important factor affecting the price of property is where it is located. A beautiful detached house in wonderful but remote countryside may be worth a lot less than a dingy little flat in a big city, just because people need to be near their place of work, and there tends to be more work in the big cities. In cities like London, where there are a lot of highly paid jobs, property prices tend to go up because people are able to get bigger mortgages. Within the same area, two apparently identical houses may sell for different prices because of subtle differences, like the level of traffic noise, how close they are to pubs, or where the bus routes go. In addition, some areas are improving economically, which will tend to push up prices, while others are decaying, which will tend to lower prices. When choosing a property you have to take all these factors into account, and the more local knowledge you have, the better your decisions are likely to be.

Types of property

The regulations and tax status of different kinds of property affect the level of commitment you must make to managing them and the potential returns. While most people only think about residential property, it is worth considering the other types as well.

Undeveloped land

Undeveloped land is simply land that has not been built on or developed in any way. Several studies suggest that it generally keeps its value in real terms; it may be interesting as a passive investment, since if you buy a field and leave it for many years and are able to sell it later for the same value, adjusted for inflation, little effort has been required. The disadvantage is, of course, that you receive little or no income from it, and if it only keeps pace with inflation you would have done better by investing in bonds. Specialist investors are more interested in selecting underdeveloped land that has the potential to rise in value; for example, if you hold land on the edge of a growing city, planning laws may eventually change to allow you to build houses on it, greatly increasing its value. Most of the increase in the value of a piece of land occurs before any construction begins. The big money lies in getting permission for change of use. You should always buy at a low or moderate price, and make sure you have the land surveyed properly to check the drainage, stability and pollution levels to avoid problems later.

Residential property

This is the category that most people focus on. As well as the freedom from capital gains tax on your primary residence, which is a major advantage, you can live in a residential property while you are renovating it. It is relatively easy to borrow money to purchase residential property (compared with other kinds of borrowing for business) and many people possess the basic skills necessary to manage renovations, maintain the building and keep tenants happy. Property auctions are a good way to pick up bargain property, but you do not have much time to do searches and surveys, and you will need to have finance in place before you buy.

In recent years the Buy-to-Let scheme has brought many amateur landlords into the market in the UK, by providing a formalized system for lenders to provide money for the purchase of rental properties – the success of the scheme at a time of rising house prices has brought fears that many participants will be forced to sell up if there is a prolonged market slump. For the determined private landlord, however, the underlying situation has not really changed; it was always possible to borrow in order to purchase a rental property, even before the Buy-to-Let scheme was introduced, and the market cycle does not appear to have fundamentally changed. The main thing to remember is that being a landlord is a business, requiring effort on your part and a higher degree of risk than passive investments. The main headache is usually the management of tenants, and the high cost of long vacant periods when there is no rental income. At present, the UK law provides for an Assured Shorthold Tenancy, for a minimum of **❝being a landlord is a business, requiring effort on your part❞**

six months, which makes it relatively easy to evict tenants at the end of the lease or in the case of rent default. The rules are strict, though, and you must make sure that you follow them carefully. For example, if you fail to serve notices at the proper time, you risk a court judgment allowing a tenant to stay in your property indefinitely, which will reduce its value. There are still some unscrupulous local authorities and charitable agencies that encourage tenants to trick landlords into making mistakes that will lead to such a court order, so be careful. Choose your tenants with caution, and make them fill in application forms giving the addresses of next of kin, employment details and income level. Specializing in certain types of tenant, such as Japanese families, military families or other groups who are thought likely to be good tenants, can be mutually rewarding. If you are unlucky enough to come into conflict with a tenant, it is usually better to accept a loss and negotiate a settlement in a friendly way rather than to get embroiled in a court battle.

As well as the Assured Shorthold Tenancy, there are other types of agreement that may be of interest. For example, letting to limited companies gives the landlord more rights, but make sure the company is genuine or the tenant may be able to get security of tenure. Licences can be appropriate for flats with multiple occupants, but you will need legal advice to make sure these agreements are enforceable. The type of agreement to avoid is the fully protected tenancy, unless you are buying a property that is already occupied by such tenants and you are sure that they will leave – usually this will involve paying them a large lump sum.

Commercial property

The law on letting business premises is less weighted against the landlord than it is for residential property, but there are other risks. For example, letting to small businesses can be risky. This is because small businesses have a high failure rate, and may go bust or not be able to pay the rent in hard times. Suppose, for instance, that you buy a commercial building with several units that can provide offices, workshops and showrooms. You let them all to small local businesses, and the place is a hive of activity – but if a recession develops a few years down the line, most, if not all, of such businesses will be under financial pressure, and you may be faced with late rent payment, tenants trying to wriggle out of their leases and others simply moving elsewhere when their lease expires. There are various ways to try to mitigate such risks, for example by getting personal guarantees from company directors, or by seeking only the best-financed, best-established business tenants, or by staggering the lengths of the leases so they do not all expire at once, but the name of the game is keeping the property fully let at all times, and this can be difficult if economic conditions are bad.

Other property strategies

Property offers many ways for the investor to specialize. Here are just a few:

Timeshare

Timeshare is a system where people buy an annual slot of time in a property (often an apartment in a holiday resort) which they can use indefinitely. The management company has to administer the system, give guarantees to buy back the timeshare, maintain the building and so on. In the USA the timeshare industry is quite well regulated and respectable, but this is less true of Europe and elsewhere. The main risk for purchasers of timeshare is that everything depends upon the quality of the management company; if it goes bust, for instance, your timeshare may become worthless. However, some investors have made money on timeshares by purchasing in a resort that booms later, enabling them to get out for a large profit.

Property development

The nineteenth-century tycoon Jacob Astor used to say 'never develop'. Development is a rough and risky ride, even for the professionals, and requires a lot of expertise. Nevertheless, some people have a natural aptitude for getting development right and have done well. Even quite small developments, like converting a house into a number of flats, are a major challenge for the amateur, but people who start small, do a good job, control their costs and keep within the numerous regulations can achieve good results over time.

Property funds

You can buy shares in publicly quoted property companies, or in funds such as REITs (Real Estate Investment Trusts) that offer some tax advantages over direct investment in property. The risks are similar to those of other types of stock market investment.

Ground rents and freeholds

In England and Wales there is an interesting trade in the freeholds of buildings that have been sold off, usually as flats, on leases. The householders pay you an annual 'ground rent', which can be raised every few years, and when the leases expire the building could revert to you, in which case you could resell the lease. It is possible to buy parcels of such freeholds at auction at prices that could give you a profit on the ground rent income. The value of any improvements the tenants make could become yours if the property reverts to you at the end of the lease. Most leases require tenants to maintain the building, which can be a substantial benefit to the freeholder. The Leasehold Reform legislation allows tenants to get together to buy freeholds compulsorily from the owner, but at a fair price that could give you a profit. It also offers opportunities for investors who purchase leases on flats and then persuade their fellow tenants to get together to purchase the freehold – once a flat has a share in the freehold, its value goes up considerably.

Property for guerrillas – using property in asset allocation

'Property is the best way, the safest way, and indeed the only way to get rich', wrote an American president nearly a century ago. This has a nice ring to it, and even quite a lot of truth! As a business, property can be much safer than other forms of business because of two unusual characteristics: the fact that you can 'gear' your investment relatively easily, and the fact that a single person on their own can easily control and manage assets worth millions of pounds.

From the point of view of asset allocation, property should almost certainly be an important element in your portfolio because it is negatively correlated to the share and bond markets. For most people it probably forms the largest percentage of their asset allocation, and this can lead to liquidity problems. For example, if you have owned a home for 10 years that has grown in value and you have only recently started investing in the stock market, your asset allocation to property could easily be more than 90 per cent of your total wealth. In the short term there is little you can do about this, but in the long term it is probably a good idea to try to invest more and more in liquid assets such as shares and bonds. If you become wealthy, it will generally be easier to balance your overall asset allocation to reduce the proportion of your wealth that is held in property. What is the ideal proportion? There can be no definite answer, but many wealthy people think that it is a good idea to keep their property holdings to under 50 per cent, or even under 30 per cent of their overall wealth, because this will tend to improve their liquidity and leave them less exposed to the vagaries of the property market.

Gold

Should you own gold? Much depends on how wealthy you are, and where you are based. For example, if you are quite wealthy and live in a politically unstable country such as Indonesia, there are good arguments for keeping a proportion of your assets in physical gold, because in times of trouble, when local currencies and shares are down, you can sell some gold to obtain US dollars. In such places, even small investors have benefited from having some gold as a 'get out of jail free card' in recent times.

The very wealthy often hold a small proportion of their portfolio in gold as a form of diversification. The idea is that gold will help to make the total returns on the portfolio less volatile because its price is not correlated to financial assets such as stocks and shares. Although gold doesn't produce growth, historically it has tended to keep its purchasing power, even in times of high inflation. Gold prices are denominated in US dollars, so many American investors see gold as a hedge against fluctuations in the US dollar exchange rate (when the dollar strengthens, gold tends to weaken and vice versa).

For smaller private investors, however, the arguments for holding physical gold are rather less compelling. The most cost-effective form of physical gold is the 400 troy ounce gold bar, which is used by dealers and banks, but at its current price per bar of £324,708 most people can't afford to hold more than one bar, if that, in addition to their shares and bonds. If you want to sell it for the best price you can't cut bits off it – you'll have to sell the whole thing – and it costs money to store it. There are, of course, smaller bars available, as well as coins such as sovereigns and Krugerrands, but then you get into a rather murky world of 'premiums', where the dealer's spreads are high – a 9 per cent spread is common for coins – and prices vary according to the condition and nature of the coins (spreads can be as high as 40 per cent on some coins).

As you can see, there is a world of difference between holding standard gold bars and storing them in one of the world's few accredited bullion vaults (the main ones are in London, Zurich and New York), where the spreads are quite low, and dabbling in coins and small bars, where you are at the mercy of the dealers.

There are other ways to 'gain exposure to gold' without purchasing it physically. For example, you can buy shares in gold mining companies, or funds that invest in gold, or, for the really adventurous, derivatives based on gold. In general, these types of investment are unlikely to produce returns that are closely related to the actual price of gold, so unless you really want to devote yourself fully to this specialized investment area it is probably best to give it a miss.

Collectibles

Most professional investors in the financial markets are cynical about collectibles, which include high-value objects like paintings and antiques. As an asset class they suffer from several undesirable characteristics, as detailed below.

A rigged market

The markets for most collectibles are controlled by professional traders or producers, who can ramp up prices or depress them almost at will. As an outsider, you are working at a considerable disadvantage.

No income

Unlike financial assets or rental property, collectibles usually generate no income. That means that to compare their returns fairly with income-producing assets, you need to take into account not only the capital gains but also the income or lack of it, and the cost of maintenance and insurance.

Example

> You buy a painting for £100,000 and a 5 per cent bond for £100,000 and you hold them for 5 years. At the end of the 5 years, you sell the painting for £130,000 and the bond expires, so you receive your original £100,000 back. Which has been the better investment? Suppose that maintenance, storage and insurance of the painting has cost you £10,000 during the period. Your total gain has therefore been only £20,000. Before adjusting for tax, your gain on the bond has been the interest, totalling £25,000, plus any compounding effect if you reinvested the interest. The bond, therefore, has been a safe, predictable investment that has given you a better return than the painting, for which the future sale price was unpredictable.

Illiquidity

It is not as easy as you might think to sell collectibles, even valuable ones. Usually, the quickest way to sell a collectible worth a substantial amount, say over £10,000, is by auction, but the right auction may not come up for six months or more.

Fashion

Changes in fashion can make even the highest quality items suddenly lose value. For example, the Victorians paid higher prices, in real terms, for the famous paintings of their own day than these items fetch now. Whether it is classic cars, primitive art or Marilyn Monroe memorabilia, the chances are that demand will fluctuate wildly, and unpredictably, in the future.

Forgery

Forgery is a very real problem in the collectibles world. There are many very talented artists and craftspeople who are unable to sell their own work, but make a good living producing convincing fakes. Almost anything can be faked, and the museums and art galleries of the world are full of them.

Now we have looked at some of the problems, we should consider whether there is any point at all in investing in collectibles. The answer is a cautious 'yes', assuming that you only spend a small part of your wealth on them. The real reasons to collect beautiful things are social; if, for example, you are successful in business and you want to meet other big wheels, dabbling in the art world is a good way of building the right profile for yourself. Or perhaps you need a home full of beautiful antiques in order to impress important clients. And you may even appreciate the stuff – it's a nice feeling to own a Van Dyck painting or Chippendale furniture. It may also be possible, as a long-term hobby, to make money by specializing in a certain kind of collectible and building up the most comprehensive, or the most interesting, collection in the field, and selling it off when the market is right. In general, though, collectibles do not seem to be able to beat other forms of investment on performance, given the disadvantage that they do not generate income, as many other investments can.

Wine

Suppose you spend £20,000 on fine wine that is enjoying a vintage year. You lay it down in your wine cellar and leave it alone for a few years until it is ready to drink. You then sell off part of your stock to cover your purchase costs, and keep the rest to drink yourself for free. That's the basic idea of wine investment, and it often works for educated buyers of the best French clarets and some vintage ports. No other wines are thought to be safe bets, not even champagne, because it is past its prime after about 20 years. The investment market in wine is limited to about 30 chateaus in Bordeaux, and you do need to know what you are doing to succeed as a buyer. The hard-headed investor is likely to remove wine from the list of potential investments.

Your own business

Some people seem to be born knowing how to run a business, but most people seem to have to learn the hard way. Business is almost always very hard work, and many people find it boring; the rate of failure in business start-ups (which is when you start a business from scratch) is very high, and it takes a lot of experience to know how to make and increase profits consistently, which is what you must do if the business is to grow and become valuable.

If you are considering starting or buying a business and you do not have much experience, you are vulnerable to predators who offer to sell you pre-packaged 'business opportunities' that are mediocre at best. Franchising, for example, where you buy the right to brand a small business, such as a fast food outlet, can work out if you are dealing with one of the well-established franchise companies, but it is poorly regulated as an industry and there are many firms eager to take a large up-front fee from you for a business that is unlikely to prosper. Worse are the pyramid schemes, where you pay a large fee to join what is basically a freelance sales force. These tend not to work well because the focus is on persuading new people to join up as sales agents, rather than actually selling the products to real customers. Sometimes known as 'multi-level marketing', many of these schemes appear to target people with little knowledge of business, let alone sales and marketing, upon which the success of the products will depend.

If you manage to swerve past those obstacles, the next one is probably the idea that you have to start your business from scratch. This is actually the hardest, riskiest, most inefficient way to get into business; a much better way is to take over an existing business as a 'going concern', which means that you already have an income and customers, because you start making money right away. If you have to buy the business outright, you will need to do a very thorough 'due diligence', as the bankers call it, to make sure that all the business accounts are accurate, and that you know exactly what you are paying for. It is easy for a vendor of, say, a shop, to exaggerate the number of customers and sales income, so you need to find out the truth. Remember, too, to separate the time you spend working for the business – which should earn you a salary, whether or not you actually draw it – and the return you will make on the capital you invest. The main aim should be to build, over time, the value of the business as an asset so that in due course you can sell it for a large capital gain.

Back in 1940, a Wall Street stockbroker wrote:

Most businessmen imagine that they are in business to make money, and that this is their chief reason for being in business, but more often than not they are gently kidding themselves. There are so many other things that are more attractive. Some of them are: to make a fine product or to render a remarkable service, to give employment, to revolutionize an industry, to make oneself famous or, at least to supply oneself with material for conversation in the evening.[1]

Fred Schwed was right – it is very easy for the independent businessperson to lose sight of the real purpose of being in business, which is to make money and keep it. Remember, businesses are not there just to provide you with a job – you could get a job anyway – so if you find that you are in business but constantly losing sight of your objective of making money, the chances are that deep down you find business very boring. If you can't devote yourself heart and soul to making money and working twice as hard as everybody else, you probably should stay away.

Pensions

Although pensions aren't strictly an alternative to investment, the situation is so complex these days that it is worth taking an overview of the central problems. People don't all have access to the same deals when it comes to pensions, and in any case their future benefits are getting squeezed in many countries, including the UK, because everyone is waking up to the fact that people are living longer and longer, and many are expecting to live a prosperous lifestyle well into old age.

Today, fewer and fewer people are able to obtain long-term employment with generous pension arrangements; good pensions are now basically limited to the higher levels of the public sector, major banks and a few multinational companies. Smaller firms are under pressure to reduce the benefits offered by pension schemes, and we often hear of cases where a firm's pension fund (these are termed 'Occupational

---

[1] Fred Schwed, Jr, *Where Are the Customers' Yachts?*, Simon and Schuster, 1940.

Pensions') is unable to meet its obligations. For this reason, those of us who do not enjoy cast-iron security in our jobs together with a very generous pension scheme need to think about other ways of funding our living costs in retirement.

Although you may get a basic State Pension if you have made sufficient National Insurance contributions during your working life, this provides barely enough money to live on; currently the basic State Pension pays £97.65 a week to a single person and £156.15 to married couples. It is possible that the value of this pension will decrease in real terms in the future.

Then there are the 'individual pensions' or 'private pensions' of various kinds that you take out for yourself, contributing to them out of your income. The main benefit they offer is that they are free of tax when you contribute to them, so, for example, a higher rate tax payer can save 40 per cent when he or she contributes to the fund (the fund claims back the tax relief on your behalf). When you start drawing your pension, however, it will be subject to income tax. Many of these pensions are 'Money Purchase' schemes, which means that when you retire the fund is used to buy an annuity (see below) that will provide you with a regular income, and you may also be allowed to withdraw a proportion of the money as cash, tax free. If you are already in a company pension scheme (an 'Occupational Pension'), then you may be able to take out an individual pension if your earnings fall below a certain level – check for current rates. There are limits to how much of your income you can contribute to your pension, and these rise as you get older.

Pension money is generally invested in unit trust-type funds, often very conservatively because the fund managers want stable growth. You can usually choose what kind of fund to invest in, but the range may be limited, depending on the scheme. As you get closer to retirement, it may be worth switching into investments with very low volatility so that you know more exactly how much your pension income will really be when you retire – it is no fun to retire just at the point when the market crashes and you find that your fund is worth 25 per cent less than you thought.

Annuities

When you retire, you use most or all of your personal pension fund to buy an annuity. This is a special kind of contract with an insurance company that takes the form of a bet; the company offers to pay you a fixed sum of money each year, either for the rest of your life or for a fixed number of years. Most annuities are not inflation protected, so their value will diminish in real terms over time, and you are locked in forever – there is no way to change your mind. The reason why it is a bet, in the case of lifetime payments, is that neither you nor the insurance company knows how long you will live, so if you live longer than their estimate, you will make extra money.

Rates offered by competing annuity providers can vary quite a lot – even up to 30 per cent – so you need to shop around. Pick the right one in consultation with an independent financial adviser. Timing is important, because the annuity is related to current interest rates: when interest rates are high, annuity rates should be higher too, but remember to estimate the possible effect of inflation on your future income.

Guerrilla investors should feel uncomfortable about annuities because, unlike other investments, they demand that you hand over capital permanently – there is no way to get it back. At the time of writing, a lot of people think that insurance companies are offering rotten annuity deals. Of course, the companies are defending themselves vigorously, saying that people are living longer, and so on, but the fact remains that you might do rather better by investing on your own than by buying an annuity. When deciding how much to save in a personal pension scheme, and how much to invest in your own investment portfolio that you will control for your whole life, you will need to consider all aspects of your financial situation. Clearly, a personal pension is better than nothing at all, and it will grow faster because of the tax benefits. On the other hand, you have a much wider choice of investments in your own portfolio; if you can obtain tax-free status for part of your life and keep the portfolio offshore (see page 190) it will not be burdened by tax either; you will, at a pinch, be able to sell some of your

> **❝you might do rather better by investing on your own than by buying an annuity❞**

investments if you need money; and finally, you will be able to pass on your capital to your heirs when you die. To decide on the optimum balance between the two you will need to take as much independent advice as possible – and don't believe everything you are told, but get second, third and fourth opinions; everything depends upon your age, income and personal circumstances, so you need to find the best solution for you as a unique individual.

Insurance

Although they are not strictly investment products, some insurance deals have an investment element and in any case investors need to consider if they need to make any insurance provision for themselves and their families. 'Qualifying life policies' have tax benefits: they are tax-free when they mature or when you surrender or assign them, and some policies have a use in inheritance tax planning as a way of keeping money out of your estate for inheritance tax purposes (see page 243).

Life insurance

The world of life insurance is full of complex jargon, and it is important to have a grasp of how life insurance works before taking out a policy. The main reason to buy life insurance is to provide for your dependants (usually your family) if you should die suddenly. If this happened, your family could be in serious financial trouble, but the insurance would provide a lump sum which would help them to adjust, for example by paying off the mortgage to reduce living expenses.

Insurance companies employ specialist statisticians called actuaries who estimate the chances of events such as an early death occurring, based on factors such as your age, whether you do a dangerous job, and whether you smoke. Prices for the insurance are mainly based on these estimates. It is important to compare prices and shop around, and also to make sure that the insurance company you pick is financially sound and has a reputation for prompt payment on claims – the cheapest cover is not necessarily the best.

As well as insuring against death, you should also think about insuring against disability, such as losing a limb in an accident, and for major medical bills. For any of these categories, buy the broadest cover you can; for example, don't just insure against one type of accidental death, but all types. Remember, though, that not everyone needs life insurance; for example, if you don't have any dependants, you usually don't need life insurance because its main purpose is to provide for them.

You usually don't need life insurance if:

■ you are supported by others, such as your parents

■ you are a child

■ you and your spouse both earn a good salary and the surviving spouse will be able to maintain an adequate lifestyle without your income

■ you are retired and receiving a pension

■ you are wealthy and can already provide for your dependants.

'Term life insurance' is the basic form of cover and is also the cheapest – it lasts for a fixed period of time. Some policies guarantee that they can be renewed, even if you are ill, which can be a valuable benefit – but check if any diseases are excluded.

The big question is how much life insurance cover to buy. First, check whether or not the payout is index-linked to keep pace with inflation – you don't want to claim, say, in the 23rd year of your policy, only to find that inflation has eaten away at its value. One way of estimating how much cover to buy is to estimate your earnings after tax for the whole period of insurance and buy an equivalent amount. Another is to work out the total cost of your major outgoings during the period (mortgage, cars, and school fees, for instance) and add it to a sum of money that would be enough to provide a reasonable income for your family at, say 3 per cent real interest a year. That sum is likely to be large; £1 million would only give your family an income of £30,000 at 3 per cent a year. A third way is to calculate the income your family would need if you died, take away from it any state benefits and pensions they would receive, and multiply it by the number of years until your spouse retires, adjusting for inflation. All these methods depend on assumptions, so they cannot protect your family completely. For example, if your family handles the money badly, the income could

soon be gone, so it is worth discussing the issue with them and persuading them that the sensible thing to do in the event of your
untimely death is to invest the lump sum for income, and not to draw
from the capital.

There are several kinds of term insurance that vary the premiums you
pay over the period, or offer a decreasing payout as time goes on (this
can be useful if, for example, you are paying off a mortgage). In general, though, plain term insurance is the best option for most people.

Whole life policies

'Whole life' polices are more expensive and complicated than life
insurance because they have an investment element. Despite the tax
benefits, they are arguably less attractive today than they used to be
when people had less access to the financial markets and thus less
choice over how to invest their money. Not many people realize that
it can take more than five years for a life policy to beat saving in a
building society and that more than a third of people who buy them
give them up within three years and lose money by doing so.

Whole life insurance guarantees to pay out a sum on your death,
whenever it occurs. There are several kinds, including:

- 'Without profits' or 'non-participating' policies – these pay a fixed
  sum when you die, but are not inflation-linked. All benefits are
  guaranteed. They are becoming increasingly rare, but some people
  still have existing policies.

- 'With-profits' or 'participating' policies – these offer a guaranteed
  sum on death plus a share of the profits from the company's life
  fund. The profit shares are usually called 'bonuses' or 'dividends'
  and may be paid annually as 'reversionary bonuses' or a cash sum,
  and on termination of the policy. You cannot lose a 'reversionary'
  bonus once it has been declared. Insurance companies choose the
  amount of bonus to pay each year based on a cautious assessment
  of the life fund's profits, and may reduce bonuses or cut them altogether in some years.

- Unit-linked policies – these policies guarantee to pay a sum of
  money (the 'assured sum') plus the value of the units that you

accumulate in the company's investment funds. The premiums you pay go to purchase units, but your investment is charged with administration fees, life insurance costs, commissions and so on. Unit-linked policies are riskier than conventional whole life ones because they are exposed to stock market volatility.

A with-profits policy may produce adequate returns, but only if you keep the policy for the full term. While locking you in like this can be a good discipline for people who are psychologically unable to save and invest for the long term in other ways, guerrilla investors may be able to beat these returns by investing elsewhere.

Surrendering policies and the second-hand market

If you give up ('surrender') a policy before it ends, you suffer penalties, which are highest in the early years – if you surrender it during the first couple of years, you may receive nothing at all. If you do have to surrender a policy, there are several things you may be able to do to reduce the pain (check the conditions before you sign up in the first place):

■ You can make the policy 'paid-up', which means that you do not have to pay any more premiums. The assured sum is reduced and the terms of what is covered may change.

■ You can borrow against the policy, often at lowish interest rates; in return, the payout may be less.

■ You can only surrender a part of the value of the policy.

■ You can sell the policy on the second-hand market for more than the insurance company will give.

The second-hand market for investment-linked policies is quite lively, and represents an investment opportunity. Insurance companies keep penalties high to discourage early surrender, so investors can make a return by offering to take over the policy, paying a higher value to the original owner than the insurance company offers. Essentially, you are profiting from someone else's inability to keep up the payments. Profits are subject to CGT but you can use your annual CGT allowance and offset losses against the gains. There are specialist firms that act as market-makers, who advertise policies for sale in magazines such as the *Investor's Chronicle*. When dealing with these firms, make sure that they:

- are regulated by the FSA

- have a compensation scheme

- have indemnity insurance.

Think of second-hand policies as a form of saving with a better return than, say, a building society deposit. The size of the gains you make may depend on bonuses, which may not be possible to estimate for certain, but the investment is limited because there will be a guaranteed minimum return, which can rise over time. Second-hand policies may well perform better than, say, medium-term gilts, and you can always re-sell the policy in the market.

Insurance for guerrillas

Guerrilla investors need to make their money work hard, so they must resist buying more insurance than necessary. As a market aimed at consumers, there is a lot of nonsense and confusing presentation of the benefits and drawbacks of specific policies, and it is hard work to cut through all this to compare values. If you have dependants, you should definitely think about taking out term life insurance, and you should familiarize yourself with the various possibilities of using insurance to minimize inheritance tax, to pay off mortgages and, in the case of second-hand policies, to increase the return on medium-term savings. Pick your companies and advisers carefully – they really are not all the same – and look for people who will work hard to get you the right cover from the right company, and will fight to get any claims dealt with efficiently.

Summary

When making decisions about asset allocation, guerrilla investors need to think about where their roots are; most of us are not like the big multinational companies, that have the freedom to choose anywhere in the world as a base for their factories and back office operations in order to take advantage of the best tax regimes and economic conditions. For example, the situations of Asian investors and UK investors are very different: in Asia, investors generally enjoy a low tax burden, but suffer from thin and volatile markets for local property and shares and must save large sums of cash to pay for medical expenses and their children's education – so Asian investors tend to overweight their portfolios with cash; in the UK, on the other hand, with its high taxes, relatively solid property market and relatively generous, if slightly wobbly, welfare system, investors need much less money for medical care and education, but tend to have little cash and a portfolio that is overweighted on property. In neither case is it the investors' fault – it is the regulatory and economic environment where they are based that forces them to build their portfolios in this way. Investors who manage to build substantial wealth acquire increasing opportunities to break out of their own local environments and develop a better balanced asset allocation; periodic rebalancing of your asset allocation is vital, as you get richer, because of the need to reduce the exposure to the risks of having most of your money sunk into one asset class.

❝periodic rebalancing of your asset allocation is vital❞

As we have seen, property is generally thought to be an important element of any portfolio, and it also offers one of the lowest risk ways of being in business for yourself, should you choose to do so. Unless you really are a businessperson at heart, there are few other businesses that have such stable long-term prospects of building up value, which is, or should be, the central aim of any business. Businesses eat up cash and are very demanding – investors need to think very carefully before getting involved, and many people who are in a position to build their wealth steadily through passive investments such as shares, bonds and property, are not cut out to succeed in business, so be careful!

Other types of 'alternative' investment generally don't perform well; collectibles and wine, for instance, are appealing if you have an interest in them, but the evidence suggests that most investors in these assets generally could have done better if they had kept to the conventional asset types. A big element in successful investing is not to confuse fun with achieving good returns – for example, recently I met a 20-year-old student who told me that he had 'invested' £35,000 in making a short film, in the hope of establishing a career as a film director. He was completely unaware that possessing £35,000 at his age would give him the opportunity, within a few years, to get established on the housing ladder and would form a good foundation for building wealth; having worked in the film industry, I informed him that unless he had much more money to invest in film projects, which he didn't, it was unlikely that his short film would really land him a director's job because the supply of would-be film directors grossly exceeds the demand, and suggested that he looked for employment in more junior positions within the industry. Of course, when you are young you are optimistic, and rightly so, while investors tend to be older and more cautious. Perhaps a 20-year-old who only wanted to build wealth would be a rather unbalanced individual. Nevertheless, some of the most famous investors have indeed been driven by the wealth motive from a very early age, such as Warren Buffett, who built a business in his teens, and George Soros, who suffered under the Nazis and was determined to escape his status as an impoverished young refugee. Really good investors have great instincts about what is really a money-making investment and what isn't.

Finally, all guerrilla investors should try to understand the world of insurance, boring and tiresome though it often is; make sure you have adequate cover for your needs and those of your dependants, and consider using specialized schemes to mitigate tax. But you should be sceptical about insurance schemes with an investment element – in essence, they are a relic of times when ordinary people couldn't get at the financial markets, and they generally do not offer the best opportunities for good returns.

11

Thinking about retirement

Your financial health in retirement depends upon many issues, and some of these are beyond your control. Your physical health in retirement and how long you will live, for instance, are unpredictable, and while it is very important to take them into consideration when making plans, it is not possible to make any exact estimates. In this chapter we will look at some of the strategic issues that crop up during retirement and consider how to optimize the possibilities, striking a balance between staying flexible, enjoying the best possible quality of life, and passing on money to your relatives after you die.

The topics covered in this chapter are:

- Where to retire?

- Changing your asset allocation in retirement

- Asset rich, cash poor?

- Making a will

- Inheritance and offshore investment

Where to retire?

These days more and more people are retiring abroad. A few decades ago, the conventional advice to British consumers was that this was very dangerous unless you were very rich, but with the advent of cheap flights, an increasing sophistication about foreign travel and the realization that countries like France currently offer a better healthcare system than is available at home, retiring abroad has become a popular, and arguably sensible, option for many people who are only moderately well-off. As mentioned in Chapter 10, there has been a rash of television programmes on how to purchase a property abroad, ranging from traditional retirement areas such as southern France and Spain, to the rather more exotic, such as the Balkans, Algeria and Thailand. Like most things in life, making such an adventure work well depends on the individual; it is perfectly possible to arrange for a happy retirement in somewhere as remote as, say, Bali, but you need to have the experience and ability to cope. The secret of success is not to rush into the move with the assumption that the system is similar to the UK's – this is never the case, even in other EU countries.

Retirement for true guerrillas

There are many books on retirement abroad that cover the practicalities in detail, but they generally discuss them in consumerist terms; guerrilla investors need to focus on the core issues. These are summed up very well by the maverick international fund manager, Marc Faber, who is based in the Far East:

> If I can give one piece of investment advice I would say...
> as an alternative to ending your days in cold London, New
> York or Munich, you could retire in a community in Thailand,
> North Africa, the Caribbean or Latin America with, say, three
> servants... Some people might say that in northern Thailand,
> for instance, you don't have the medical attention that you
> have in New York, but I don't care... maybe you have better
> attention in the sense that you have a doctor who is nice to
> you and some nurses who are nice to you, whereas if you go
> into a hospital in the West, nobody cares...[1]

This is strong stuff, but essentially it is accurate, and a strategy that really determined guerrilla investors should consider; it is quite a challenge, and many people find that in the end family ties and personal taste outweigh the very real advantages that retiring in an exotic location can offer. Before dismissing the idea out of hand, though, you

---

[1] Gough, *Trading the World's Markets*, Wiley, 2001.

should consider the potential benefits. Retiring in the developing world can often give you:

- much better value for money in terms of housing, food, personal service and leisure pursuits

- a better climate

- a more interesting and lively society where the elderly are more respected than they are in the West.

The traditional objections to retiring to an exotic location have been the lack of medical care, the cost of travel home and potential problems locally from corrupt officials, punitive legislation and inefficient bureaucracy. Today, many newly developed countries have improved out of all recognition from how they were, say, 30 years ago and these difficulties are much less serious than they used to be. Good medical care is widely available (although often at a relatively high cost), air travel is currently cheap, and the global economy has caused many countries to be more efficient and transparent in the way they treat foreign investors. Taking Marc Faber's example of northern Thailand, for example, the cost of a return flight to the UK is only a few hundred pounds, local hospitals are good for minor ailments and world-class hospitals are available in Singapore, a short flight away.

The most serious financial issues for people retiring abroad are likely to be:

- Ensuring that you have good title to any property you purchase. Some countries only allow foreigners to purchase short leases on properties, while in others it is very difficult to prove you really own a property.

- Ensuring that local property can be sold easily and that the money can be repatriated, either by you because you want to return home, or by your heirs in the event of your death. Remember to check how the inheritance process works, and plan in advance how to minimize any legal delays, for example by holding the property through a foreign company.

- Minimizing the taxation of local assets when you die.

In most cases, these issues can be solved one way or another, for example by renting rather than buying a property, and keeping the bulk of your financial assets elsewhere. The key is to ensure that you are extremely well-informed about the local situation before you make a major commitment. Building a house for half a million pounds on the coast of Southeast Asia, seeing it washed away by a tsunami and then discovering that it was uninsured, for instance (which has happened), is surely an avoidable disaster for the well-prepared.

Most people, of course, opt for less challenging places like France and Spain. As fellow EU countries that are nearby, these can be successful choices, but you still need to be aware of all the differences that are likely to affect you, such as planning regulations and inheritance taxes. The property market may be very different from the UK, too – it may be easy to buy a house, but it could be a lot more difficult to sell it later. These days, the verdict on retiring abroad is broadly positive, but remember to do your homework!

Changing your asset allocation in retirement

Can you live off your assets after you retire? Will you be condemned to a life of miserable poverty? It all depends, and there are imponderables that nobody can really forecast with any certainty. For instance, we know that the UK is heading for a long-term crisis in pension arrangements, but we don't know what future governments will do about poverty in old age. We don't know how long we will live, how sick we will get, or how much, if anything, we will have to pay for medical treatment in the future. It does seem clear, however, that most people in the UK will not have accumulated sufficient personal savings to live off the interest alone; they will need to supplement them with any pension rights they have accumulated, including state pensions, and they may have to downsize and move to a cheaper home in order to liberate more capital. Even if you have accumulated a really quite large chunk of capital – say £1 million – the average annual real return on it, if you invested it all in gilts, would only be £13,000, which would put you near the poverty line. For some, the answer to this is to dip into their capital each year and live the high life; I've known people who have done this successfully, but it carries the obvious risk that the money will run out before you do, leaving you destitute in very old age.

Nevertheless, the conventional advice to the newly retired is to adjust your asset allocation by weighting it more heavily in favour of bonds rather than equities. At the time of writing (early 2011) top-quality government bonds are producing a real return of less than 1 per cent, which is a little less than the long-term average for UK bonds, and is unlikely to supply you with all the income you will need to survive in retirement. Even so, the advice still stands. There are two main reasons for this.

First, most people are likely to receive a lower income in retirement than they do when they are working full time. Many retired people need to use some or all of the returns they make on their investments to supplement their pensions and other income. Bonds and similar financial instruments provide the safety and regular payments that people in this situation need; in contrast, equities cannot do this because of their greater volatility. Even though the returns on gilts are low, they are at least reliable and predictable.

Second, we do not know how long we are going to live. If we did know this, we could decide, for instance, to spend a proportion of our capital each year until it ran out just after we died. Since this is not the case, the preservation of capital is important; most people want to retain or increase the real (inflation-adjusted) value of their investments indefinitely so that they can be assured of a regular income from them (another reason for this is to pass on their assets to their children). Although equities offer the best chance for capital growth in the long term, they can go through extended periods where they drop in value. If you die during one of these periods, you may be passing on a much reduced portfolio to your children. Of course, if your children are experienced investors and are not in need of cash – and the investments are basically sound – this might not be a bad thing, since inheritance tax would be lower and the portfolio would be likely to rise in value in the long term. Many people, however, feel that their beneficiaries are likely to make suboptimal decisions when they come into their inheritance, and that it is best to try to keep the portfolio's value stable by weighting it towards bonds and cash.

While these arguments are not unreasonable, they are based on notions of the average retired investor, and may not apply to you as an individual. Suppose, for instance, you have sufficient income from other sources, such as pensions, to live on, so you do not need to spend any of the returns you make on your portfolio. This does not necessarily mean that you are very rich – you may simply be happy to live frugally. Some retired people are able to go on working and earning, and people who have had senior positions in large companies or the civil service may enjoy pensions that are sufficiently large that they can save from them to add to their investments. A retired person who does not need to draw down investment income can continue to seek capital growth for as long as he or she is mentally fit enough to manage the portfolio. In many cases, this could give 20 or 30 years in which the portfolio can continue to grow after you have retired, which could be as long, or longer, than the length of time you held your portfolio before retirement. If you are in the fortunate position of not needing to withdraw anything from your portfolio then it makes sense to allocate your assets to optimize potential capital growth (this generally means heavily weighting it towards equities) and continuing to reinvest all investment income.

Example

Just to labour the point, let's imagine two contrasting situations for retired people.

John and Grace are a married couple and have £500,000 invested exclusively in bonds, which provide them with, say, £5,000 annually. Their pensions are low and the money they receive from their bonds is an essential part of the income they need to live on, so they do not reinvest it. Since they are spending all the interest from their investments, the real (inflation-adjusted) value of their capital is gradually shrinking. An adviser has suggested to John and Grace that they could reinvest some of the interest in order to mitigate this, but they are unwilling to do so. The problem is that if they do not do so, there may come a time when their capital has shrunk so far that the investment income it provides is substantially less than it is today.

John's sister Lucy, on the other hand, is in a better position. She receives a good pension, lives frugally, and can actually afford to continue saving. She also has a portfolio worth £500,000, and as an experienced investor who wants capital growth, she keeps most of her portfolio in equity funds, periodically rebalancing it but minimizing trades. She hopes that her portfolio will show substantial capital growth in the long term. As Lucy ages, she is conscious that she may reach a point where she is no longer able to take good decisions about how to manage her portfolio. If this occurs, her plan is to switch to a more conservative portfolio of cash and bonds to keep its value stable.

Asset rich, cash poor?

It is common for people in retirement to become increasingly asset rich and cash poor. Typically, the value of their home will be growing, but, like John and Lucy, the value of their financial investments will be shrinking because they are not reinvesting the income. Using the asset allocation model, we can describe this as a process of their assets becoming unbalanced in favour of property, which is undesirable chiefly because the investor increasingly has less and less cash available for emergencies. The problem is that it is not easy to rebalance the asset allocation because one cannot usually sell off a piece of one's house to invest it in financial securities. In addition, living costs could actually increase in old age because of a greater need for healthcare. While it may be true that the UK provides a safety net to the elderly, many people do find it necessary to pay for medical treatment (for example, to bypass waiting lists) and they may be forced to pay high fees for nursing home care. If you are living abroad, the cost of medical treatment may be higher (although currently some EU countries, such as France, have a better, almost-free national health service than the UK); nursing costs, on the other hand, are low in developing countries such as Thailand.

A drastic, sudden downgrading of one's lifestyle can cause physical and psychological harm; for example, moving home can often be very upsetting for the elderly if they have not planned for it for a long time. In making your retirement plans, therefore, it is advisable to factor in these kinds of eventualities and to consider ways in which you could cope with them. Financial planning needs to be kept flexible – you need to keep your options open so that you can change your strategy according to changing circumstances. Making unbreakable long-term commitments to one type of investment is almost certainly a bad idea. For example, putting all your money into annuities (see page 218) is probably not advisable because you are giving up all control in return for an income which could diminish in real terms.

Making a will

A surprisingly large number of people die without making a will (this is known as 'intestacy'). You might think that people fail to make a will only when they have little or no assets, but this is not the case; for example, in 2003 a Taiwanese billionaire, Wen Say-ling, died intestate, leaving his estate liable to 50 per cent inheritance tax and much speculation about how the money would be divided. From a financial point of view, it is a very bad idea not to make a will for the following reasons:

■ Most countries have rules on how a person's estate (their assets) must be split up if they die intestate. Usually there is a rigid formula that prescribes shares to various relatives. Little can be done to mitigate taxes at this point. Legal and administrative costs can be very high.

■ An administrator is appointed by a court to share out the estate, and the deceased person's wishes are not really considered. Some of the estate may go to people whom you would not wish to help.

■ The process of administering the estate is much slower and more expensive than it would be if the deceased leaves a will and appoints executors to handle the process. This can make life very difficult for a spouse, for example, who may have to wait for years before receiving any money.

■ If a person dies intestate abroad, the delays and costs are likely to be even greater because two countries' rules will have to be followed.

In essence, if you have any assets at all and you do not make a will, you are virtually guaranteeing that a substantial amount of money will be wasted on unnecessary fees and taxes. It is cheap to have a solicitor draw up a will for you; although you are allowed to draw up a will without legal help, this is inadvisable because the solicitor will help to ensure that there are no ambiguities or potential legal difficulties or disputes.

The key dos and don'ts for making a will are:

■ DO appoint executors whom you know and trust. Executors are people who agree to take responsibility for seeing that the legal formalities of dividing up an inheritance are done properly. This work can be done by any reasonably competent person – no professional is required. Pick two or more executors, in case one of them is unable to do the work when the time comes.

■ DO NOT appoint a professional as an executor. Some people appoint bank managers, accountants or solicitors as their executors.

These professionals will charge fairly high fees, and will work slowly and cautiously, causing avoidable delays and substantially increased expense. In the rare cases when they do need professional help on a technical matter, the executors can simply engage a professional to do the work at a fraction of the cost.

■ DO think about estate planning. Inheritance tax is often called a voluntary tax because it can be substantially reduced by careful planning. The current rules for inheritance tax in the UK are discussed on page 243.

■ If you are planning to retire abroad, DO make sure that your will can be enforced. Remember, in many countries you are not allowed to choose the people to whom you want to bequeath assets and the state has fixed rules on who inherits what. This could be a serious problem if, for instance, you bought an expensive chateau in France that you want to leave to an only child: under French law, an only child only gets half the estate, with the rest going to other relatives. There are often legal ways to get around these problems, but make sure you take the necessary steps before you invest your money. Of course, if you retire to a run-down shack in the Pyrenees, say, and you keep the rest of your assets in the UK, it may not be worth the effort to avoid French inheritance law because of the low value of your French property.

Inheritance and offshore investment

If you have substantial financial assets, it may be worthwhile to keep them in a low-tax or no-tax jurisdiction (the so-called 'tax havens') to mitigate the effects of taxation (see Chapter 9). This is never a straightforward option, however. One important consideration is how to ensure that the assets you hold can be transferred easily to your beneficiaries when you die. Some people have found it extremely difficult, or even impossible, to claim money they have inherited that is held in a tax haven, even when they have successfully gained probate at home. The safest ways to pass on money held offshore to your beneficiaries are either to transfer it to them while you are still alive or to make them joint account holders. Doing this, however, may incur tax liabilities at home, so you need to take specialist advice. If you are no longer regarded as resident in the UK for tax purposes, you may be able to avoid inheritance tax altogether. Another possibility is to use a trust (see page 244), but this can be expensive to manage and you need to make sure that there will be little delay in handing over the assets to your beneficiaries after your death.

Summary

Creating a happy and enjoyable retirement is a very personal thing, and financial security is only one ingredient in the recipe, albeit an important one. In this chapter we have looked at the most important issues from what are hopefully some fresh angles, with the aim of thinking about the new possibilities that retirement opens up, and how to avoid the pitfalls.

- Retiring abroad – this has become much more feasible than ever before for most people, but do your homework thoroughly. Retirement abroad can potentially give you a much better quality of life than you can ever achieve in the UK.

- Asset allocation – if you are relying on your investment income to live on, it is advisable to weight your portfolio heavily towards bonds. If you have sufficient income from elsewhere, such as a pension, it may well be worthwhile to continue to weight the portfolio towards equities in pursuit of further capital growth.

- Try to avoid becoming asset rich and cash poor. This is easier said than done, but the effects can be mitigated by careful planning, regular reviews, and keeping your financial plans as flexible as possible. Consider downsizing your home to release cash for your financial portfolio.

- Make a will – it is cheap to do this, and will save a lot of heartache and expense later. Avoid appointing professional executors – good, trustworthy friends can do the job, often more quickly, cheaply and sensitively. Plan to mitigate the effects of inheritance tax (see page 243).

- Money offshore – if you hold substantial sums offshore, go to great lengths to ensure that it can be passed on quickly and inexpensively to your beneficiaries. Double check everything you are told and get second opinions.

12

UK taxation

Tax is a burden on everyone in society, from the richest to the poorest, and although governments often say that tax revenue is spent on providing essential services to the public, one might be forgiven for suspecting that a lot of our tax money is wasted or goes to the wrong places. From an investor's point of view, the real difficulty with tax systems is that they are constantly changing, and the rules are highly complex and often contradictory, which makes it very hard for the investors to plan how to legally minimize their tax liabilities.

It is important to use an accountant, even if you don't have very much money, to stop you getting into a mess – sometimes they can even save you money. The key is to stay within the law: many impatient people prefer to try to break the rules rather than to take the trouble to find ways of using them, legally, to their best advantage, but ultimately it really isn't worth the trouble – stay legal!

There is quite a lot of scope to save tax if you are prepared to study the rules. Although this chapter can only scratch the surface of all the possibilities, it should give you some food for thought. Remember, though, that since the rules are always changing you will need to factor in the possibility of future changes into any long-term plans you make – and for this, you will need to pay for the best accountants and tax advisers that you can afford.

In this chapter we will look at:

▇   Income tax

▇   Tax avoidance and tax evasion

▇   Capital gains tax

▇   Inheritance tax

▇   Trusts

An overview

The UK tax system operates a range of taxation methods, and if your circumstances have recently changed – for example, if you have just inherited some money – it is worth reminding yourself of the main UK personal taxes:

▇   Income tax – this is paid on your earnings, pension income and some state benefits such as the Jobseeker's Allowance, Carer's Allowance and Incapacity Benefit. If you have an income, you also have to pay National Insurance contributions (NICs). Interest from savings accounts, share dividends and rents from property are also subject to income tax. There are many exemptions and reliefs on how much you pay.

▇   Capital gains tax (CGT) – this is a tax on assets you sell, such as shares and property. The tax is on the profit you make, and again there are numerous reliefs.

▇   Stamp duty – this is a tax on property and shares that you buy. If you invest in a fund, the fund manager pays the tax, which is reflected in the bid/offer spread.

▇   Inheritance tax (IHT) – when you die, if the value of your estate (the total assets you leave behind) is above a certain level (currently £325,000) you have to pay tax. If you have given away money and assets during the preceding seven years, these may be subject to tax too.

▇   Purchase taxes – many things that you buy are taxed at flat rates. For example, VAT is charged for many goods and services, there is fuel duty on petrol and excise duty on alcohol and tobacco.

Tax on investment income

Investment income is principally the money you receive as interest and dividends. Interest is usually taxed at source, which means that whoever is holding your money, such as a bank or building society, deducts 20 per cent of your interest and pays it directly to the Inland Revenue. If your total income, including investment income, puts you into the higher tax band (currently 40 per cent) you have to pay the rest later. People with no income or very low incomes may be able to claim back the tax or to register to prevent the tax being deducted at source.

There are three different tax rates on dividends you receive from UK companies:

▪ Basic rate taxpayers and people who pay no other income tax pay 10 per cent on dividends.

▪ Higher rate taxpayers pay 32.5 per cent on dividend income that falls above the basic rate limit of £37,600 (see taxable bands, below).

▪ Additional rate taxpayers pay 42.5 per cent on dividend income that falls above the higher rate limit of £150,000.

Income tax

Income tax rates change frequently, so always check the current rates. The system is based on 'personal allowances', which are sums of money you are allowed to earn before any tax is applied. The main allowances for 2011/12 are:

Personal allowance	£7,475
Allowance if you are aged 65–74	£9,940 (limited to income of £22,900)
Allowance if you are aged 75 or older	£10,090 (limited to income of £22,900)

The money you earn above these allowances is then divided into 'taxable bands' and taxed at different rates. This means that if your income is high and reaches all the bands, different parts of your income will be taxed at different rates. For 2011/12 the tax bands are:

Starting rate for savings only (10% tax)	£0–£2,560
Basic rate (20% tax)	£0–£35,000
Higher rate (40% tax)	£35,001–£150,000
Additional rate (50% tax)	Over £150,000

Example

Fiona is a 30-year-old software developer earning £46,000 in the 2011/12 tax year. How much tax will she have to pay?

Income	£46,000
Less personal allowance	£7,475
Taxable income	£38,325
Tax on the basic rate band	20% of £35,000 = £7,000
Tax on the higher band	40% of £3,325 = £1,330

Total tax to pay = £7,000 + £1,330 = £8,330

Tax avoidance or tax evasion?

One is legal and one isn't, but do you know which? Tax avoidance is legal; this is where you make efforts to reduce or avoid paying tax by taking advantage of the complexities and confusions in the tax rules. Tax evasion is trying to do the same thing, but this time breaking the law. Sometimes, especially in very complex cases, it is not always possible to tell the difference, but most of the time we know if we are legally avoiding tax or illegally evading it. The right to avoid tax is very well established, and, to paraphrase Lord Clyde's comments in a famous tax case in 1929, a person does nothing wrong by arranging his or her affairs to take advantage of the rules, so long as they are not broken. The extraordinary complexity and unfairness of tax legislation does mean that many people do occasionally encounter situations where they cannot tell whether or not a certain action would break the rules, so it is important to pay for the best possible professional advice and to do all that you can to stay within the law.

❝expatriates probably have the greatest scope for mitigating tax❞

Expatriates probably have the greatest scope for mitigating tax. In certain circumstances you may be able to avoid a large capital gains tax liability by becoming non-resident, but the rules are getting tougher. Tax planning is essential if you are to make full use of the opportunities to save money, and you will definitely need professional help to achieve this.

Residence outside the UK

If you are not 'resident' or 'ordinarily resident' in the UK, you are not subject to UK income tax, except in a few exceptional cases. Low-tax jurisdictions and tax havens charge their residents little or no tax, and wealthy people have often found it necessary to move to such places for that reason. Residence, as defined by HMRC, has nothing to do with nationality or what passport you hold.

There is scope for reducing your tax liabilities if you are enterprising enough to work abroad for a few years, or if you have a foreign spouse, but it isn't easy to arrange this on your own – hire a specialist accountant, and possibly a specialist tax lawyer, to make sure that you get it right.

The rules for residency can only be covered briefly here, and in any case they are constantly changing, so make sure you double check with your advisers. Currently, there is no single test for UK residence, and it is has become harder than it was for a UK resident to lose this status. If you spend more than 183 days in the UK in a tax year, however, you will be deemed resident in the UK for that year. If you work for a whole year abroad and you have a full-time contract of employment, you can be deemed non-resident, and if you stay outside the UK for three full tax years you may also be deemed non-resident, but recent court judgments have emphasized the need to show that you intend to make a clean break with the UK.

Ordinary residence

'Ordinary residence' is a strange concept, quite different from residence. As it is the main criterion for capital gains tax, it is important to persuade HMRC to agree with you that you are not 'ordinarily resident' before you make a capital gain if you wish to avoid CGT. According to the rules, you can be resident in more than one country at the same time but 'ordinarily resident' in only one county at a time. If you are leaving the country permanently, it is relatively easy to persuade HMRC to accept that you will no longer be ordinarily resident, but if you are going for a shorter period you may have to produce a strong argument supported by detailed evidence – you'll need a specialist to help.

Domicile

Domicile is another strange concept, and again is completely different from 'residence' and 'ordinary residence'. You can only have one domicile at a time. There are two kinds:

- Domicile of origin – this is usually the country where your father was domiciled when you were born. If you have a domicile of origin outside the UK, you may be able to live in the UK for a long time without having to pay UK tax.

- Domicile of choice – this is more tricky. You have to be resident in a country and have 'the intention of permanent or indefinite residence' there. If you want to change from a UK domicile, you must intend never to return except for brief, infrequent visits, or HMRC will say that you have not changed your domicile.

Domicile does not have to be the same thing as residence or nationality – for example, you may have lived in the UK for decades, and still be domiciled elsewhere.

Summary – avoiding tax by working overseas

If you work full-time abroad you may still have to pay tax in the country where you are working; there are however, many countries that have low taxes and prosperous economies, for example in the Far East. If you go abroad but do not have a full-time job, under the current, rather nebulous, rules, you will need to show that you intend to make a clean break with the UK; so, for instance, spending a lot of time in your holiday villa in Spain, but keeping a house in the UK and giving money to your children while they are at university in the UK is unlikely to be treated as being non-resident.

In essence, it is possible to avoid UK tax by getting a full-time job abroad. Ideally, this will be a well-paid job in a low-tax or no-tax jurisdiction, and you will be able to save a substantial amount of your income, which you will invest through an offshore centre. By the time you return to the UK, you will have accumulated a lump sum much more quickly than you could have done if you had stayed at home, even if you were earning the same salary.

Capital gains tax

Capital gains tax (CGT) is a tax on the profits made from selling an asset, such as shares or a building. The tax is assessed on the market value of the asset, so if you try to avoid CGT by giving it away or selling it too cheaply, you will still incur a liability on the profits you would have made.

Each year you have an annual exemption; in 2011/12 this is £10,600, which means that you can make capital gains up to that amount without paying CGT.

There are also a number of exemptions from CGT, including the sale of:

■ your main home (but check for special conditions)

■ your car

■ gilts

■ personal belongings up to £6,000

■ betting gains

■ assets which are given to charities

Also, you are able in some cases to offset capital losses against other capital gains. You can transfer assets to a spouse or a partner in a civil partnership free of CGT.

From 23 June 2010, CGT is charged at 18 per cent and 28 per cent (the rate depends on total taxable income and gains), and 10 per cent if you are eligible for Entrepreneurs' Relief, which applies when you sell all or part of a business.

Investors may have to pay CGT if they sell shares. There are special rules applying to shares because often you have bought shares in the same company at different prices over a long period. The sums aren't particularly easy but if you have an accountant or a stockbroker, they can help you work it out correctly. There are also special rules for shares held through an employee share scheme, and in general you pay less CGT on these.

The rules on CGT are very complicated, but it is possible to mitigate CGT on large gains by careful tax planning; for example, you may be able to sell an asset while you are working abroad and exempt from UK tax. Specialist advice is needed.

> **❝it is possible to mitigate CGT on large gains by careful tax planning❞**

Inheritance tax

Inheritance tax (IHT) is due on the assets you leave behind when you die, known as your 'estate', and also on some gifts that you may have given while you were alive. For 2010/11, you pay IHT on the amount of the estate over £325,000 at 40 per cent.

The main exemptions and reliefs are:

■ The estate can go to a spouse or civil partner free of IHT.

■ Most gifts you make seven years before you die are exempt.

■ You can in any case give away £3,000 a year free of IHT, and wedding gifts from parents are exempt up to £5,000 each.

■ Gifts above the annual limits are known as 'potentially exempt transfers' (PETs), and are taxed on a sliding scale, depending how long before your death the PET was made.

■ There are some very generous reliefs on businesses and agricultural property, but, as you might expect, the rules are very complex and you will need specialist advice.

If you have any money and you care at all about the people you will leave behind when you die, it is very careless not to make a will, because, as we saw in Chapter 11, if you die intestate (without a will), there will be a great deal of expense and delay in transferring the money to the beneficiaries. Normally most if this will go the spouse, and some to any children. If there are no children, the estate goes to other relatives, and some of it may go to the Crown! The real problem, other than delay and expense, is that the money may go to the 'wrong' person, from your point of view, so take the trouble to spend an afternoon with a lawyer and get a will drawn up – your beneficiaries will thank you for it after you are gone.

One useful way to use wills to mitigate IHT if you are married is to leave a sum equal to the annual exemption (currently £325,000) to your children or others, and give the rest to your spouse free of IHT. Other methods of reducing IHT include:

■ Making large PET gifts regularly; if you survive more that seven years after making the gifts, they will be exempt.

■ Investing in the Alternative Investment Market (AIM), discussed on page 153. If you hold these shares for more than two years, they will qualify for 100 per cent business property relief and be free of IHT. There is a risk that the shares perform poorly.

■ Take out a life assurance policy to cover the potential tax liability.

IHT is sometimes called a voluntary tax because there are many ways to reduce it. The best way is to move to a low-tax/no-tax jurisdiction before you die. This may sound a little extreme, but suppose your estate is worth £15.325 million; some people might think that making a relatively small sacrifice of moving abroad in order to save 40 per cent of a hard-earned £15 million is worth the effort. If you do think that your estate may be liable for IHT, make plans early and review them annually with a professional adviser so that you can adapt them to any changes in the rules.

Trusts

Trusts separate the control over assets, the entitlement to capital and the entitlement to income. They were invented centuries ago as a way of protecting assets, for example from people who might unduly influence immature or irresponsible beneficiaries (the people who receive money from the trust). They are best understood as a kind of slow motion gift, where the giver, known as the 'settlor' puts money into a trust that is administered by the trustees, and the trustees pay out some or all of the money to the beneficiaries according to the conditions of the trust, which can last for up to 100 years. Once the settlor has put money into trust, it no longer belongs to him or her, but to the trustees. A settlor can be a trustee, but this can make the trust liable for certain taxes. The settlor can also be a beneficiary of a trust.

A settlor can retain some control over a trust by keeping the right to appoint new trustees, or by making the trustees gain the settlor's consent before taking certain actions. The trustees have a legal duty to act in the best interests of the beneficiaries and have many other heavy obligations. In practice, this can mean that trusts that last for three generations have poorly performing portfolios, because trustees sometimes tend to be overly conservative in their investment policies; 80 years' worth of cash and bond investment, avoiding equities, can produce surprisingly bad results.

The main reasons to use a trust are:

- to provide for someone who is too young to look after money

- to provide for someone who is too old or ill to look after money

- to pass on a valuable asset, such as a large farm, while making sure that it is not broken up and sold off too quickly

- to mitigate IHT.

Successive governments have progressively tightened the rules on trusts based in the UK to the point where their use as a tax shelter has become increasingly unattractive, especially when you take into account the costs of administering the trust (if you use professional trustees, they will need to be paid), but they still may be useful in reducing taxes in certain circumstances. The good news is that many offshore centres allow trusts, so it may be possible for the wealthy to arrange their affairs to take advantage of much greater tax savings, although this would generally mean that the settlor was a non-UK tax payer at the time the trust was created.

Let's look at some of the various types of trust it is possible to create:

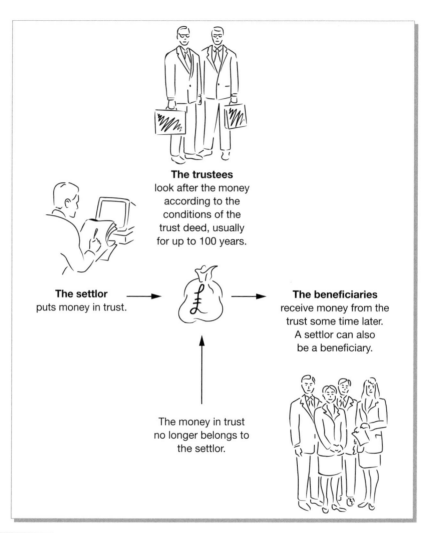

The trustees
look after the money
according to the
conditions of the
trust deed, usually
for up to 100 years.

The settlor ⟶
puts money in trust.

The beneficiaries
receive money from the
trust some time later.
A settlor can also
be a beneficiary.

The money in trust
no longer belongs to
the settlor.

Figure 12.1   The trust concept

Bare trusts

In a bare trust, the trustees act as nominees who hold the assets for someone else, who still legally possesses them. Bare trusts can be useful to higher-rate taxpayers who want to accumulate money for their children. For example, a child can possess the assets of the trust, while the trustees reinvest the income generated from investments. This income is tax free up to certain limits.

Fixed-interest trusts

The beneficiaries receive income from the trust, and this is subject to income tax. If the trust deed allows it, the trustees can suspend payments if the beneficiaries behave in ways that the trustees disapprove of.

Discretionary trusts

The trustee has the power to decide how much money a beneficiary will receive, and can make interest-free loans to a beneficiary. This can be useful if, for instance, your spouse needs to go into a nursing home after your death, because the trust's assets are not counted as part of the spouse's estate, so they may be eligible for state aid.

Accumulation and maintenance trusts

These are designed to hold assets for beneficiaries until they reach the age of 25, and have IHT advantages. The rules changed in 2008, and these trusts have now largely been replaced by '18 to 25' trusts, which currently enjoy a low tax rate if the beneficiary receives the trust property between the ages of 18 and 25.

Trusts – a summary

Trusts can be expensive to run and are vulnerable to future changes in the tax regulations. They are not the solution to all financial headaches, and do require very able trustees to administer them, so it is important to consider whether there are other ways of achieving your goals. UK trusts still offer some tax advantages, but these need to be considered very carefully in the light of possible rule changes in the future, especially if the trust is likely to last a long time.

Summary

All governments need to raise money to pay for the servies they operate, and in the most developed countries this is done mainly by quite high taxation. Taxation is a problem for investors in that it hampers the process of accumulating wealth, and then can take large chunks out of money that investors want to pass on to their heirs. Political change can lead to sudden, and unfair, adjustments to what are already highly complex tax systems, and are a major challenge to wealthy people who want to increase their wealth over many generations. In practice, great fortunes rarely last for many generations, arguably because they represent an IOU from society at large that it will eventually find ways to destroy through taxation and other methods of expropriation. Guerrilla investors must be realistic; it is possible to mitigate tax legally when accumulating wealth, and it is also possible to reduce the tax liabilities when passing it on by careful tax planning, but few, if any, fortunes prove indestructible in the very long term.

13

An overview of the financial crisis

'It's the death of capitalism!' exclaimed a radical academic happily at a dinner party I went to in early 2008, just when it had become plain that the financial crisis that had begun in the previous year was really very serious indeed. So far it looks as if she was completely wrong, but there is no doubt that the financial crisis, which is still ongoing at the time of writing, was a big one, and that guer-

... try to understand how it happened and what
r investing in the future.

look at:

n

o Europe

nd the financial crisis

in the long term

'gan

early 2000s the USA was enjoying a runaway boom in the housing market, as were many other countries, including the UK, Spain and Ireland. House prices in the US increased by 124 per cent in the period 1997–2006 (S&P/Case-Shiller national home-price index), well ahead of inflation. There had, of course, been housing bubbles before, but what made this one unusual in the USA was the immense scale of the lending, in particular to new uncreditworthy borrowers (the 'sub-prime' market) and to home owners who remortgaged on the basis of the increasing equity value in their homes and promptly spent the cash. Interest rates were very low and many sub-prime borrowers were able to obtain mortgages offering low initial repayments that would increase later to market-based rates.

At the same time, a 'shadow-banking' system had grown up in the USA and Europe which was largely unregulated, and did all kinds of banking business in the wholesale markets. The participants were legitimate financial entities, such as investment banks, hedge funds and finance companies, that played a major role in the markets for a wide variety of complicated financial instruments such as securitized products, commercial paper, asset-backed commercial paper, repurchase agreements, and derivatives. Innovations in these instruments were becoming increasingly important as a source of profits for many financial institutions. As they were largely unregulated, it was difficult to get any clear estimate of how much risk any player was exposed to, although in the upbeat mood of the time the obvious dangers of this lack of transparency were generally dismissed. Financial innovation, we were told, was a wonderful boon to humanity because it enabled the experts to control their risks with much greater precision than ever before, and it was all far too complicated for lesser mortals to understand – although from time to time some of the expert practitioners have admitted that they didn't fully understand it either!

One popular financial innovation in the shadow banking system was securitization, which involves pooling a large number of debt contracts, such as mortgages, credit card debts and car loans, and selling them on to investors (usually financial institutions from all over the world) as a financial product called a 'structured debt'. One of the key ideas was that this type of product reduces the risk, compared with that of the individual contracts in the pool, to investors. It was argued that a large pool of similar debts would behave predictably – for example, it was thought that one could accurately estimate the default rate on such a pool. Often, the assets were transferred into a

Special Purpose Vehicle (SPV), which issued the products to investors, frequently in tranches, or categories, of different levels of risk: the top, or 'senior', tranches would have a high credit rating. As a largely unregulated field, shadow banking did not enjoy the formal system of support from central banks and governments that the traditional banking receives, and was very highly geared and over-reliant on short-term borrowing. Shadow banking was thus potentially very vulnerable to a large-scale financial crisis.

In 2005 and 2006 the US housing market began to drop, following rises in the base interest rate, and defaults on sub-prime loans began to increase. In early 2007, US sub-prime loans totalled $1.7 trillion. By the end of the year, some 16 per cent of sub-prime mortgages were seriously behind in their repayments or were already the subject of foreclosure proceedings; by the spring of 2008, this figure had risen to 25 per cent. During 2007/08, almost a million homes in the USA were repossessed, with California and Florida being the most affected areas.

As the severity of the crisis began to become apparent, evidence of serious misdeeds began to emerge, as is often the case in a crash. Some aggressive lenders had encouraged naive borrowers to obtain mortgages, knowing that they would be unable to cope with the repayments, and had even encouraged them to fraudulently exaggerate their incomes in order to obtain the loans. Some lenders had abandoned assessment of creditworthiness altogether, confident that their associates on Wall Street would be able to securitize the loans anyway, and there is even evidence that some Wall Street firms encouraged the lenders to lower their standards in order to generate more business. It emerged that Fannie Mae (the Federal National Mortgage Association, FNMA) and Freddie Mac (the Federal Home Loan Mortgage Corporation, FHLMC), two large and powerful government-backed organizations originally intended to facilitate home ownership by providing liquidity in the wholesale markets, had lowered their underwriting standards and had become heavily involved in sub-prime lending.

Then people began to examine the securitized mortgages, and ask why the major credit rating agencies, such as Moody's and Standard & Poor's, had rated the senior tranches of structured debt as AAA when now these debts were defaulting at a high rate. Financial journalists Bethany McLean and Joe Nocera argued in their book *All the Devils Are Here* that the credit rating agencies had knowingly rated the sub-prime structured debt too highly in order to earn more fees for themselves and help boost the market, as many institutional customers for these products were prohibited from investing in anything less than AAA rated debt.

In 2010, the Financial Crisis Inquiry Commission, a Congressional panel set up to investigate the development of the crisis, was told by the former head of Clayton Holdings, an independent firm that analysed mortgage-backed securities, that Clayton had analysed 911,000 structured loans between January 2006 and June 2007 on behalf of large banks such as Morgan Stanley, Citigroup and Deutsche Bank and had found that 54 per cent of the loans did not meet the banks' lending criteria.[1] Using this period as a sample (it covered about 10 per cent of the total number of mortgages Clayton had analysed), representatives of the firm said that despite being given this information, the banks nevertheless chose to include a large proportion (varying from bank to bank) of these sub-standard loans in the structured products they sold on to other investors. Clayton had approached the major credit rating agencies with detailed information on the sub-standard loans, and had been ignored.

It is only now, when the world has moved on to face much more serious problems, that the whole sorry tale of sub-prime lending is beginning to become clear. Initially, much of the blame had been put on the large investment banks which had created the structured products to sell on to other investors; it was thought that, in their endless quest for profits, the banks had cooked up the scheme on their own. Now it is becoming plain that other players had also consciously played a role in bending the rules, including: the lenders who are now accused of unfair business practices, false advertising and even the falsification of mortgage documents; the rating companies who are now accused of knowingly rating the structured products too highly; Fannie Mae and Freddie Mac, once known for only backing sound loans, for having given their seal of approval to the sub-prime market

---

[1] 'Raters Ignored Proof of Unsafe Loans, Panel Is Told', *New York Times*, 27 September 2010, page B1 of the New York edition.

by investing in it substantially, and for having too close a relationship with politicians (many senior executives moved through a 'revolving door' between these firms and government posts in Washington); and finally, various politicians who helped squash attempts to prevent fraud and slow down the bubble (discussed below).

It was not, however, really a conspiracy of 'Wall Street against Main Street', as some have suggested; for example, some banks even purchased the dodgy sub-prime debt for their own portfolios, as gung-ho employees in one department bought the securities being produced by another department without performing the due diligence that would have uncovered the problems. It is typical of all booms, in whatever type of asset, that as they approach their peak participants of all kinds become greedier, more impatient, and ever more willing to break the rules. In the sub-prime crisis, many market players certainly failed in their duties, but it was also a failure of the state to prevent the excesses, to protect millions of vulnerable borrowers, and to limit the damage that the crisis was to have on the world's financial system.

The banking crisis

The sub-prime crisis was bad, but at first it seemed that it could be contained. HSBC, a long-established international bank, had purchased a sub-prime lender, Household International, in 2003 in order to enter the US market. In February 2007 HSBC made the first profit warning in its 150-year history, stating that housing loan defaults in the USA had been higher than expected. This announcement hit the firm's share price, and alerted investors to the sub-prime problem, but did not appear to presage any wider crisis. Over the next few months a number of sub-prime lenders in the USA got into financial difficulty, and some filed for bankruptcy. In June, several highly geared hedge funds that were exposed to the sub-prime market collapsed, and Merrill Lynch seized assets worth $800 million from two troubled hedge funds managed by the investment bank Bear Sterns.

It was not until August 2007, however, that it became clear that many major banks around the world were being hurt badly by the sub-prime market. On 9 August, the French giant BNP Parisbas announced that it was suspending redemption in three of its funds that had invested in the sub-prime market because 'the complete evaporation of liquidity in certain market segments of the US securitization market has made it impossible to value certain assets fairly, regardless of their quality or credit rating'; however, it believed that 'the valuation of these funds and the issue/redemption process will resume as soon as liquidity returns to the market'.[2] In hindsight, this was the beginning of the credit crunch in international banking, as a torrent of announcements of losses and write-downs followed. Commentators suggested, probably correctly, that the major banks were nervous about doing business with one another because they were unsure of the degree to which the others were exposed to the 'toxic assets' in the sub-prime market. Central banks, including the European Central Bank, the US Federal Reserve and the Bank of Japan began to intervene by pouring billions into the banking market to improve liquidity.

In mid-September 2007, one of the UK's top mortgage lenders, Northern Rock, had to obtain emergency support from the Bank of England in order to make its loan payments. To obtain the funds it needed to lend to house buyers, Northern Rock had relied heavily on short-term borrowing in the wholesale money markets, and it now found that other banks were no longer willing to lend it the money it needed. When the news became public, savers rushed to withdraw their money from Northern Rock, causing the first run on a British bank in over a century. The escalating crisis began to spread to other areas, such as the specialist 'monoline' insurers, who insured highly geared structured debt products against default, and now suddenly found that they were being downgraded by the credit rating agencies, ruining their capacity to write new business.

During the first half of 2008, as stock markets around the world fell from their peaks in the previous year, banks continued to announce major losses and the US government announced measures to prop-up the collapsing housing market. In March Bear Sterns, now almost completely out of cash and on the point of bankruptcy, was purchased for a song by JP Morgan with some of the money being supplied by the

---

[2] 'Press Release: BNP Paribas Investment Partners temporarily suspends the calculation of the Net Asset Value of the following funds: Parvest Dynamic ABS, BNP Paribas ABS EURIBOR and BNP Paribas ABS EONIA', BNP Paribas, Paris, 9 August 2007.

Federal Reserve; Ben Bernanke, the chairman of the Federal Reserve, explained that 'the sudden failure of Bear Stearns likely would have led to a chaotic unwinding of positions in those markets and could have severely shaken confidence'.

In September 2008 Fannie Mae and Freddie Mac were put into 'conservatorship' (a less stringent form of receivership) by the US government to ensure that they could meet their obligations on their debts of some $5 trillion dollars.[3] The following week brought more startling news, as Lehman Brothers collapsed in the biggest banking failure since the demise of Drexel Burnham Lambert during the junk bond scandal of 1990. Although it had been known after the sale of Bear Sterns that Lehman, which was similarly exposed to the property markets, was likely to be under extreme pressure, many thought that the bank was 'too big to fail' and that, as with Fannie Mae, Freddie Mac and Bear Sterns, the government would find a way to keep Lehman out of bankruptcy. Just before the collapse, officials from the Federal Reserve told agitated senior bankers that 'there is no political will for a federal bailout', and that it would create a 'terrible precedent', since other troubled banks would expect the government to save them too.[4]

Lehman, as an investment bank, had not been subject to the same regulatory limits on its gearing as commercial banks, and it is estimated that at the time of its collapse its borrowings to assets ratio was more than 30:1. That meant that a relatively small drop in the valuation of the property assets underlying its complex portfolios could wipe out their value altogether. Furthermore, Lehman had obtained much of its funding from very short-term 'Repo 105' transactions, where the bank sold securities in return for cash with a guarantee to buy them back at a fixed price a short time in the future. According the Chairman of the SEC, Lehman accounted for Repo 105s as sales, rather than financial transactions, which had the effect of reducing its leverage in its reports to the authorities and the public.[5] By funding itself in this manner

---

[3] Order Code RS22950 15 September 2008 'CRS report for Congress Fannie Mae and Freddie Mac in Conservatorship', Mark Jickling.

[4] *Wall Street Journal*, 15 September 2008, 'Ultimatum by Paulson sparked frantic end'.

[5] Testimony Concerning the Lehman Brothers Examiner's Report by Chairman Mary L. Schapiro U.S. Securities and Exchange Commission Before the House Financial Services Committee April 20, 2010.

Lehman was very vulnerable to a loss of confidence, and the immediate cause of its bankruptcy was that, as with Northern Rock, other banks became unwilling to lend it short-term money.

The US government's signal that it was prepared to allow a major bank to fail provoked a panic. Merrill Lynch quickly sold itself to Bank America. On 16 September a giant insurance company, AIG, which was heavily exposed to the credit default swaps market, was bailed out by the Federal Reserve, eliciting howls of outrage from bankers. Around the world, stock markets were in turmoil. By the end of the month, it was plain that European banks were in trouble too. In Iceland, the government nationalized the country's third largest bank, Glitnir. The Benelux countries (Belgium, Netherlands and Luxemburg) nationalized Fortis bank. The German government said it would rescue a property financier, Hypo Real Estate, but the plan eventually failed. In Ireland and Australia, the governments promised to guarantee their financial sector's debts. In the USA, the government passed the Emergency Economic Stabilization Act in early October, which enabled it to purchase distressed securities and lend money to troubled banks.

The crisis spreads to Europe

The crisis was now no longer the preserve of banking insiders and had become the major political issue in the Western world. There seems little doubt that government intervention was necessary, given that a collapse of the international banking system, which was a real danger in late 2008, would have had a drastic effect on the world's real economy, although even this notion has been challenged by the heterodox 'Austrian School' of economics (see below). For conventional economists, the big question was, and at the time of writing still is, how best to intervene. Paul Krugman, a Nobel Prize-winning economist at Princeton, has consistently argued in favour of an internationally co-ordinated plan, warning of the danger of another Great Depression, and demanding a profound reform of the banking system. In the USA, Barack Obama was elected President in November 2008 amid hopes that he would avert the country from recession by major government-sponsored programmes. Republicans have continually voiced objections in principle to government intervention in the market, which will naturally increase the country's deficit, at least in the medium term. Meanwhile, the flamboyant right-wing historian Niall Ferguson has been warning that the crisis is really a sign that America's 'imperial hegemony' is coming to an end. Some Republican critics of intervention have drawn on the ideas of the Austrian School of economics and one of its early leaders, Friedrich Hayek, that central banks give false signals to the economy by promising to be lenders of last resort, adjusting interest rates and quantitative easing (printing money), and that a free banking system (where there is no central bank) is actually preferable. Non-intervention enthusiasts point to the experience of Japan, which has been providing fiscal stimulation to its economy with little positive effect for more than 20 years, and to the strength, during the financial crisis, of the offshore banks in tax havens around the world which, because they have no central bank to rely on, have had to run their businesses much more conservatively than the onshore banks in the US and Europe that are now having to be bailed out.

Leaving the intervention debate aside, it is clear that government intervention costs money, and the money ultimately comes from the taxpayer and public spending cuts, which is why the question became a burning political issue during 2009 and 2010. At the time of writing (early 2011), it is not at all clear how successful the various interventions by wealthy governments have been; time will tell, but in the meantime people in the UK are nervously anticipating long years of low public spending, high unemployment, high taxes and a stalled property market.

A central problem, however, was that no one knew the precise size of the losses in the banking sector. In October 2008 the Bank of England estimated the total losses, worldwide, at $2.8 trillion, double its estimate of May of that year. In January 2009 the economist Nouriel Roubin opined that the US losses alone might be $3.6 trillion. In April 2009 the IMF estimated the total global losses at $4 trillion, but a year later it had reduced this figure to $2.8 trillion owing to a modest improvement to the global economy which reduced write-downs. Shifting the responsibility for the debts to governments by nationalizing the banks, however, soon caused new calamities to appear in Europe during 2010 that illustrate why we should be cautious about accepting economic data at face value.

In early 2010 a report by the European Commission's office of statistics, Eurostat, stated that Greece had misreported, sometimes deliberately, much of its economic data since 1997, which had had the effect of disguising its mounting deficit (one of the highest in the world). Eurostat said that 'the present institutional setting, which has showed [sic] its weakness, inefficiency and permeability to political interference throughout the years, does not guarantee the professional independence and full accountability' of Greece's office of statistics.[6] There was a danger that Greece would default on its debt payments, which would have forced it out of the eurozone and the risk of a flight of investors from the euro. For this reason EU finance ministers and the IMF agreed on a bailout but forced the country to take austerity measures, including large public sector cuts and changes to its generous pensions and early retirement schemes.

In May 2010 Olli Rehn, the European Commission's economy commissioner, said that 'Greece is indeed a unique and particular case in the EU. Greece has had particularly precarious debt dynamics and Greece is the only member state that cheated with its statistics for years and years'.[7] In fact, several countries had massaged their figures from time to time in order to conform to the eurozone's fiscal rules, and it became known that Wall Street banks had provided dozens of complex financial deals to various European governments, including that of Greece, with the deliberate aim of circumventing the eurozone's deficit regulations. Throughout 2010 a major worry was that other EU member states with high deficits might also run into the danger of defaulting, including, in order of the relative size of their deficits, Ireland (14.3 per cent of GDP), the UK (12.6 per cent of GDP), Italy (12 per cent of GDP), Spain (11.2 per cent of GDP) and Portugal (9.4 per cent of GDP). Hence the new UK Conservative government's tough talk on deficit reduction during 2010.

Iceland, which has applied for membership of the EU, was hit extremely hard by the financial crisis. Soon after the nationalization of Glitnir bank in late 2008, mentioned above, the two other largest

---

[6] European Commission – January 2010 Report on Greek Government Deficit and Debt Statistics, Brussels, 8 January 2010.

[7] http://euobserver.com/9/30015 'Rehn: No other state will need a bail-out'.

banks in the country, Kaupthing and Landsbanki, had to be national-ized as well. Iceland's external debts in late 2008 were estimated to be more than six times its GDP, a staggering imbalance, and the govern-ment resigned in January 2009. The problem had been that Iceland's three commercial banks had, after their deregulation in 2001, jumped recklessly into the exciting new world of international finance, bor-rowing massively in the short-term money markets to finance a rapid expansion. When this kind of borrowing became tighter, the banks then sought deposits from savers abroad, particularly in the UK and Netherlands, to fill the gap, offering unusually high interest rates and easy-to-use online deposit accounts through Icesave, a brand of the Landsbanki bank. When the Icelandic government said that it would not guarantee the deposits made by foreign account holders there was an ugly spat with the UK government, which froze Icelandic financial assets in the UK using anti-terrorist legislation. Some £840 million had been invested in Icelandic banks by local authorities in the UK, which complicated the political furore. To date, the 'Icesave' dispute has yet to be resolved, although UK depositors were able to receive compensa-tion via the Financial Services Authority in the UK. Iceland, perhaps understandably, given its dire economic situation, has attempted to wriggle out of its obligations, for example by arguing that any deposit guarantees it had made were not intended to cover 'wholesale' inves-tors such as local authorities in the UK. In March 2010 a referendum in Iceland overwhelmingly rejected a plan to repay £3.4 billion in compensation to the UK and the Netherlands, demonstrating how ill-prepared the country had been to participate responsibly in the global financial markets. The IMF has bailed out Iceland, but it delayed pay-ments, as did Finland and Sweden, to the country during 2010 because of Iceland's unwillingness to acknowledge its international financial obligations in the Icesave saga.

During 2010 much attention was paid to the so-called 'PIIGS' (Portugal, Ireland, Italy, Greece and Spain). This was an unsatisfactory category, since there were other EU member states, including the UK, Belgium and Latvia, that were severely affected by the crisis. However, it was argued by many commentators that while Greece had been brought under control by the IMF bailout early in the year, the other PIIGS were the EU states most likely to need bailing out too, and as they were all in the eurozone, the future of the euro continued to be in doubt. In November 2010 Ireland had to seek financial help from the IMF and the EU after banking losses and political unrest against austerity measures became too much for it to cope with on its own. At the time of writing (early 2011), it is not at all clear whether the other PIIGS have evaded the worst of the crisis. For the EU, the central problem is a potential collapse of the single currency, which would be a very major setback for the EU as a long-term political project. On 16 November 2010 the German Chancellor Angela Merkel told a political convention that 'if the euro fails, then Europe fails', which many have interpreted as an indication that Germany is determined to prevent such a failure. However, in spite of all its economic strength, Germany cannot save the euro on its own, and much depends on the kinds of measures that EU politicians, some of whom are notorious opponents of the free market, decide to take. In December 2010 a think-tank, the Centre for Economic and Business Research (CEBR), said that it believed that for the euro to survive in its present form, the PIIG countries would have to slash consumer spending by 15 per cent, Germany's growth would have to exceed 3 per cent a year for four years, the weaker EU states should cut public spending by 10 per cent and a bailout plan for Italy and Spain should be ready to go. The CEBR argued that these cuts were comparable to wartime and would not be possible to implement, and therefore gave the euro a one in five chance of surviving in its present form. It is not inconceivable, however, that the euro may be able to survive in some other form, with the worst affected economies removed from it.

This has been a summary of the main events of the financial crisis so far. As yet, the crisis has not severely damaged the economic powerhouses of the Far East, China and India, who, some say, will be the ultimate beneficiaries of what is still essentially a crisis of the West. The developing world has suffered a slowdown owing to its dependence on aid and trade from the West, but will recover when economic growth returns, say the pundits. A glance at the economic forecasts from national and international bodies will tell you that economic growth is the main measure they use to decide if things are getting better or worse; a 'recession' often being defined as two consecutive quarters of negative economic growth and a 'depression' as either a drop of more than 10 per cent in GDP or a recession that lasts for more than two years. It is clear that there was a recession in the USA and the UK during 2008 and 2009, but, according to the IMF, there has not been a worldwide recession since 2001/02.

In the next section we'll consider the question of economic growth, and the controversies that surround it. We will also look at whether there is some deeper phenomenon underlying the the financial crisis; for example, is it a symptom of the coming end of Western global supremacy, as doomsayers like Niall Ferguson suggest?

Economic growth and the financial crisis

In 2007 Nigel Lawson, a former chancellor of the exchequer, gave evidence to a parliamentary committee on climate change. In the course of talking about the difficulties of achieving global co-operation on limiting carbon emissions, he pointed out that estimates of long-term global economic growth made by the Intergovernmental Panel on Climate Change (IPCC), a body set up by the UN to assess climate change, implied that in a hundred years' time the world's population would be seven times better off than it is today, even taking into account the worst-case economic effects of climate change. Of course, the IPCC, and even Nigel Lawson, may have been wrong in their analysis (although they are certainly more serious and reliable sources than many other analysts); even so, the concept is remarkable. It suggests that the world may continue to enjoy a rapid increase in material progress, as it has been doing for the last 200 years or so, long into the future.

Let's consider for a moment just how much our lives have improved in the last few generations. Worldwide, infant mortality dropped by two-thirds between 1950 and 2002. In the last 60 years, literacy has almost doubled, and today nearly three-quarters of the world's population can read and write. During the same time period, life expectancy in the developing world (that's the poor part) has increased by 25 years. All this has occurred while taking into account the very serious problems of hunger, overpopulation, disease and lack of clean water that still beset parts of the developing world, notably Africa. Remember that India, China, and much of the rest of the Far East were in as bad a condition as Africa 70 years ago in many respects. In fact, as little as 50 years ago, most of Asia, Africa and Latin America suffered from one of the key indicators of poverty: very high infant mortality (ranging from 10 per cent to 38 per cent) combined with large numbers of children per mother (4–8 children). Today, outside sub-Saharan Africa, the overwhelming majority of the world enjoys a much lower infant mortality (under 10 per cent) combined with a far more manageable number of children per mother (4 children or fewer), and it is thought that this has a strong correlation to the economic growth that these countries have experienced. With the possible exception of two or three sub-Saharan countries, depending on whose figures you believe, there are now no countries in the world with a life expectancy lower than the countries that had the highest life expectancy (around the age of 40) in 1800 – this, surely, is incontrovertible evidence of a desirable improvement in the human condition since 1800!

If we turn to the developed part of the world, different kinds of improvements are more noticeable, such as improvements in living standards, diets and the variety of goods available to us. For instance, today I can buy a wide range of exotic fruits fresh in my local supermarket, such as lychees and pomegranates, that were unheard-of luxuries when I was a child. I can buy a plane ticket for a fraction of the cost of restaurant meal and fly for the weekend to remote parts of Europe that used to take a couple of days just to reach. It is now considered perfectly normal to take holidays in Thailand, Mexico and Egypt, when a few decades ago it was considered pretty exciting to go for a fortnight to the south of Spain. And then there is all the new technology, like computers, mobile phones and the internet – even if you are a technophobe, you would have to admit that they are pretty useful things. Of course, basic measures, such as life expectancy, are up in the West too, but not as dramatically as in the developing world. In the UK, for instance, average life expectancy 'only' improved from 74.3 in 1980 to 79.8 in 2010. That's still quite a bonus, a free gift of 5 extra years of life just for living during a time of economic progress. On average, we live longer, and are better fed, taller, and richer than most of our ancestors. And if Nigel Lawson and the IPCC are right, our descendants in a hundred years' time are going to be able to look back at our era and shudder in horror at what will seem to them to be the appalling material and physical hardships of the early twenty-first century.

If Martians landed on Earth for the first time and were presented with this evidence, they might legitimately ask why we are so worried about the world. After all, over the last 200 years, life, on average, has just got better and better for more and more people. So what's the problem? Most of us would probably start telling the Martians about all the things that are wrong with the world. We would be right to do so. Measuring economic growth, average life expectancy and the like does not capture the full story of the last 200 years. For instance, no one (I hope!) needs to be reminded that there has been an enormous amount of suffering for a vast number of people during this period, or that there is still a great deal of suffering in the world today, much of which looks as if it could be avoided if governments would only take the necessary steps.

There are other things, too, that trouble us. Two centuries of development has destroyed large parts of the world's natural environment, and wiped out many species of animals and plants. It has led to the disappearance of many languages and cultures, and made much of the landscape considerably uglier to look at. It has produced technology that has the potential to destroy all human life once and for all. It has failed to eliminate exploitation and injustice. It has failed to make the better-off happy, in spite of all their material gains. It has allowed new social ills to appear on a large scale, such as obesity. Obesity, remember, was a sign of prosperity for most of human history, but now in the West it is more common among the poor – rich people can afford to spend money on dieting and exercise to keep their weight down. And we no longer feel as optimistic about the future as we did, say, in the 1950s. Instead of believing that things are just getting better and better, we contemplate nightmarish visions of the future – just think of all the movies and books about post-apocalyptic worlds. And we are deeply, and probably rightly, sceptical about the benefits of all the consumer products and services that are incessantly advertised at us.

This is not to make a moral judgement about these phenomena – I may hate going to shopping malls, for instance, but there are millions of people, especially in the developing world, who think they are terrific and who like nothing better than spending a whole day wandering around a mall talking non-stop on their mobile phones and eating processed foods stuffed with excessive quantities of sugar, salt and fat. Nevertheless, it is a fact that dissatisfaction with aspects of the last two centuries of development has become a mainstream issue. Fighting climate change, for example, is now a major political concern. There is now a constant public debate about all the things that may possibly go wrong with the world, from future epidemics and the growth in hidden long-term unemployment to GM foods and the rapidly ageing populations in Europe and Japan. We fear that we may somehow hit a limit to economic growth, and that the whole edifice of modernity will suddenly unravel.

Economists, who naturally try to measure and predict this wide variety of phenomena, have developed many new theories to try to understand these problems. 'Sustainability', for instance, has become a buzzword both in business and in the humanitarian aid sector. People now think, not unreasonably, that any kind of economic project should take all the possible consequences into consideration, and strive to ensure that it can be sustained indefinitely, rather than just use up resources and create a wasteland. For example, it may be quick, cheap, and profitable to harvest tropical hardwoods to use as packaging (this really does happen), but it would be better for the world as a whole to manage what is left of the world's jungles responsibly. Similarly, building lots of new multi-lane highways through your third-world city and forgetting to build anything to allow pedestrians to cross the road (again, this really does happen) is not exactly a triumph of town planning.

Traditional growth measures, such as GDP, only tell us about economic activity. They do not tell us about standards of living, sustainability, the underground economy, improvements in quality, or the effect on the environment, wealth distribution, or happiness. We need to find better ways of measuring these things too, if we want to understand what is really happening to the world.

Investment survival in the long term

So how does all this relate to the financial crisis that began in 2007? Clearly, we can use GDP growth rates to determine when and where recessions have occurred, and to try to develop policies that help manage our economies. If growth rates in the UK improve, for example, public spending, access to credit, and the availability of jobs are likely to improve too. But such an improvement will not remove other worries about the nature of economic progress that have been discussed above. A major question remains: was the recent financial crisis just the latest example of greed and folly getting out of control during a boom, or is it a sign of some deeper underlying trend?

Many respectable academics are now suggesting that it is. They point to the fact that there have been 'hegemonic shifts' (which is when one state or region replaces another as the dominant world power) in the past. For example, Britain was the dominant world power for much of the nineteenth century, but lost its position to the USA during the twentieth century. Some argue that the rise of European economic and political power during the last 500 years should be seen as a hegemonic shift (previously, most of the wealth and power had been in the East), and that we are now witnessing a shift of power back to the East. There is much speculation about what the world would look like if China and India became the dominant political and economic powers. For instance, would the West lose its democratic system, its human rights, or its ability to grow economically? Would global capitalism stop being biased in favour of the USA and the West? Would the major financial institutions be based in Beijing and Delhi rather than New York and London? Would life expectancy start to fall in the West as it became impoverished? The truthful answer is that nobody knows for sure.

One of the most difficult things to grasp about investment is that the future is genuinely uncertain. All of us – hopefully – understand that life is uncertain, but we have the natural human tendency to look for security and reassurance. In the UK, one of the more stable countries in the world, this tendency has been raised almost to an art form because we live in such a highly ordered society: we may expect and demand that the health system cures all diseases, even though we know deep-down that this is impossible; we may worry about our pensions, even though we may not live long enough to claim them; we may expect government agencies of one kind or another to sort out any problems that come up, even though we know they can't solve everything. In spite of all the sophisticated systems that we have, the truth is that no one, no organization, and no system really knows what the future holds, and this is no different in investing.

Imagine you were living at the time of Jesus Christ and you were able to invest in a fund that was likely to produce an average annual real return of 4 per cent. Let's further suppose that you found the elixir of life and that you were still alive today. How rich would you be? The answer is that you would be so rich that your wealth would exceed the number of atoms estimated to exist in the universe – an impossible sum. So what is wrong with this picture? The answer is, and it is a shocking thought, that investment returns, even modest ones, are unlikely to grow steadily for any great length of time, and the same is true for the economies of countries. Everything we assume to be true about investment is based upon the study of much shorter timeframes – really no farther back than the nineteenth century, when advanced countries began to industrialize. As we saw in Chapter 1, investment as we understand it today is based upon the notion that societies are, or should be, organized economically on a capitalist basis, with capital markets providing a means for the people who have some money (investors) to put it into organizations (companies) that can use this money productively. Although we can find such mechanisms in earlier times, before the industrialization of the globe, they weren't terribly efficient or widely available.

The 'doomsayers', then, are not completely wrong. The chances are that the present system will not last for ever, and that at some point there will be a period in which much of the world's wealth is destroyed. On a shorter timescale, we know that this has occurred in various places in the world several times since 1900. Here are just a few examples: before the 1917 Russian Revolution, Russia was the favourite investment destination of the French, but in 1917 these investments were completely wiped out; Shanghai and Manchuria once enjoyed 90 per cent of all foreign investment into China, but all these were seized by the communists in 1949 (note that Shanghai has been coming back during the last few years); in 1945 Egypt had the third largest stock market in the world but in 1956 Nasser nationalized everything, and all shares became worthless. Going back further in time, it is perhaps surprising to think that 250 years ago, two of the most economically important cities in North America were Charleston and Savannah, or that 2,000 years ago the third largest city in the Roman Empire was Antioch, now a sleepy provincial town in Turkey.

Nothing, it seems, is really a permanent store of value, and periodically there have been upheavals that have destroyed huge amounts of capital. To this extent, the doomsayers are right, although they are not very good at predicting when or how this might come about. They, like the rest of us, have to live with uncertainty.

It is important to recognize that good times do not last for ever, and to have some kind of back-up plan for what you would do if the markets went into a death spin – that is one of the reasons why asset allocation is important, since it reminds you to spread your wealth across different types of asset, some of which may survive better than others during bad times. But we should try to see things in proportion, and there are strong arguments for remaining moderately optimistic as an investor – if, for instance, you are so gloomy that you keep all your money in gold, your investment returns are not likely to be good over the long term. A moderately optimistic investor keeps a substantial proportion of his or her money invested in the stock markets at all times (jumping in and out of the stock market is probably not going to produce superior returns) because it is the best chance – although not an absolute certainty – of earning a good return. Even if it is the case that in a century's time the West will no longer be the richest and most powerful part of the world, it doesn't necessarily mean that Western investors won't be able to profit from a rise of the East.

Summary

Successful investment, as we have seen, is largely about improving our chances of obtaining a reasonably good return at an acceptable level of risk. Risk is the currency of investment decision-making; we can reduce the risks that we don't want, but we can never completely eliminate them. The more we educate ourselves about the intricacies of investment, the more we are able to identify opportunities that may improve our returns at an acceptable level of risk, and the longer we stay in the game, the more we improve our chances of doing this. What we cannot do, however, is follow a mechanical system of investment that is certain to produce marvellous results whatever the circumstances – we need to remain flexible in the face of the unexpected. So the strategies that seem sound today, such as index investing, may not be appropriate in 25 years' time. Guerrilla investors need to be alert to how the world is changing, and to be willing to adjust their investment strategies accordingly.

In the next chapter we will look at how you can develop a financial plan as a guide to your investing strategy, and how you can integrate this with the rest of your life.

14

Making investing part of your life

We have covered a lot of ground in this book, and as budding guerrilla investors there is much to consider before taking the plunge into investment. In this chapter we go back to basics and take another look at how and why you need to develop a set of good financial habits before starting to invest, and introduce the idea of 'life stages', which can help you to identify the real priorities in your long-term financial plans.

We look at:

■ Making and reviewing your financial plan

■ Taking into account the stages of life

Making and reviewing your financial plan

Most people hate doing it, but making a financial plan, sticking to it and updating it periodically is a very, very effective way of keeping your finances under control and ensuring that your investment programme continues. If for, instance, you have been investing for a few years but have not kept the rest of your finances in good order, you might suddenly have to sell all your shares to generate emergency cash, spoiling all the good investment work you have done.

There are many books available that can guide you through money management in detail, but to get you started, here's a brief step-by-step guide to financial planning:

1 Make a list of realistic goals for the next 10 years. Depending on your age, these might include things such as clearing your credit card debts, buying a house, or starting a pension plan. Ask yourself questions such as:

■ How much money would I need to live on if I stopped working next week?

■ Do I want to own my own home?

■ Would I like to own a bigger home?

■ Do I want to renovate my home?

■ Do I want to retire in another country? Would I like to buy a home abroad?

■ When will I need a new car? Could I buy it for cash or should I borrow?

■ Do I want to have plastic surgery?

■ Would I like to take holidays more frequently?

■ Would I like to pay off all my debts? Which ones would I most like to pay off?

■ How much money would I like to leave my family after my death?

■ Do I want to get married and start a family?

■ At what age do I want to retire? How much income would I need to live comfortably?

■ Would I like to take time off from work to pursue further studies?

■ How much money would my family need to live on if I died suddenly?

■ If I become ill or disabled, how much would I need to live on?

■ What would happen if I lost my job and it took me a year to find another one?

2 Try to estimate how much each of these goals would cost in today's money – take the trouble to find out accurate prices.

3 Next, put these goals in the order you would like to achieve them – this will be different for every individual. For example, plastic surgery might be very high on one person's list and very low on someone else's. In general, though, it is a good idea to try to prioritize goals which will serve as building blocks to reach other important goals – for example, getting rid of expensive credit card debt, if you have it, should come before saving for a deposit on a house.

4 Now you have a list of goals, you need to start thinking how and when you can achieve them. Some of them may require taking out insurance or starting a pension plan; others may simply require you to save cash. Group the goals into timeframes – short, medium and long term – so you can focus on achieving high-priority short-term goals, and think about what you have to do now to work towards achieving goals that will take longer to reach.

5 Make a list of your income and expenditure – it is not pleasant to do, but it is necessary. Are you spending everything you earn and more? If so, you need to set a goal of reducing your expenditure (and, hopefully, increasing your income) to the point where you generate extra money you can save. Keep a dated copy in a file and every 6 or 12 months make a new list and compare it with the old one. Are things improving? If not, what can you do to change this?

6 Use your income and expenditure sheet to help you work out whether any of your goals are affordable, and the effects of any big changes in your life that you may make. For instance, if you are thinking of moving to another town to start a new job, how might this affect your outgoings? If you move to London from the provinces, for instance, you will find that the cost of living is much, much higher.

7 Aim to get to the point where you have a surplus of income over expenditure. However, it is probably sensible to start the saving habit even if you have not yet reached this target, because psychologically it is easier to treat regular saving like a living expense – in other words, to pay so much a month into a deposit account or an investment fund that allows regular saving in small amounts, so that it seems like just another monthly bill. Try it – this works well for a lot of people.

8 Review your net worth, once every six months to a year. Your net worth is your total assets minus your total liabilities (debts). For many people in the UK, net worth is essentially the equity they have in their homes plus a few thousand in savings. Property prices go up and down, so it is important to make a realistic assessment of what your house is currently worth. Most people in the UK don't have as much liquid assets (cash, bonds and shares) as they need, so one of your goals should probably be to increase your liquidity. This will help you cope with financial emergencies.

Doing all this gives you the basic tools for financial control, so you can begin to develop your knowledge and skills as an investor. Armed with this knowledge, you can start talking to financial advisers. Your adviser can help you to calculate how much you need to save at a given rate of return to achieve your medium- and long-term goals. Longer-term investments have time to recover from losses and so have a better chance of meeting expectations. This is especially true of investments lasting more than 20 years, so making long-term invest-ments to meet a long-term goal, such as a target retirement income, has a good chance of success.

Taking into account the stages of life

A useful approach to investment planning is to consider how your needs are likely to change during your life. This helps you to make better decisions, and not to beat yourself up for not becoming a mul-timillionaire at the age of 25, for instance. Real investment is about maturity – wild speculation is really for the juvenile at heart, whatever their real age.

Everybody is unique, but most of us go through stages in our adult lives that are to some extent predictable, and this can help us to plan our finances more realistically. There are four basic stages:

1 The young adult

2 Having a young family

3 Middle age

4 Retirement.

Stage 1 – the young adult

Once you have finished your full-time education your main focus is likely to be on getting established in a career. This may involve trying out many different types of job. With so many things to do and places to go, there is usually a strong pressure to spend everything you earn and more. This is not necessarily a bad thing, but at this stage many people do not have good money management skills, and they can easily get into debt, especially expensive credit card debt, which can take years to pay off. Once you have settled into a job, you may start thinking about buying a house, and you will probably need to start saving towards the deposit. If you have the discipline, now is a great time to start contributing to a long-term pension or investment scheme, because although your contributions may be small, they will have many, many years to grow.

Your financial objectives could include:

- paying off debts
- a regular saving scheme towards a deposit on a house
- small, regular payments to a long-term investment scheme, such as a pension or an investment fund.

Stage 2 – having a young family

By the time you have reached your 30s, you may have started a family. Although you will probably be earning more than before, your outgoings for your family, and/or your home, will be higher too, and it will still be difficult to save. If you have dependants, you will certainly need life insurance, and it is a good idea to make a will. If you have bought a home, well done! Owning a home is a kind of long-term saving, because its value will grow as prices gradually rise and you pay off your loan. You will probably need some cash savings to cope with unexpected emergencies, and although retirement is still a long way off, you really do need to start planning for it now.

Your financial objectives could include:

- life insurance
- regular payments to a cash fund for emergencies

■ make and update your will

■ regular payments to a long-term investment scheme, such as a pension or an investment fund.

Stage 3 – middle age

In your 40s, 50s and 60s, you are generally reaching the top of your career and the peak of your earning power. Your money management skills should have improved, and you may have substantial equity in your house. You may have the capital, intellectual interest and skills to take a much more active approach to stock market investment. However, retirement is not so far away, so for most people the really important priority is to convert as much of your income into long-term investment capital as possible.

Your financial objectives could include:

■ maximizing your rate of saving – the more you put into your long-term saving and investment schemes, the better

■ active investment in the stock market – you could weight your asset allocation as heavily as possible towards investments in shares, because they are likely to outperform other asset classes in the long term

■ if you do not enjoy the volatility of stock market investing, you could focus on achieving a target income in retirement, and weight your portfolio towards less volatile investments, such as bonds

■ saving up to buy a retirement home, perhaps in another country.

Stage 4 – retirement

For most people in the UK, retirement means a lower income and lower expenditure. If your pension income is sufficient, you can focus on achieving more capital growth in your investment portfolio, which is a desirable situation to be in but it generally depends upon how successful you have been earlier in your life in accumulating capital. Most people need to use at least some of the returns from their investments to live on in retirement. This means that your portfolio will grow more slowly, or even begin to shrink gradually.

Your financial objectives could include:

- reallocating your investment portfolio towards less volatile assets, such as bonds

- focusing on flexibility – the more you keep your options open, the more able you will be to respond to adverse changes such as tax increases and inflation shocks.

Life stages summary

It is good to think about life stages because it reminds you of two really important issues. First, although it is harder to save when you are young, if you can start a disciplined habit of saving you will achieve substantial growth in the long term. Second, retirement is a very big change in life, and you need to plan for it years in advance; become an expert on all the issues that could affect you, and don't rely on the state to look after you, or, indeed, to keep many of its promises. This doesn't have to be all doom and gloom – retirement can, and should – be fun, but you do need to face facts and act responsibly.

The goals of saving from your income and building up your assets should be the backbone of your lifelong investment programme, but you will also need to buy expensive things from time to time – if you plan for them and save for them in earmarked funds that you keep separate from the rest of your money, you are much more likely to get most or all of them.

Summary

This book has been about investing in the stock market, but we cannot look at shares in isolation; successful investing is all about developing good financial habits that are well-known and well-established, and sticking to them over the long term. Investors are up against many pressures, social and economic, that push them towards consuming as much as possible to the detriment of their long-term investment goals. Guerrilla investors need to learn to resist these pressures, and this involves doing things other people don't do, and not doing things that other people do, like running up massive credit card bills.

Guerrilla investors can spend and enjoy life, but they need to stay out of debt and keep saving regularly; this doesn't mean you have to be a miser, but it probably does mean that you will come into conflict with friends and partners over spending, because we live in a world where people are encouraged to spend much more than they can afford. We are all different, and we learn to cope with this problem in different ways, but one thing is certain: careless spendthrifts are unlikely to become successful investors!

In Appendix 1 we look at some basic concepts in finance, such as the effect of compounding, that will help you understand why unexciting habits like regular saving will probably do much more for your wealth in the long term than the exciting bits in investment, like seeing shares that you own suddenly double, are ever likely to. By all means enjoy the fun parts of investing, but remember to keep up your good habits, and you are much more likely to achieve your goals.

Appendix 1

A little financial maths

People don't like doing sums, but if you are going to be a successful investor you will have to learn how. This section introduces a few important notions which you need to be familiar with.

Payback

Payback is a remarkably simple rule-of-thumb method of assessing investment propositions. It is used in the boardrooms of large companies to help decide whether or not to go ahead with, say, the introduction of a new product or the building of a new factory.

Suppose the cost of purchasing a widget-making machine is £5 million. How long will it take for the profits on the widgets it makes to reach £5 million? That's the 'payback'time – the time it takes to recoup the initial investment. Companies like to see a short payback period, preferably under five years.

Simple and compound interest

Interest is the amount that you pay when you borrow money from someone else for a given length of time. It is also the amount that someone will pay you for borrowing your money. If you put money into a bank or a building society, you are lending it money, so make sure that you receive some interest!

Since the amount of interest paid is related to the length of time that the money is borrowed, interest is calculated as a percentage of the sum borrowed per a fixed time period, usually a year. Thus, if you lent a building society £1,000 and it is paying 10 per cent interest per annum, you could get your money back at the end of the year with the interest as well: 10 per cent of £1,000 is 100, so you would have £1,100.

If only life were so simple! Unfortunately, governments have found out about interest, and like to take some of it in tax, so your building society might have to offer, say, a gross rate of interest of 10 per cent, which only non-taxpayers can get, and a net rate of 7.5 per cent for most taxpayers. The remainder is taken by the government directly from the building society.

Another complication is that your £1,000 might not buy as much at the end of the year as it would have done at the beginning – this is because of inflation. The 10 per cent interest that you earned should compensate you for the reduced buying power of your £1,000, but the inflation has taken another bite out of your profit. Out of the gross interest of 10 per cent, you might have made only 2 per cent profit after tax and inflation on your original £1,000. The £1,000, by the way, is the 'capital' that you have lent.

The interest rate offered to you will vary, taking tax and inflation into account. A point to notice is: Interest rates are usually quoted as the interest you will get or give for a year's lending or borrowing, but not always, so you should check. The kind of interest we are talking about at the moment is called 'simple interest'.

Example

If you lent £1,000 for five years at 10 per cent simple interest per annum (p.a.), you would earn £100 per year:

£1,000 at 10 per cent a year simple interest

Year 1	£100
Year 2	£100
Year 3	£100
Year 4	£100
Year 5	£100
Total	£500

At the end of the fifth year you would have your original £1,000 back, plus the £500 interest, totalling £1,500. The value of what you lent at the beginning (£1,000) is the 'present value', and what you will get at the end of five years (£1,500) is the 'future value'.

Compound interest

If you were getting £100 in simple interest every year, you could also lend that, and get interest on it.

Example

If you lent a bank £1,000 for five years and received 10 per cent interest a year, you could re-invest the 10 per cent (£100) each year and earn interest on that too. If you did this by leaving the interest in a deposit account, the £100 that you received in the first year would earn £10 in the second year, so by the end of the second year you would have:

The capital	£1,000
10% interest on capital in Year 1	£100
10% interest on capital in Year 2	£100
Interest in Year 2 on Year 1's interest	£10
Total	£1,210

Interest plus the interest on the interest is called 'compound interest'. How much compound interest you get depends on how often the bank gives you the interest. If you deposit £2 million in a bank at 10 per cent per annum and it only gives you the interest at the end of the year, you would have £200,000 in interest at the end of the year, but what if it calculated the interest every six months? The annual interest rate would be the same, but the interest you earned in the first six months (half of £200,000 = £100,000), would earn interest in the second half. You would earn an extra £5,000, which is half of 10 per cent of £100,000. The intervals between the times when the bank calculates the interest is called the 'conversion period'. The shorter the conversion period, the more the interest will be compounded, and the more money you will make for a given annual rate.

Why compounding is so important

Compounding is one of the great joys of investment, and is likely to be the largest part of the investment gains that you make over the long term. The longer you invest at a positive rate of return, the more significant the effect of compounding becomes.

The secret of successful investing is patience. The longer you hold an investment, the more it is likely to grow, simply through the effect of compound interest.

In the stock market, which is a risky type of investment in the short term, shares have consistently outperformed cash and bonds over the long term. If you hold shares for the long term, either directly or through managed funds like unit trusts or investment trusts, the risks of volatility (violent changes in price) are ironed out.

Example

Here's what would happen if you invested a lump sum of £25,000 in the stock market and achieved an annual rate of return of 8 per cent and 10 per cent:

Years invested	8%	10%
1	£27,000	£27,500
5	£36,700	£40,300
10	£54,000	£64,800
15	£79,300	£104,000
20	£116,500	£168,200
25	£171,200	£270,900

The longer you hold your investment, the more it grows – and in the later years, the growth becomes remarkably large. Notice that the apparently small difference in the rate of return – only 2 per cent – makes a huge difference in the long run. In the table, an 8 per cent return produces £171,200 after 25 years while a 10 per cent return produces £270,900.

Liquidity

You can distinguish assets from one another by their liquidity, which simply means how fast the asset can be turned into cash.

While shares and bonds are highly liquid – although you may not be able to sell for the price you paid – property and businesses are not. In the case of a property, you might expect to sell it within a few months, while a business could take years to sell.

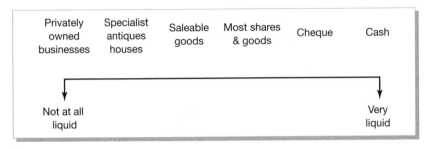

Liquidity scale

You need some liquidity to give you the freedom to adapt to sudden changes in your circumstances. For example, if you have a house worth a million pounds and no money in the bank, you'll be in a panic if you suddenly have to pay for a new roof.

You often, but not always, get better returns on illiquid assets than highly liquid ones. Keeping all your money in an instant access account will give you great liquidity, for instance, but not much hope of a good return. In the long run, in fact, you might even get a negative return!

Shares in heavily traded companies are highly liquid, since you can sell them with one phone call or internet message, but they may also produce good returns if you hold them for many years.

A useful rule of thumb that is well accepted in the USA, but less talked-about in the UK, is that it is a good idea to keep a percentage of your assets in cash on short-term deposit at all times; 5–10 per cent of your net worth is usually considered appropriate. For eager share traders, this is particularly useful since it prevents you from selling your shares too soon in order to pay for some emergency living expense.

More on inflation

Inflation can be defined as a general increase in prices. It's a chain reaction where price rises are passed on from one supplier to the next until they reach the consumer, who has to pay up. In times of high inflation, people on fixed incomes tend to suffer because their cash can buy less than it could previously.

Inflation figures are published regularly in the national press, and it is worth keeping an eye on them. Increasing inflation can eat into your investment returns – you may be delighted at a return of 15 per cent one year, but what if inflation was at 16 per cent? You would actually be making a loss.

To monitor the effects of inflation, adjust your investment returns downward by the annual rate of inflation that year, from the published figures. This will give you the 'real', or 'inflation-adjusted', return, which is more accurate.

Example

> On 1 January Joe invests £100,000 in a one-year fixed term deposit that pays 10 per cent. At the end of the year he receives £110,000 back. If inflation during that time was 2 per cent, his £110,000 would only have the 1 January buying power of £107,800, so his inflation-adjusted return is 7.8 per cent, not 10 per cent.

Coping with inflation

Inflation is genuinely unpredictable over the medium to long term, but there are many investment products designed to protect against inflation shocks.

The people who are hurt most by rising inflation are those who have little room for manoeuvre, either because their money is tied up or because they have retired and are no longer earning an income. In the famous Weimar inflation in Germany in the 1920s, respectable old ladies literally starved because their bonds were inflated into worthlessness.

You can protect against inflation to some extent by diversifying your assets – some assets tend to increase in value during inflationary periods. Diversification is discussed in more detail in Chapter 5.

How long will it take to double your money?

To work out approximately how long it will take your money to double from an investment producing a given rate of return, simply divide the annual rate of return into 72.

Example

> You are contemplating an investment that will yield 10 per cent a year.
>
> $72 \div 10 = 7.2$
>
> Your money will double approximately every 7.2 years.

...And to treble your money?

Divide the annual return into 115 to find out roughly how long it will take for your money to treble.

Example

> You are contemplating an investment that will yield 10 per cent a year.
>
> $115 \div 10 = 11.5$
>
> Your money will treble approximately every 11.5 years.

Compounding again!

The doubling and trebling rule is another way of looking at the compounding effect.

Example

> If you invest £100,000 to produce an inflation-adjusted average return of 10 per cent a year:
>
> After approximately 7.2 years it will be worth £200,000
>
> After approximately 14.4 years it will be worth £400,000
>
> After approximately 21.6 years it will be worth £800,000
>
> After approximately 28.8 years it will be worth £1,600,000

Most people don't start investing with a lump sum, so they add to their investments out of saved income over many years, but the same effect applies.

Introducing risk

Investment is not a one-size-fits-all process. We are all different, with different needs and aspirations. Part of the art of successful investing is in tailoring your plans to suit yourself. To do this, you should consider your own attitudes towards risk.

Nothing is 100 per cent certain and there is no such thing as zero risk. This is another way of saying that nobody, not even the Treasury, can predict the future with much certainty. In the investment business, you will come across many pompous individuals who pretend to be able to forecast the future. If you pressed them, they would admit they they don't know for certain, but it is easy to get the impression from watching television or reading the papers that these prophets are certainly correct. They are not! It is not possible to predict the future with absolute confidence.

In practice, we have to rely on probability. It is very *unlikely* that extra-terrestrials will conquer Birmingham this year, but it is very *likely* that the sun will come up tomorrow morning.

In investment, we assess risk constantly. Some risks are much easier to judge than others, and it is often possible to calculate likely outcomes given certain assumptions. For instance, gilts, which are bonds guaranteed by the British government, are considered to be completely safe. Over the centuries, the British government has always honoured its gilt obligations, so we make the assumption that gilts carry zero risk. Given that assumption, it is possible to predict accurately the return on gilts held for the life of the loan by simply doing sums.

An ordinary building society account is also considered to have virtually no risk because it is protected by a compensation scheme. Various kinds of investment schemes are structured to give you more risk in return for the chance of getting a better return. Shares are more risky, but they may give you an even better return.

As a general rule, the more risk you are willing to accept, the higher your returns may be. That's why cash deposits in banks and building societies don't pay you a high rate of interest – there is little or no risk of losing your money.

Appendix 2

Compound interest table

The effect of compound interest is the principal reason why long-term investments perform better than short-term investments. It's a simple mathematical process that produces remarkable results. The secret of successful investing is patience. The longer you hold an investment, the more it is likely to grow, simply through the effect of compound interest.

Looking at Table A2.1, you can see that in the first few years the increase in the value of an investment is not very much, even at a high rate of return. After many years, however, the effect of compounding becomes much stronger, and you see a really substantial difference between a rate of return of, for instance, 2 per cent and 4 per cent after 25 years. Although investments like bonds generally pay a consistent rate of interest, other investments, such as shares, are much more volatile, and the returns (the combination of an increase in the price and the dividends the company pays, which are the equivalent of interest) will vary from year to year. With volatile investments, you have to work out the average annual return, adjusting for inflation, over a period of years. Nevertheless, the principle remains the same across all types of investment: the longer you keep an investment, the faster it will grow in later years, all thanks to the principle of compounding.

Table A2.1 Value of £1 invested over 1–25 years

	1.00%	2.00%	3.00%	4.00%	5.00%	6.00%	7.00%	8.00%	9.00%	10.00%
1	1.01	1.02	1.03	1.04	1.05	1.06	1.07	1.08	1.09	1.10
2	1.02	1.04	1.06	1.08	1.10	1.12	1.14	1.17	1.19	1.21
3	1.03	1.06	1.09	1.12	1.16	1.19	1.23	1.26	1.30	1.33
4	1.04	1.08	1.13	1.17	1.22	1.26	1.31	1.36	1.41	1.46
5	1.05	1.10	1.16	1.22	1.28	1.34	1.40	1.47	1.54	1.61
6	1.06	1.13	1.19	1.27	1.34	1.42	1.50	1.59	1.68	1.77
7	1.07	1.15	1.23	1.32	1.41	1.50	1.61	1.71	1.83	1.95
8	1.08	1.17	1.27	1.37	1.48	1.59	1.72	1.85	1.99	2.14
9	1.09	1.20	1.30	1.42	1.55	1.69	1.84	2.00	2.17	2.36
10	1.10	1.22	1.34	1.48	1.63	1.79	1.97	2.16	2.37	2.59
11	1.12	1.24	1.38	1.54	1.71	1.90	2.10	2.33	2.58	2.85
12	1.13	1.27	1.43	1.60	1.80	2.01	2.25	2.52	2.81	3.14
13	1.14	1.29	1.47	1.67	1.89	2.13	2.41	2.72	3.07	3.45
14	1.15	1.32	1.51	1.73	1.98	2.26	2.58	2.94	3.34	3.80
15	1.16	1.35	1.56	1.80	2.08	2.40	2.76	3.17	3.64	4.18
16	1.17	1.37	1.60	1.87	2.18	2.54	2.95	3.43	3.97	4.59
17	1.18	1.40	1.65	1.95	2.29	2.69	3.16	3.70	4.33	5.05
18	1.20	1.43	1.70	2.03	2.41	2.85	3.38	4.00	4.72	5.56
19	1.21	1.46	1.75	2.11	2.53	3.03	3.62	4.32	5.14	6.12
20	1.22	1.49	1.81	2.19	2.65	3.21	3.87	4.66	5.60	6.73
21	1.23	1.52	1.86	2.28	2.79	3.40	4.14	5.03	6.11	7.40
22	1.24	1.55	1.92	2.37	2.93	3.60	4.43	5.44	6.66	8.14
23	1.26	1.58	1.97	2.46	3.07	3.82	4.74	5.87	7.26	8.95
24	1.27	1.61	2.03	2.56	3.23	4.05	5.07	6.34	7.91	9.85
25	1.28	1.64	2.09	2.67	3.39	4.29	5.43	6.85	8.62	10.83

Further reading

Jules Abel, *The Rockefeller Millions: The Story of the World's Most Stupendous Fortune*, 1967

Peter Bernstein, *Against the Gods*, Wiley, 1996

Rowan Bosworth-Davis, *Too Good to Be True*, Bodley Head, 1987

J Carswell, *The South Sea Bubble*, Cresset Press, 1960

Simon Cawkwell, *The Profit of the Plunge*, Rushmere Wynne, 1995

Elroy Dimson, Paul Marsh and Mike Staunton, *Triumph of the Optimists: 101 Years of Global Investment Returns*, Princeton University Press, 2002

Richard Eels and Peter Nehemkis, *Corporate Cultures*, Macmillan, 1984

Eugene E Fama, 'Random Walks in Stock Market Prices', *Financial Analysts Journal*, September/October 1965

Kenneth Fisher, *100 Minds that Made the Market*, Business Classics, 1995

Phillip Fisher, *Common Stocks and Uncommon Profits*, John Wiley, 1996

JK Galbraith, *The Great Crash*, Penguin, 1975

John Giuseppi, *The Bank of England: A History from its Foundation to 1964*, Evan Bros, 1966

Leo Gough, *The Financial Times Guide to Business Numeracy*, Financial Times Management, 1994

Leo Gough, *Going Offshore*, Financial Times Management, 1995

Leo Gough, *25 Investment Classics*, Financial Times Management, 1998

Leo Gough, *Trading the World's Markets*, Wiley, 2000

Benjamin Graham, *The Intelligent Investor*, HarperPerennial, 1973

SL Hays, AM Spence and DVP Marks, *Competition in the Investment Banking Industry*, Harvard University Press, 1983

Michael Joseph, *The Conveyancing Fraud*, Michael Joseph, 1989

JM Keynes, *The General Theory of Employment Interest and Money*, Harcourt, 1936

Richard Koch, *Selecting Shares that Perform*, Financial Times Management, 2008

Edwin le Fevre, *Reminiscences of a Stock Operator*, John Wiley, 1994

LH Leigh, *The Control of Commercial Fraud*, Heinemann Educational Books, 1982

Michael Lewis, *Liar's Poker*, Penguin, 1990

Michael Lewis, *The Big Short: Inside the Doomsday Machine*, Norton, 2010

Andrew Lo and Craig Mackinlay, *A Non-Random Walk Down Wall Street*, Princeton University Press, 2002

Ferdinand Lundberg, *The Rich and the Super Rich*, Thomas Nelson & Sons, 1969

Roger Lowenstein, *The End of Wall Street*, Penguin, 2010

Peter Lynch, *One Up on Wall Street*, Penguin, 1989

Burton G Malkiel, *A Random Walk Down Wall Street*, WW Norton, 1991

Mark Mobius, *Mobius on Emerging Markets*, Financial Times Management, 1995

James Morton, *Investing with the Grand Masters*, Financial Times Management, 1997

C Northcote Parkinson, *Parkinson's Law*, John Murray, 1958

Patrick Philips, *Inside the Gilt-Edged Market*, Woodhead-Faulkner

Robert Prechter, *At the Crest of the Tidal Wave*, New Classics Library, 1995

W Proctor, *The Templeton Touch*, Doubleday, 1983

Jim Rogers, *Investment Biker*, Random House, 1994

David E. Rye, *25 Stupid Mistakes You Don't Want to Make in the Stock Market*, McGraw-Hill Professional, 2001

Anthony Sampson, *The Money Lenders*, Random House, 1968

Jack Schwager, *Market Wizards*, HarperCollins, 1993

Fred Schwed, Jr, *Where Are the Customers' Yachts?*, Simon and Schuster, 1940

Adam Smith, *The Money Game*, Vintage, 1976

Ralph Lee Smith, *The Grim Truth About Mutual Funds*, Putnam, 1963

George Soros, *Soros on Soros*, Wiley, 1995

Kathryn F Staley, *The Art of Short Selling*, Wiley, 1997

Michael Stolper, *Wealth, an Owner's Manual*, HarperBusiness, 1992

Tolley Publishing Company, *Tolley's Tax Guide*, annual

John Train, *Preserving Capital and Making It Grow*, Penguin, 1983

John Train, *The New Money Masters*, Harper & Row, 1989

Charles Vintcent, *Be Your Own Stockbroker*, Financial Times Management, 1995

Useful websites

The academic understanding of finance and investment has developed in leaps and bounds over the last 30 years, and there is a vast wealth of theoretical information about investment available on the internet; for beginners, however, much of this material is just too complicated to make sense, so most people tend to use the websites purveying 'dumbed-down' consumer information. This may be all right as far as it goes, but senior figures in the industry – and especially the financial regulators – now believe that financial education for ordinary investors has become extremely important. As a guerrilla investor, you need to take advantage of the new moves towards providing better financial education for all investors. This section provides some websites that offer reliable information, research and good links to other, more specialized sites.

Financial regulators

The Financial Services Authority (FSA)

The FSA is the UK regulatory body for the financial services industry:

http://www.fsa.gov.uk/

The FSA also runs a compensation scheme for investors who lose money when firms go broke:

http://www.fscs.org.uk

The Securities and Exchange Commission (SEC)

The SEC is the USA's main stock market regulator. It provides a massive amount of information about US companies and also many multinational firms that have a listing in the US (this includes many well-known UK firms):

http://www.sec.gov/

The SEC requires listed firms to provide a huge amount of information about their activities (much more than in the UK). Most of this is publicly available through the SEC's EDGAR database:

http://www.sec.gov/edgar.shtml

Market data

Market data, which includes share prices, interest rates, indices and charts of all kinds is quite widely available. Here are two of the most useful sites:

Bloomberg

Useful, comprehensive, easy to navigate – and free!

http://www.bloomberg.com/markets/stocks/wei.html

Yahoo finance

Not my preferred site for serious work, but useful for quick price checks:

http://finance.yahoo.com/

Major markets

Most of the money invested in shares goes through only a handful of the major exchanges, which are listed here. All the stock exchanges of the world have websites, but unless you are specializing in quite unusual forms of investment you will not need to use them – in any case, it is probably best to familiarize yourself with the major markets before branching out into obscure markets, which are often quite expensive to access as a private investor.

The London Stock Exchange

Useful for annual reports and price data on UK shares, and now provides much improved educational material on funds, saving for retirement, finding a broker and so on:

http://www.londonstockexchange.com/en-gb/

The New York Stock Exchange

The first port of call for investing in the USA – many of the blue chips are listed here. Excellent investor education material:

http://www.nyse.com/

The American Stock Exchange (AMEX)

Lists a very wide range of US companies and provides various other services such as options trading:

www.amex.com

NASDAQ

NASDAQ is an electronic 'screen-based' market that lists many 'hot' companies in new industries. During the dotcom boom, for instance, many internet firms got themselves listed on NASDAQ. The website is orientated towards the needs of frequent traders, and does not provide a lot of educational material:

http://www.nasdaq.com/

Other useful sites

The UK Debt Management Office (DMO)

The UK government website for gilts (UK government bonds):

http://www.dmo.gov.uk/

The Motley Fool

A consumer-oriented personal finance site, quite useful for UK-specific money issues:

http://www.fool.co.uk/

Paul Krugman

A brilliant maverick economist, Krugman's writings are a useful antidote to what you read in the financial press:

http://pkarchive.org/

Proshare

A not-for-profit organization that provides backup for UK investment clubs, where ordinary people get together to invest as a group and to learn about the markets. A good way of getting into investment if you are the socializing type:

http://www.proshareclubs.co.uk/

The Investment Management Association

Well-organized site providing information on UK funds, and how to pick them:

http://www.investmentuk.org/

Glossary

Account Fortnightly, or sometimes three-weekly, trading period on a stock exchange.

Actuary A statistician, usually employed by an insurance company, who calculates risk.

Advisory broker A stockbroker who advises clients on their investments as well as buying and selling on their behalf.

Agency brokers In the UK, broker/dealers who act as agents between market makers and investors.

Allotment price In a tender for gilts, the price allotted to successful tenders. In a gilts auction, non-competitive bids are allotted a price that is the weighted average of successful competitive bids.

Annual charge Management fees levied on investments, often as a percentage of their value.

Annual Percentage Rate (APR) A standardized way of expressing interest rates which make them comparable with one another, and include hidden charges and other extras.

Anti-trust Anti-monopoly legislation, originally aimed at US trusts used to create monopolies.

Arbitrage Taking advantage of the difference in price of the same product or rate in different places.

Arbitrageurs ('ARBS') Generally, but incorrectly, used to mean speculators who buy shares in a company in the hope that it will be taken over. This is not strictly arbitrage, since some time elapses between purchase and sale, and in theory one should not know the future price. If you do, it's cheating!

Asset Anything that has a monetary value.

Auction For gilts, an auction is where new issues are bid for in one of two forms: competitive or non-competitive.

Audit The process of inspection of a company's books by independent accountants.

Averaging 'Averaging' a particular shareholding is achieved by buying more on a fall or selling some on a rise in value.

Back-to-back loan Hedging against interest rates changes by borrowing in one currency against the security of a deposit in another currency.

Backwardation This is when the spot or near-term price of a commodity is higher than its forward price, sometimes caused by shipment delays.

Balance of payments The difference between the total value of money entering a country and the total leaving it in a year.

Balance of trade The difference in total value between a country's annual imports and exports.

Balance sheet A statement of a company's financial situation at the end of the last financial year.

Bargain A transaction on a stock exchange.

Basket currency An invented currency based on several national currencies, such as the ECU and special drawing rights.

Bear Someone who thinks the share market will go down.

Bearer bonds Bond certificates that can be held anonymously and used almost as freely as cash.

Bed and breakfast operation Selling shares and then buying them back to mitigate capital gains tax. Now no longer possible because of a rule change.

Bell-wether share A share in a company that is regarded as likely to move in line with market trends.

Beneficial owner The true owner of a security who may not be named in the register of ownership.

Bid price The price at which a unit trust manager or market maker is willing to buy shares.

Blue chip The top 100 or so companies on the stock market, reputedly stable investments.

Boilerhouse operations Firms who use high-pressure tactics to obtain investments of doubtful value.

Bonds Securities, usually paying a fixed rate of interest, which are sold by companies and governments.

Bonus issue The issue of additional shares by a company to its shareholders at no cost; also called a 'scrip issue' or a 'capitalization issue'.

Bretton Woods The place in New Hampshire, USA, where the post-war system of foreign exchange was agreed in 1944.

Bull Someone who thinks the share market will go up.

Bulldog bonds Bonds issued by governments in sterling, other than British government gilts.

Call option The right to buy shares at an agreed price within a certain time.

Capital gains tax (CGT) A tax on the increase of value of assets realized in a particular year.

Capitalization The total value at the market price of securities issued by a company, industry or market sector.

Capitalization issue See 'bonus issue'.

Cash and carry When a dealer buys a commodity for cash and sells the futures contract at a profit, possibly when the spot price is more than the forward price, interest, storage and insurance costs.

Central Gilts Office (CGO) The Central Gilts Office in the UK is where trade in gilts is processed on computer.

Central Moneymarkets Office (CMO) The Central Moneymarkets Office in the UK is where trade in money market instruments is settled on computer.

Chartist Someone who studies charts in the hope of predicting changes in stock market prices.

Chinese Walls The attempt to keep confidential information from passing from one department of a financial organization to another.

Churning Trading with a client's portfolio in order to generate extra commissions dishonestly.

Clean price The price of a gilt, not including rebate interest or accrued interest.

Closed-end fund A fund where the size of the total investment is fixed. All investment trusts are closed end.

Commercial bank A 'high street' bank which deals mainly with the public.

Commodity Any raw material.

Common stocks The US name for ordinary shares.

Concert party An informal group of investors who try to obtain control.

Consideration The value of a share transaction before the costs of dealing are paid.

Contango The normal situation in the futures market where the spot price is less than the forward price.

Contract note Written details of an agreement to buy or sell securities.

Contrarians Investors who act against consensus views.

Conventional option Options that are not traded.

Conventional stocks/bonds Bonds with fixed interest rates and repayment dates.

Convertible loan stock A security paying a fixed rate of interest which may be changed in the future for ordinary shares.

Corporate governance A jargon term for the fashionable issue of how companies should be run, in the context of society as well as the law and best practice.

Corporate issue A bond issued by a company.

Coupon The nominal interest rate on a fixed-interest security (bond), or a warrant which is detached from a bearer bond or bearer share certificate to be used to claim interest.

Cum The Latin word for 'with'. For instance, 'cum dividend' means 'with dividend'.

Currency hedging Trying to reduce or eliminate exchange rate risks by buying forward, using financial futures or borrowing in the exposed currency.

Dealing costs The cost of buying and selling shares, including the broker's commission, stamp duty and VAT.

Debenture A bond issued by a company, paying a fixed rate of interest and usually secured on an asset.

Deep discount Bonds that have been issued in the UK after 14 March 1989 at a discount of more than 0.5 per cent per annum or 15 per cent in total are said to have a 'deep discount', and the discount is to be taxed as income. No such bonds have yet been issued.

Derivative These include options, forward contracts, and the like. They are often said not to be 'real' assets, because they may expire and become worthless.

Designated territory The UK's Department of Trade and Industry (DTI) terms certain tax havens 'designated territories', meaning that they operate proper controls over their financial industries. They include the Isle of Man, Luxembourg, Jersey and Guernsey.

Devaluation The formal reduction in the value of a high currency against other currencies.

Dirty floating The practice of a state intervening to influence or manipulate exchange rate movements.

Discount broker A stockbroker who deals for clients but gives little or no advice and charges low commission rates.

Discounted cash flow A way of estimating the value of an investment in today's money by adjusting future returns to get their present value.

Diversification The act of spreading capital across different investments in order to reduce risk.

Dividend A regular payment out of profits by companies to their shareholders.

Domicile The country where you are resident for tax purposes; it is difficult, but not impossible, to change your domicile.

Double dated stock UK gilts that can be redeemed by the government between two specified dates.

Double taxation treaty Treaties between countries to offset a person's tax liabilities in one country against those in another.

Dragons The economies of Thailand, the Philippines, Malaysia and Indonesia.

Earnings The net profit of a company that is distributed to its shareholders.

Earnings per share (EPS) The profits of a company, after tax, divided by the number of shares.

Enfacement The process by which a UK bond passes from a CGO member to a non-member. *See also* 'Central Gilts Office'.

Equities Another name for shares.

Eurobond A stock that is issued by a syndicate of banks and is usually bought and sold outside the country in whose currency it is denominated.

Eurocurrency Deposits of a currency that are held outside the country in which the money is denominated.

Eurodollar US dollars held outside the United States.

Euromarket The market in currencies and securities outside the countries in which they are denominated.

Eurowarrant A certificate linked to a Eurobond which entitles the holder to buy a given number of shares at an agreed price and time.

Ex dividend date The date when a holder of a UK bond receives the next interest payment.

Ex dividend stock UK bonds that are sold to a buyer who does not receive the next due interest payment because the deadline for registration of the transfer has passed.

External bonds Bonds issued in the market of one country that are denominated in the currency of another.

External Names Names at Lloyd's who do not work there.

Federal Reserve The central banks of the United States.

Fixed assets A company's assets that are not being processed or bought and sold, such as buildings and machinery.

Flat yield Also called 'running yield' or 'interest yield', it is the income you earn in a year if you bought £100s' market value of a bond. The figure is calculated by dividing the coupon by the market price and multiplying by 100.

Floating charge A right to priority payment from the assets of a person or company.

Floating exchange rates Currency exchange rates that change their rate according to the activity in the market.

Floating rate note Bonds and other debt instruments that carry a variable rate of interest, usually linked to a reference rate such as the London Inter-Bank Offered Rate (LIBOR).

Flotation When a company first issues its shares on a stock exchange.

Force majeure A supplier usually has a clause in delivery contracts allowing them to break the contract when there is force majeure which is a major external event such as a strike or major catastrophe.

Forward exchange contract An agreement to buy an amount of a currency at an agreed exchange rate on a fixed date.

FT Actuaries All-Share Index A stock market index, divided into 40 sections, covering all shares quoted in the UK.

FT Industrial Ordinary Share Index An index of the ordinary shares of 30 top companies.

FTSE 100 Index The 'Footsie', the principal index for the share price of shares quoted on the London stock market.

FTSE stocks The 100 companies whose shares are represented in the FTSE 100 Index. Generally regarded as 'blue chip'.

Fundamental analysis The assessment of the value of a share on a company's actual earnings, assets and dividends.

Fungible stocks UK bonds that are issued after an identical issue and merged with it.

Futures The right to buy or sell a financial instrument at an agreed price at some future time.

Gearing The ratio between a company's share capital and its borrowings. High gearing means a proportionately large amount of debt and low gearing means a small amount of debt.

GEMM A Gilt-Edged Market Maker.

General Agreement on Tariffs and Trade (GATT) A group representing most nations which supervises international trade.

Gilt-edged Securities issued by the British government, usually at a fixed interest rate. US gilts are called Treasury bonds.

Holding company A company that controls one or more other companies.

In play When a company is thought to be the target of a bid, it is said to be 'in play'.

Index fund An investment fund that invests in all the shares used in a given market index, mimicking the performance of the index.

Inflation A general increase in prices.

Insider dealing Trading in shares when in possession of price-sensitive information that is not known to the market. Insider dealing is illegal to some degree in most markets.

Institutions The large, managed investment funds, including pension funds, insurance funds, unit and investment trusts are known as institutional funds and are the major players in the stock market.

International Monetary Fund (IMF) The international lender of last resort, set up by the Allies in 1944.

Investment bank Called a 'merchant bank' in the UK, a bank that works as a financial intermediary, offering such services as takeover and merger assistance, and the placing of new share and bond issues.

Investment trust A company that manages share portfolios and whose own shares are quoted on the stock exchange.

ISAs Individual Savings Accounts. These provide a tax-free shelter for UK taxpayers.

Junk bonds Company bonds that are not rated by credit-rating agencies. They are 'low quality' and offer a higher rate of interest than other bonds.

Kerb trading Trading that occurs after the stock market has officially closed for the day.

Kondratiev wave A theoretical economic cycle lasting approximately 60 years.

Less developed country (LDC) A polite way of saying an underdeveloped or poor country.

Liquidity The degree of ease with which an asset can be turned into cash.

Lloyd's of London An insurance market.

London Inter-Bank Offered Rate (LIBOR) The rate of interest offered by commercial banks to other banks on the London Inter-Bank Market.

Longs British government securities that are to be redeemed in 15 or more years' time.

Management charges Fees taken by fund managers to cover their overheads. These can be too high.

Margin In the market, a cash deposit against a sum invested on credit.

Market maker Formerly 'jobbers', these are dealers in securities in their own names on a stock exchange.

Marketability The degree of ease and speed with which a security can be sold.

Maturity date The day the bond expires.

Mediums British government securities that are to be redeemed in between 5 and 15 years' time.

Merchant bank *see* 'investment bank'.

Money supply The available money in a system and the rate at which it circulates.

Mutual funds The US name for unit trusts.

Name An investor at Lloyd's of London.

Negotiability The freedom to trade a financial instrument with third parties.

Net asset value (NAV) The net assets of a company divided by the number of shares it has issued gives the net asset value per share.

Net margining system Used by some stock exchanges in the United States, this system reconciles the total margins due to each broker so that the difference, rather than the total, is passed to the clearing house.

Net present value (NPV) A figure that represents the total of future cash inflows from a project, less cash outflows, inflation, and/or a required rate of return.

Net worth The value of an individual's assets after all debts have been subtracted.

NIC A newly industrialized country, for example South Korea.

Nominal value The value of a security printed on its certificate. Also called 'par' or 'face value'.

Nominee A person or company that is registered as the owner of a security in order that the true owner's identity is kept secret, or to make dealing easier.

Non-competitive bid In a gilts auction, a bid for between £1,000 and £500,000's worth of stock which will receive an allotment at a price that is the weighted average of the successful competitive bids.

Offer price The price at which a unit trust manager or market maker will sell a stock or share.

Open-ended A fund that has a variable amount of capital and doesn't have to match its buyers and sellers. See also 'unit trusts'.

Open outcry A system of face-to-face trading where brokers shout their bids and offers out loud; now only used in some commodity and derivatives markets.

Option The right to buy or sell a security at an agreed price within an agreed timespan.

Ordinary share The most usual type of share, called 'ordinary' to distinguish it from other kinds, such as 'preference' shares which pay a fixed dividend.

Organization of Petroleum Exporting Countries (OPEC) An association of some of the major oil-producing countries that tries to regulate oil production and prices, thus affecting the world oil market.

Over the counter (OTC) Any market that does not work through an exchange-based system.

Par value The nominal value of a share or bond, as stated on its certificate. This is not its market value.

Pari passu Latin for 'at the same rate', 'equal ranking'.

Pit trader A dealer who works on the floor of an exchange, usually a futures exchange, that uses the 'open outcry' system.

Portfolio A collection of securities held by one investor or fund.

Preference shares Fixed dividend shares giving preference, as a creditor, over ordinary shareholders but behind bond holders.

Price/earnings (p/e) ratio The market price of a share divided by its earnings (e.g. profits) gives the p/e ratio, which is the most commonly used measure of the 'value' of a share.

Prior charges Interest paid on loan stock and debentures that is settled before the distribution of dividends to shareholders.

Private placing An issue of new shares to institutions and large private clients rather than to the general public.

Programmed trading Investors who give standing instructions to their brokers to buy and sell at pre-ordained price or growth levels.

Proxy A person who votes, with permission, in the place of a shareholder at company meetings.

Put option The right to sell a security at an agreed price within an agreed time limit.

Quotation The price of a security currently fixed by a stock exchange market maker.

Rating of bonds This is done according to risk: the least risky bonds are rated AAA and the highest risk bonds are rated D. Junk bonds are too risky to be rated.

Redemption yield Any one of several methods of calculating what interest rate is necessary for the market price of a bond to equal the net present value of the remaining interest payments and redemption value.

Reserve currency The currency that is most used by governments and institutions for holding cash reserves. Currently, it is the US dollar.

Reverse auction When a bond issuer invites bond holders to sell their bonds back to the issuer.

Rights issue When a company offers new shares pro rata to its own shareholders, usually at a discount.

Saitori Members of the Tokyo Stock Exchange who work as intermediaries between brokers. They are not allowed to deal on their own accounts or for non-members of the exchange.

Savings and loan (S&L) The US equivalent of British building societies.

Scrip issue See 'bonus issue'.

Seat Having a seat on an exchange means being a member of the exchange.

Securities These are any financial instruments traded on a stock exchange, such as shares and bonds.

Self-regulating organizations (SROs) These are financial organizations that regulate, with varying degrees of effectiveness, the activities of their members.

Shell company A quoted company that has few or no trading activities.

Shorts Short-term bonds.

Special drawing right (SDR) A basket currency used by the International Monetary Fund (IMF) which consists of weighted amounts of major currencies and US dollars.

Speculation Gambling on the change in the price of a security.

Spread The difference between the prices of a share at which a market maker will buy (bid) and sell (offer).

Straddle Making contracts to buy and sell an option or future at the same time in order to protect against big price changes.

Swap An agreement to exchange a stream of future payments.

Tap issues In the UK, the name for an issue of government bonds that is not fully subscribed. In such cases, the broker keeps the remainder and 'dribbles' them into the market slowly.

Technical analysis The attempt to predict share price movements on the basis of past patterns of movement.

Tigers The economies of Hong Kong, Taiwan, Singapore and South Korea.

Tombstone A newspaper advertisement that set out the details of a bond issue or major loan, and the banks that have underwritten it.

Underwriter One who provides insurance cover or guarantees a financial transaction.

Unit trusts UK savings schemes run by specialists for small investors; funds are invested in securities. In the USA they are called mutual funds.

Warrants A certificate, usually attached to a bond, that gives the holder the right to buy shares at a given price and date.

Widows and orphans Mythical creatures, a metaphor for clients who are very risk averse and financially unsophisticated.

Working Name An investor at Lloyd's who also works as an agent or underwriter there.

Yearlings These are short-term bonds, usually with a one-year life.

Yields The annual return on an investment, excluding capital growth.

Zaibatsu The Japanese word for 'financial clique'; the original zaibatsu was a group of powerful families who industrialized Japan in the nineteenth century.

Index